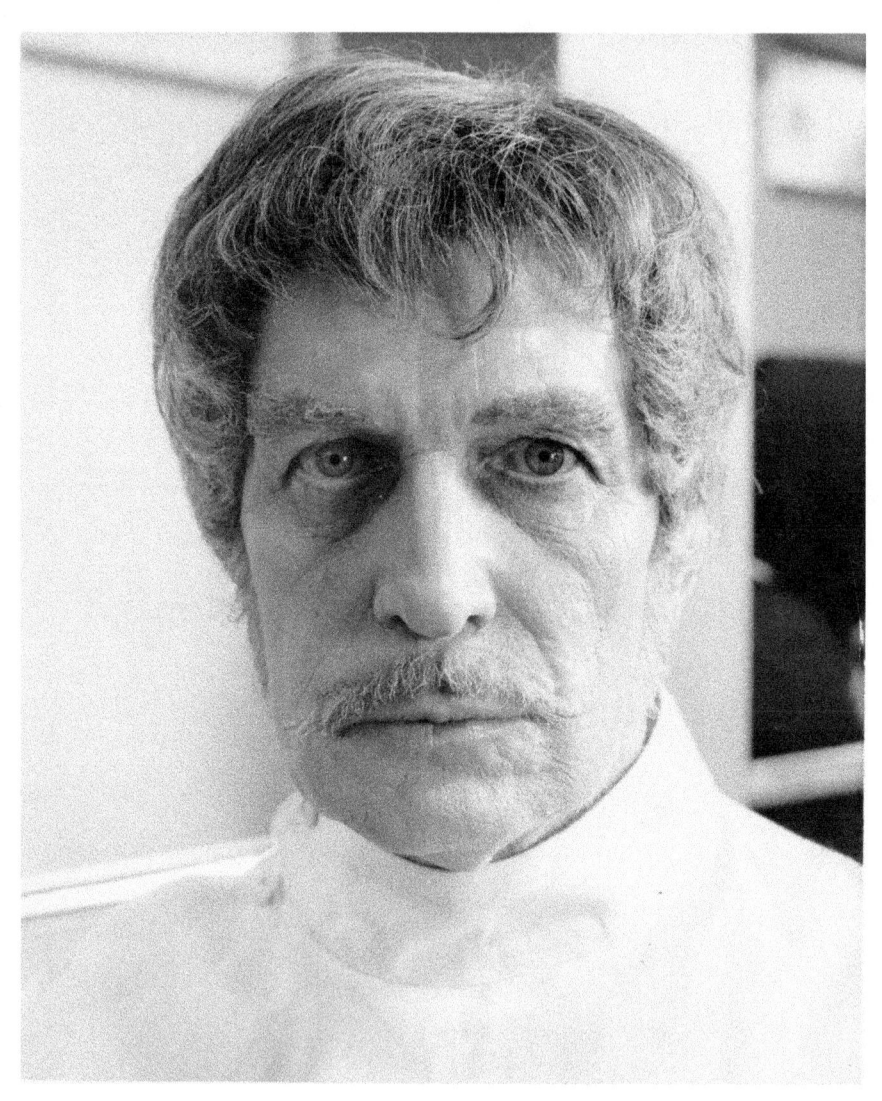

The Dr. Phibes Companion:

The Morbidly Romantic History of the Classic Vincent Price Horror Film Series

By Justin Humphreys
With Contributions by Mark Ferelli, Sam Irvin, and David Taylor

The Dr. Phibes Companion: The Morbidly Romantic History of the Classic Vincent Price Horror Film Series
Justin Humphreys
Copyright © 2018- Justin Humphreys. All rights reserved. Essays by William Goldstein, Mark Ferelli, Sam Irvin, and David Taylor are copyright © their respective authors. No part of this book may be reproduced in any form or by any means, electronic, mechanical, digital, photocopying, or recording, except for inclusion of a review, without permission in writing from the publisher or Author.

Published in the USA by:
BearManor Media
P O Box 71426
Albany, Georgia 31708
www.bearmanormedia.com

ISBN: 978-1-62933-293-2
BearManor Media, Albany, Georgia
Printed in the United States of America
Book design by Robbie Adkins, www.adkinsconsult.com

JUSTIN HUMPHREYS

For Robert Fuest (1927-2012)

ACKNOWLEDGMENTS:

The late, great Bob Fuest made this book possible. Though he wasn't given to discussing himself, Bob was unfailingly informative, friendly, loving, and supportive. Several other key contributors to the Phibes series also passed away since I interviewed them: James Whiton, John Gale, and Brian Clemens.

Thanks to Dick Klemensen of *Little Shoppe of Horrors* magazine for initially printing "The Kind of Fiend Who Wins" and putting together his excellent Dr. Phibes issue. My fellow contributors, David Taylor, Sam Irvin, and Mark Ferelli deserve a big hand, too. They not only supplied chapters for this book, but also interviews with Bob Fuest and John Cater (Irvin), many photos (Taylor), and rare images from John Jay's estate (Ferelli). Many thanks to Phibes' creator William Goldstein for providing this book's foreword and much information about Phibes' life, past and present.

The author would also like to thank the following people for their invaluable assistance with investigating Dr. Phibes and his nefarious deeds: the Fuests, the Eatwells, Fiona Lewis, Ronald Dunas, Peter Lennard, Laurie Ede, Lem Dobbs (Thanks for the photo of Goldstein and Whiton!), Stephen Wathen, Juan Camacho, Derek Nice (quote from Brian Eatwell's letters), Denis Meikle, Jason Frederick, Donald MacKenzie, Alan Spencer, Damon Goldstein, Robert Skotak, Bruce Hallenbeck, Mary Stone and the House of Phibes Yahoo Group (Interview with Brian Eatwell and a Fuest quote), Michael Orlando Yaccarino, Tom Weaver, Marcus Hearn (*Dr. Phibes* bluray audio commentary with Fuest, *The Vincent Price Collection*, Scream Factory), John Brosnan, Anthony Petkovich, Lucy Chase Williams, Dave Elsey, Lisi Tribble, Stanley Weiser, Dave Tompkins, Graeme Cochrane (for rare articles on Virginia North), Terry Gilliam, Mr. Darrow (for the handbill), Perseverence Records (Interviews with Fuest and Kirchin re: *Dr. Phibes* score), Ed Naha, Thomas Kuntz, Grant Moninger, *Parade* magazine (Tim Burton quote- March 21, 2010 issue), Johnny Trunk, Chris

Stavrakis (for finding Basil Kirchin), David Lady, Mike Hines, and Lou Arkoff.

Special thanks to Cathey Flickinger for her cover design!

Thanks to May Routh, Joanna Eatwell, Nicolas Roeg, Ilya Salkind, Derek Nice, Tony Richmond, Thomas Jerome Newton, David Weston, and Si Litvinoff for their help with my research into Brian Eatwell's life and work. (I would also like to thank Laura Edie again for writing so eloquently about Eatwell's work in her excellent *British Film Design*.)

Thanks to Quentin Tarantino and the staff of the New Beverly Cinema for programming *Dr. Phibes* five wonderful times in a very short timespan just as I was completing this book, and for letting me introduce three of those screenings. Thanks to Grant Moninger and the staff of the American Cinematheque for letting me and Bill Goldstein host a *Dr. Phibes* double-header at the lovely Aero Theater.

I am *always* looking for new and unusual information about *The Abominable Dr. Phibes*, its sequels (filmed and unfilmed), and Robert Fuest. I am especially interested in contacting anyone directly involved with the series, like choreographer Suzanne France, and actors Sean Bury and Julie Mendez. If you have anything that you would like to see added to this book, please contact me at, and direct all corrections, comments, and hate mail to, testamentoforpheus@gmail.com.

SELECT BIBLIOGRAPHY & SOURCES:

Several chapters in this book have been previously published in shorter forms: "The Kind of Fiend Who Wins. . .," "Abandoning the Obvious. . .," and "The Unphilmed Phibes. . ." appeared in *Little Shoppe of Horrors* magazine #29. Thanks to its editor/publisher, Dick Klemensen, for giving us his blessings on publishing them here. "The Irreplaceable Mr. Fuest. . ." appeared in *Video Watchdog* magazine #168. Thanks to its editor/publisher Tim Lucas for wholeheartedly approving of its use here.

Anderson, Michael. Correspondence with Justin Humphreys.
Arkoff, Lou. Interview with Justin Humphreys.
Arkoff, Samuel Z. with Richard Trubo. *Flying Through Hollywood by the Seat of My Pants*. Birch Lane Press, 1992.
Author Unknown. "The Changing Face of Vincent Price." *The Evening Standard*, January 6, 1972.
Author Unknown. "Last of the Ghouls." *Newsweek*. June 14, 1971. Quotes related to the Museum of Modern Art screening of *The Abominable Dr. Phibes*.
Author Unknown. *Variety*. June 19, 1969. Announcement that Ronald Dunas would be producing *The Survivors*.
Author Unknown. "Virginia North: Entre de Dracula y Mark Spitz." Periodical unknown. South America, circa 1970.
Brosnan, John. *The Horror People*. MacDonald's and Janes, 1976. Robert Bloch interview.
Burton, Tim. Quote about *The Abominable Dr. Phibes*. *Parade* magazine. March 21, 2010.
Cassyd, Syd. "Backstage." *Boxoffice* magazine. February, 22, 1971. Interview with Robert Fuest.
Clemens, Brian. Interview and correspondence with Justin Humphreys.
Dante, Joe. *Film Bulletin* [circa 1971]. Review of *The Abominable Dr. Phibes*. Reprinted on www.trailersfromhell.com.

Dunas, Ronald. Interview with Justin Humphreys.
Earnshaw, Tony. "Father of Phibes." *Fangoria* #314. Pp 16-18, 86. Robert Fuest interview.
Eatwell, Joanna. Correspondence with Justin Humphreys.
Ede, Laurie N. *British Film Design*. I.B. Tauris. 2010.
Frederick, Jason. Interview with Paul Lewis. YouTube. 2017. Re: Working with John Gale on the *Dr. Phibes Rises Again* score.
Fuest, Robert. Interviews with Justin Humphreys.
Gale, John. Interview with Justin Humphreys.
Goldstein, William. Interviews with Justin Humphreys.
Goldstein, William and James Whiton, with Robert Fuest (uncredited). Robert Fuest's annotated copy of *The Abominable Dr. Phibes* shooting script (titled "The Curses of Dr. Phibes"). Author's personal collection.
Hearn, Marcus. Audio commentary with Robert Fuest. *The Abominable Dr. Phibes* BluRay in *The Vincent Price Collection* set. Scream Factory.
Irvin, Sam. John Cater interview. *Bizarre* magazine. #4.
Irvin, Sam. Robert Fuest interview. *Bizarre* magazine. #4.
King, Stephen. Facebook post. January, 2018. Quote about *The Abominable Dr. Phibes*.
Koetting, Christopher. "AIP's Third Man: Part Two: The Other Guy, Deke Heyward." *Ultra Filmfax* magazine. August/September, 1997. #62.
Knight, Chris and Peter Nicholson. "On the Set of Phibes II." *Cinefantastique* magazine. Vol. 2, #2. Summer, 1972. Interview with Valli Kemp.
Lennard, Peter. Interview with Justin Humphreys.
Lewis, Fiona. Interview with Justin Humphreys. 2018.
Litvinoff, Si. Correspondence with Justin Humphreys.
Meikle, Dennis. "A Date With Dr. Phibes." *Little Shoppe of Horrors* #29. p 74-76.
Muschietti, Andrew. Twitter. September, 2017. *It* movie official page. Tweet about *The Abominable Dr. Phibes*.
Naha, Ed. *Horrors: From Screen to Scream*. Avon Books. 1975. Quote about *The Abominable Dr. Phibes*.

Nanjiani, Kumail. Twitter. July, 2017 and May, 2018. Tweets about *The Abominable Dr. Phibes*.

Nasr, Constantine. "Remembering Vincent: A Conversation With Tim Burton." *Little Shoppe of Horrors #29*. p 28-31.

Nice, Derek. Correspondence with Justin Humphreys.

Petkovich, Anthony. Robert Fuest interview. *Psychotronic Video* #41. pp 34-40.

Petkovich, Anthony. "Robert Quarry- Count Yorga Rises Again!" *Psychotronic Video* #33. pp 32-40.

Pirie, David. Correspondence with Justin Humphreys.

Price, Vincent. Papers- The Library of Congress. Screenplays of *The Abominable Dr. Phibes* and *Dr. Phibes Rises Again*; production paperwork on both films; letter from a young fan; and various press clippings. Boxes 129 and 133.

Richmond, Tony. Interview with Justin Humphreys.

Roeg, Nicolas. Interview with Justin Humphreys.

Ross, Robert. *The Complete Terry-Thomas*. Richmond, Surrey, UK: Reynolds and Hearn. 2002. P. 175. Interview with John Cater re: *Dr. Phibes Rises Again*.

Routh, May. Interviews with Justin Humphreys.

Salkind, Ilya. Interviews and correspondence with Justin Humphreys.

Spencer, Alan. Interviews and correspondence with Justin Humphreys.

Stone, Mary and the House of Phibes Yahoo Group. Interview with Brian Eatwell.

Tompkins, Dave. *How to Wreck a Nice Beach*. Brooklyn, NY: Melville House Publishing. 2010. Information about Dr. Phibes' connection to hip-hop music and the Vocoder.

Tribble, Lisi. Correspondence with Justin Humphreys.

Uncredited. *Boxoffice*. June 7, 1971. p 7. Report on Pantages premiere.

Weaver, Tom. Interview with Robert Blees.

Weston, David. Interview with Justin Humphreys.

Yaccarino, Michael Orlando. Vincent Price interview. *Scarlet Street* magazine. #7, Summer, 1992.

CONTENTS:

Acknowledgments vii

Select Bibliography & Sources. ix

Table of Contents. xiii

Foreword by William Goldstein xv

Introduction: *Non Omnis Moriar* by Justin Humphreys. xix

1- The Kind of Fiend Who Wins: The Making of 1
The Abominable Dr. Phibes by Justin Humphreys

Vulnavia Interlude 125

2- The Coffin Hasn't Been Built That Can Hold Him: 133
The Making of *Dr. Phibes Rises Again* by Justin Humphreys

3- The Unphilmed Phibes: From *The Fingers of Dr. Pibe* 182
to Somewhere Over the Rainbow by David Taylor and Sam Irwin

4- The Irreplaceable Mr. Fuest: A remember of Robert Fuest . . 211
by Justin Humphreys

5- Abandoning the Obvious: The Brilliant Life and Art of . . 227
Brian Eatwell by Justin Humphreys

6- John Jay: Photographer of Phibes by Mark Ferelli 241

7- Phibes and the Arts: Phibes Risen by Mark Ferelli. 245

FOREWORD

By William Goldstein

Pushing up from its northeastern corner Nob Hill and its geologic partners - Telegraph and Russian Hills - landmarked San Francisco for generations of adventurers high and low. The view, more than anything else in this city of many vistas, is the driving engine of the real estate markets. And for the hill-dwellers on those peaks, the view is always splendid. For those less fortunate there is always the Mark Hopkins where, from its rooftop lounge, one can look across the bay at Oakland-- and all of America stretching beyond that.

Eight miles away down the diagonal that demarcates the north and south parts of this city-- Market Street-- rises another tall hill. Devout San Franciscans make their annual Easter climb to the top of this Mt. Davidson to celebrate and to consecrate.

On Mt. Davidson's northside downslope through the Mt. Sutro Urban Forest a pasty tan aggregate of buildings rises to announce the presence of the University of California Hospital and Medical School. Half a block further downhill in a similarly tan private residence, Anton Phibes, the man and his legend, took shape over a few months in the spring and summer of 1964.

It was an easy, almost automatic writing buffered by the fog that pours through the Golden Gate and up from Ocean Beach, three miles away at the west end of America.

Phibes' is a simple story-- a love story inside a horror story-- about a man who loses his wife, and tries for the rest of his life to revivify her; retribution to all who would stand in his way.

Phibes first saw the light of day (or more accurately, the dark of a movie theatre) seven years later at the Hollywood Pantages, a red carpet affair complete with probing searchlights, popping flash bulbs and the Hollywood Glitterati out in full force-- all this for a horror flick, one that has grown into today's Dr. Phibes Cult Classic Series.

Writing is solitary. Filmmaking is by committee. Those who contributed to this book are the same talented artists who constructed the gorgeous sets, the ephemeral costumes and the crisp pacing of *The Abominable Dr. Phibes* and of its pyramidic sequel, *Dr. Phibes Rises Again*. Don't be surprised if you are entertained, really really entertained. It's OK to clap because there is an encore!

Dr. Phibes—In the Beginning is both the back-story and the continuation-- in Gotham-- of Anton Phibes' quest. In *Vulnavia's Secret*, he restores his mute assistant - badly burned at the end of the first film - to her original beauty. *Dr. Phibes' Androbots* takes his band and their diva, Sophie, on a cross-country concert tour. Hailed in the press as "The Band That Can Play Forever", these diminutive musicians and their music offer a haunting tribute to Phibes' mastery of nano-acoustics.

Can love triumph over death?

Anton Phibes has made this most prosaic, most profound theme his *Forever Mission*. Readers may want to watch it unfold on THE OFFICIAL DR. PHIBES BLOG SPOT.

-William Goldstein
Beverly Hills, California
July, 2016

Vincent Price and director Robert Fuest rehearsing Dr. Phibes Rises Again, *their expressions clearly reflecting their working relationship.*

Introduction:
Non Omnis Moriar

By Justin Humphreys

"Non omnis moriar." ("I shall not wholly die.") - Horace

"He's had years to hide, to plot this damnable thing. . . It's the psychic force that holds this man together, this maniacal precision!"

By the time I finished this book, those lines of Joseph Cotten's from *The Abominable Dr. Phibes* semi-accurately described the process of writing it.

When I was thirteen, I would've killed for the book you're reading. Back then, my inner world was Dr. Phibes's ballroom, in all its Art Deco/Art Nouveau splendor. *The Abominable Dr. Phibes* was my favorite film, and I watched and re-watched it religiously. Phibes was my role model—a worldly, suave, impeccably dressed, and independently wealthy aesthete/polymath. *Dr. Phibes* was also truly my gateway drug to a lifelong obsession with 1920s-1930s jazz, swing, and big band music. At that age, I was starved for elegance, and *Dr. Phibes* was just the ticket.

As an adolescent, I wouldn't have killed *nine* times, like Dr. Phibes himself, to have all the rich background information in this book about one of my all-time favorite fictional characters and the arcane imaginations that brought him to life, but I would have maybe knocked *one* person off to get it. And, as I matured, I realized that, though murder wasn't required to thoroughly understand and appreciate the undead genius Anton Phibes, a lot of digging *was*.

In the pre-Internet era, as I sought out the few substantial articles or interviews related to *The Abominable Dr. Phibes* and its sequel, *Dr. Phibes Rises Again,* that were available, I found scattered material that seldom even remotely answered my questions. Those articles usually focused almost exclusively on the films' star, Vincent Price. I can't quibble but so much since Price was a magnificent actor and human being, but there were many other major contributors to the Phibes films whose work remained an enticing mystery to me. *Who the hell are Robert Fuest and this genius art director, Brian Eatwell? I kept wondering. And why hasn't anyone done a long interview with Trevor Crole-Rees, the makeup artist who gave Phibes his unique*

Dr. Phibes with one of his trademark Art Nouveau designs. Art director Brian Eatwell brought one of these silkscreen designs home, according to his daughter.

The author and Phibes' papa William Goldstein pose with a Phibes bust by makeup artist John Goodwin.

skull-like look? And these screenwriters, William Goldstein and James Whiton—have they just vanished?

Sigh . . .

So I hunted and scavenged and scoured, seldom finding what I was after. I squirreled away what little information on the series I could find for years, stunned by their lack of comprehensive coverage. (A notable exception is a respectable article in *Monsterscene* magazine from the late 1990s.) So I eventually befriended *Dr. Phibes*' director (and uncredited co-screenwriter) Bob Fuest and his collaborators and picked their brains as much as I could about the series' minutiae. Over time, I also began making archival visits that revealed fascinating new layers of the real-life Phibes saga.

In 2012, I discovered that editor Dick Klemensen was planning a Dr. Phibes issue of his *Little Shoppe of Horrors* magazine and immediately emailed him about writing a making-of article on the original film. Dick green-lighted the piece, and I was off and running. Bob Fuest had passed away before I began the article in earnest, but screenwriters Goldstein and Whiton graciously assisted me in my research, and other *Phibes* vets followed suit.

I also discovered that my deep affection for Dr. Phibes wasn't unique. The doc's other fans included directors Ken Russell, Frank Darabont, and Tim Burton, screenwriters Stanley Weiser and Alan Spencer, and even the late Marty Feldman and Peter Sellers. Quentin Tarantino programmed *The Abominable Dr. Phibes* five times in April and May, 2017 at his theater, the New Beverly; several times, it played with *The House That Dripped Blood*, recreating the double bill that Tarantino initially saw it on. In the Academy Award-nominated comedy hit *The Big Sick* (2017), star/co-author Kumail Nanjiani built a scene around introducing and showing *Dr. Phibes* to his girlfriend in the film. In July, 2017, Nanjiani Tweeted with director Edgar Wright: "Once both our insanities are done, we host Phibes screening. We'll pre-record audio of intro & stand still holding stethoscopes to our necks"—a reference to Phibes' signature neck-jack. In September, 2017, Andrew Muschietti, director of the enormously successful horror film *It* (2017), Tweeted that "every shot in *Dr. Phibes*" were among the most terrifying things he saw as a child. Stephen King joked on Facebook in January, 2018 that the phrase "doctor recommended" in commercials always called Dr. Phibes to mind for him. The *Telegraph* recently voted *Dr. Phibes* #17 on its list of the Greatest Horror Films Ever Made. The Museum of Modern Art screened *Dr. Phibes* in February, 2018. Perhaps most delicious of all—literally and figuratively-- in 2015, Vincent Price's daughter, Victoria, toured with the film throughout the Alamo Drafthouse chain, offering "*The Abominable Dr. Phibes* Feast"—a meal at each screening to tie-in with the re-release of her parents' cookbook. Phibes remains a key role model to folks with a respect for healthy dementia everywhere. End of digression.

My original *Dr. Phibes* article ran in *Little Shoppe of Horrors*' Phibes issue, #29; that piece was later a runner-up for a Rondo Award for best magazine article, and it led to my providing the audio commentary for the American BluRay release of *Dr. Phibes*, part of the Rondo Award-winning *Vincent Price Collection* box set. Just as importantly, it helped draw other hardcore Phibes enthusiasts out of the woodwork; as the estimable film historian Preston Jones says,

"The best way to start researching a film book is to publish it." If you build an Art Deco palace with a clockwork band, they will come.

Here you have the dark fruits of my labors—an expanded version of my original article, a new article on the making of *Dr. Phibes Rises Again*, an extended version of David Taylor and Sam Irvin's article on the unfilmed Phibes sequels, two short pieces by Phibes enthusiast Mark Ferelli, and longer versions of my previously-published Fuest and Eatwell profiles. Since my making-of article originally ran, I've acquired many rare and unpublished images related to the good doctor, some of which are reproduced here for the first time, to my knowledge, in print.

Even after endless viewings and research so far-reaching I'm convinced I'm as batshit crazy as Dr. Phibes himself, I never tire of *The Abominable Dr. Phibes*. Its bizarre vision of an exquisite Jazz Age dreamworld, its flawless cast, fantastic musical score, volcanic romance, and seamless blending of pathos and farce make it a masterpiece, in my book—literally: THIS book. That the film's creators became dear and trusted friends makes my appreciation of and affection for Phibes all the sweeter. I hope that everyone who loves the good doctor's elegant mayhem as much as I do will enjoy this book immensely.

And though I don't spend nearly as much time fantasizing about Dr. Phibes' ballroom as I did when I was thirteen . . . I'd still love to live there.

-Justin Humphreys
Highgate Cemetery
2018.

Chapter I
The Kind of Fiend Who Wins: The Making of *The Abominable Dr. Phibes* (1971)

By Justin Humphreys

"... He becomes almost a figure out of some remote past; of tragic dignity and of immeasurable suffering."
– *From James Whiton and William Goldstein's screenplay* The Curses of Dr. Phibes.

AUTHOR'S NOTE: I almost never write articles as exhaustive and labor-intensive as this one, but *The Abominable Dr. Phibes* merits special attention for personal reasons. This article originally appeared in *Little Shoppe of Horrors* magazine #29 (October, 2012). Prior to that, much had been written about the film, but most of it was basically fixated on Vincent Price and Vincent Price alone. Long before I agreed to write this piece for *Little Shoppe*, I was already writing it, intent as I was on preserving the film's history. It seemed as if no one would cover the fascinating details of the film's production design or follow the windy path of its script's development (and they are probably the saner for it). (Some major exceptions to this are Lucy Chase Williams' *The Complete Films of Vincent Price* and English author Laurie Ede's phenomenal essay on the *Dr. Phibes* films in her *British Production Design*. Luckily, I was able to get a copy of Edie's essay to *Dr. Phibes*' director, Robert Fuest, only weeks before his death in 2012– neither he nor his family, nor the family of his art director, Brian Eatwell, had ever seen it. I tried to let Ede's prose set the tone for this article.)

Judging by the outstanding reader response, I am satisfied with this piece. I was deeply gratified to receive comments like the following from Price's biographer Lucy Chase Williams: "Justin Humphreys' exhaustive mini-book on *The Abominable Dr. Phibes* is, and will remain, the definitive work on the subject."

Screenwriter Stanley Weiser (*Wall Street*, *W*): "Your magazine-- or, more aptly, book-- on *Dr. Phibes* is quite remarkable. I've rarely seen such a definitive study of a movie anthologized and written with such passion and painstaking detail . . . I did see *Phibes* again about a month ago and it is one of those films that always yields some new delightful pleasures upon viewing again."

Dave Elsey: "This book is an absolute must have item for anyone interested in the Dr. Phibes movies! These unique Vincent Price films are a carnival ride of Comedy, murder, art Deco and revenge. And if that list sounds like an incredibly rich mixture, it is!

"There's some very strange people practicing medicine these days, Find out just how strange in this incredible celebration . . ."

Dr. Phibes' co-creator/co-author William Goldstein's praise was equally effusive: "Wow . . . Wow . . . and WOW!!! What a fine piece of work. You have done Dr. Phibes proud, Justin! . . . Your article matches the top level scientific journals in its attention to detail - without sacrificing the flow of the narrative."

I have expanded the original with more new *Phibes* material to feast on. Enjoy!

A FURTHER NOTE TO THE READER: I recommend that anyone who hasn't seen *The Abominable Dr. Phibes*, or hasn't seen it recently, watch the film before reading this article. Many spoilers lie ahead...

The Abominable Dr. Phibes is an anomaly of the best kind. No film has a mood quite like it. In a way, it's like Mozart: heavy, but light. Its story veers wildly between black comedy, romance, and Grand Guignol gore in bizarre and delicate ways that shatter the constraints of the horror film. It plays like an experimental combination of *The Phantom of the Opera* and Poe's "The Raven," conceived by a French New Wave director. (But *The Abominable Dr. Phibes* couldn't be French-- it's *so* British.) *Dr. Phibes* (as it will be referred to from hereon in) is an Art Deco horror comedy– a sub-sub-genre as distinctive and rare as the film itself, and, in its own perverse way, one of the most romantic films imaginable.

For those unfamiliar with *Dr. Phibes*, its plot goes like this: in 1925 London, an independently wealthy, suave, brilliant, and severely deranged organist/theologian/inventor, Dr. Anton Phibes, vengefully murders the medical team that he blames for failing to save his wife, Victoria, on the operating table four years earlier. Phibes' background in theology gives him a twisted inspiration. He has nine intended victims, which, including Phibes himself, adds up to ten– the same number of biblical curses visited upon one of the Pharoahs (thought to be Ramses II). Those curses, the G'Tach, become the theme of Phibes' series of skewed killings. With faultless precision, Phibes and his assistant Vulnavia eliminate the doctors, baffling Scotland Yard every gory step of the way. His rampage builds to a final confrontation with the medical team's chief surgeon, Dr. Vesalius, and the revelation of Phibes' own hideously disfigured face.

Dr. Phibes may seem like a pastiche– of its star, Vincent Price's, films (particularly *House of Wax*), and the various versions of *The Phantom of the Opera* and *Ten Little Indians*, among other things. It has elements of Sax Rohmer's Fu Manchu novels, ranging from its title (akin to *The Insidious Dr. Fu Manchu*, etc.) to its titular murderous mastermind's ability to cleverly exterminate his enemies, outwit the police, and escape in the end.

The film might seem like some kind of homage, but its director, the late Robert Fuest, and its co-author and creator, William Goldstein, deny having any such conscious intentions. It was made at a time when directors predominately forged their own images rather than cherry-picking other directors' work, and though *Dr. Phibes* definitely plays on familiar horror tropes, it represents something wildly fresh, distinctive, and unprecedented. What Fuest had helped do for the espionage genre in tv's "The Avengers," he did for horror with *Dr. Phibes*.

Few films, horror or otherwise, have barrage audiences with such an endless string of never-before-combined (and never-again-combined) ingredients, such as a life-size clockwork band, gorgeous Art Deco sets, Mendelssohn blasting from a red neon organ, a doctor impaled on a brass unicorn head, archaic stag movies, John Donne's love poetry, and the sexiest assistant any mad doctor ever had. *Dr. Phibes* is an antiquarian's madcap dream-- a wildly romantic, singularly bizarre conglomeration of elements culled from some of the best of 20th century design and the collective pulp unconscious. It's a ridiculously funny *Weird Tales* story illustrated by Max Ernst, or like Rube Goldberg collaborating with Edward Gorey. (Ernst's presence in particular is deeply felt in the film. "Of course Bob loved Max Ernst," director Robert Fuest's widow says. "He didn't choose to go down that particular road himself, but you can imagine how much he was influenced by him in his films." Ernst's collages of monsters, mayhem, and lust invading polite English drawing rooms are very much in-synch with *Dr. Phibes'* innately irrational set pieces.)

Dr. Phibes is a film of wild polarities-- full of deep pathos and pure farce, utmost refinement and grotesque violence, Brontean romance and lurid horror-- but one that does justice to all of these extremes. Its mood swings are reminiscent of similar frantic shifts in tone in Francois Truffaut's *Shoot the Piano Player* (1962). Like *Dr. Phibes*, Truffaut's film wittily, comically toyed with the conventions of its genre– in its case, gangster movies-- while still remaining true to its story's central heartbreaking romance.

Dr. Phibes is closer still in spirit to Georges (*Eyes Without a Face*) Franju's *Judex*– the two movies would make a perfect double feature. Set in a similar '20s milieu, *Judex* deals with a masked, vengeful mastermind. Both films are loaded with curveball plot twists and even prominently feature scenes where their elegantly dressed protagonists wear ornate bird masks to costume balls. Judex's masked ball has the dreamlike, delicate beauty of the brief interludes where the Dr. Phibes' lovely girl Friday, Vulnavia, dances gracefully across his ballroom.

In one of his final interviews, Vincent Price himself eloquently described *Dr. Phibes'* tone, which kidded his own onscreen persona: "It's like operetta," Price told Michael Orlando Yaccarino. "Gilbert and Sullivan couldn't have existed if 'serious' opera hadn't because it's a take-off, a send-up of Grand Opera. Their operettas are hysterically funny, but divinely beautiful at the same time."

But perhaps what really lodges the film in viewers' minds is its uncompromising commitment to weirdness. Almost all of its ingredients contribute to its all-pervading abnormality, from the loony accoutrements of Phibes' murders, to the costumes (Phibes' bizarre hooded cloaks/robes; Vulnavia's saris), to its characters' unforgettable names: Vesalius, Kitaj, etc. *Dr. Phibes* is lavish, melancholic, visually stunning, unique, dark, stylish, musical, haunting, and hilarious. It succeeds at simultaneously being so many things because of its exceptional cast and crew, including its stars (particularly Price and Joseph Cotten); screenwriters James Whiton and William Goldstein; cameraman Norman Warwick; art director Brian Eatwell; composer Basil Kirchin; and others . . .

But none more so than its director, Robert Fuest.

THE DIRECTOR:

The thread that bound every aspect of the late Robert Fuest's life together was art. After serving in the military and studying art at Wimbledon and Hornsey, every job that he took was somehow artistic. While in his twenties, his paintings were exhibited to some acclaim, and he taught at the Southampton College of Art. Among his major influences as a painter were Ben Shahn, who Fuest described as "My god" during his art school days, and Edward Hopper. Among filmmakers, Fuest admired John Cassavettes, particularly his loose style, and his films' calm stretches, which masked deep darkness.

Fuest began his career in film as an art director for London's ABC TV between 1957 and 1962. It was there that he first befriended Brian Eatwell, who in time would contribute immeasurably to Fuest's feature films. Fuest's first real breakthrough was as a designer on "The Avengers"– the series' inventive stylishness would set the tone for much of his directorial career. It also forced him to use his limited budgets judiciously, but in wildly creative ways– the show demanded minimalism at its inventive best. Fuest left the series, and designed and directed TV commercials (several of which were photographed by future director Nicolas Roeg, and others directed by Richard Lester). He later returned to "The Avengers" to direct.

In a February, 1971 interview Fuest, told Syd Cassyd: "Using television as my training ground, I learned my lesson of handling the camera, the crew, and castas tools of production. We had a ten-day schedule and I used the rehearsal method with the cast, sending the crew off until we were set, and then shooting."

Fuest's feature film career began with a very stylish and little-seen sexy British pop comedy, *Just Like a Woman* (1967). He followed that with one more aligned with the future progression of his career– a sunstruck thriller, *And Soon the Darkness* (1970), produced by Brian Clemens of "The Avengers" and his partner, Albert Fennell. But Fuest's breakout hit was an adaptation of Emily Bronte's *Wuthering Heights* for American International Pictures.

Fuest offered a much-needed infusion of new blood to AIP's talent pool. When AIP hired Fuest, director Michael Reeves (*Witchfinder General*) was dead. The studio's one-time horror mainstay, Roger Corman, had long since departed from the genre, and was about to part ways with AIP itself. Two of AIP's few horror specialists at the time were the talented Curtis Harrington and the almost inevitably bland Gordon Hessler, whose films, Fuest said, were "As subtle as an air raid." Under Hessler's direction, AIP's seemingly endless Edgar Allan Poe series was limping to a close. With his jungle of hair, loony (and infectious) sense of humor, frantic energy, and vast artistic talent, Fuest was about to reanimate the studio's horror output.

In 1960, Corman had lifted AIP's artistic reputation by filming Poe's work to great popular and critical acclaim, and, in 1970, Fuest performed the same service with his *Wuthering Heights*. Unlike AIP's standard fare, *Wuthering Heights* had no chain-whippings or acid-tripping– all of its hell-raising was strictly literary and, like its deceptive G-rating, was acceptable to more refined audiences. "In one fell swipe," critic Stefan Kaufer wrote in *Time*, "[AIP] has disavowed its sleazy origins, bypassed the grindhouses, and landed the distributors' dream." The film was "a moderate hit," according to Samuel Z. Arkoff's son, Lou, and became AIP's first film to play at Radio City Music Hall.

Lou Arkoff continues: "[AIP's staff] were always looking for trends to create franchises." In this case, they hoped to cash in on the success of Franco Zefferelli's *Romeo and Juliet* (1968) and potentially create a series of romances for young audiences based on literary classics. That they didn't have to pay the classics' authors a dime was a major incentive. "Starting with Poe," Lou Arkoff says, "public domain was gold."

Though AIP produced his breakthrough films, Fuest had very mixed feelings about the studio, and was cynical about their cultural aspirations. "Listen," Fuest said, "the thing is ... If [AIP] were making [money on] hubcaps, they'd make more hubcaps ... When I made *Wuthering Heights*, the producers at AIP hadn't read the book. They'd read the comic, but they hadn't read the book."

Fuest learned an important lesson on *Wuthering Heights*: AIP had no interest in making lengthy films, and the film passed the two-hour mark, so they sheered over forty minutes off it. Neophyte director that he was, Fuest didn't realize that the film would appear overlong to his producers. His subsequent AIP movies were all significantly tighter. (Sadly, a *Wuthering Heights* restoration seems unlikely. Fuest, for one, didn't own a complete print.)

Though Fuest was badly disappointed by AIP's cut of his film, he remained philosophical. "He hated it," Jane Fuest recalls. "He was very upset about it because he thought he'd made a really good film ... He was upset about it, but he wasn't a bitter person. It happened. He lived his life– things happen. It was one of the most wonderful things about

James Whiton and William Goldstein, photographed by R.B. Kitaj. (Courtesy of Lem Dobbs.)

him and also one of the most annoying things about him: he didn't get angry about stuff... Because he thought, 'I've done that. I'm the hired gun,' he'd say. 'It's their thing'... He wasn't interested in power at all. He was like that with his paintings. Once he'd finished something, it went out– people would buy it and he was happy if it made them happy and he was pleased to know who they were and everything, but it was theirs, then."

Around that time, AIP wanted Fuest to write and probably direct an adaptation of Hawthorne's *The House of the Seven Gables*, perhaps as a youth romance, or maybe a vehicle for their resident horror star Vincent Price, or both. (The project was announced in AIP's 1971 preview book, along with *Dr. Phibes*.) "Smashing story," Fuest recalled. "I got paid– I did a screenplay for that, which was never made ... Good story. Wonderful ... It was a nice script, actually, and had some nice little tricks in it, sort of twists, which I was very fond of. Never mind-- they paid me ...These things that they do ..." Fuest noted, perhaps facetiously, that his producer at AIP hadn't read Hawthorne's novel either.

Wuthering Heights, however, though successful, didn't pan out as the hit of Shakespearean proportions that AIP hoped it would be. "It was too British" for many American viewers, Lou Arkoff says. "It didn't resonate with the kids." Samuel Z. Arkoff often complained that many movies were killed popularly by their second act, when character development often overtakes exploitable action. To AIP, *Wuthering Heights* was *mostly* "second act." Fuest's *The House of Seven Gables* was never to be, nor were other films in a potential series of p.d. titles like *Les Miserables*, *Camille*, and even *Return to Wuthering Heights*. Something far more important was, though.

But as indelibly as Fuest would impact *Dr. Phibes*, in the beginning, were the words ...

THE SCRIPT

In 1969, *The Curses of Dr. Pibe*, a recently-completed script by novice screenwriters James Whiton and William Goldstein, reached American International Pictures through a real estate developer-cum-producer named Ronald Dunas. James Whiton took the

*William Goldstein (as "Rex Lode") poses on the cover of his and James Whiton's pre-*Dr. Phibes *satire.*

script to agent Paul Leserman. "He and Ron were friends," Goldstein says. "Ron, early on, became involved as one of the producers to put money into it." (Prior to that, Whiton says, his former agent, Red Hershon, had taken the script to AIP earlier that year and they had turned it down. Goldstein doesn't recall this.)

"George A. Bloom," Whiton writes, "the A for Arthur, was the singular Columbus in the discovery of *Phibes*. A very fine fellow with a great antic wit and a marvelous mind, Bloom was the one who brought *Phibes* to life at AIP . . . The script had been previously rejected when Contemporary Artists represented it. It was then submitted again by agent Paul Leserman. And Bloom had just come onboard as the new story editor. He loved it and put it on the fast track.

"Without George A Bloom there would have been no Anton Phibes."

"What happened was," Dunas recalled, "I was working with an agent, and the agent brought me the script. And I was very enthusiastic about it. And it felt to me like it was an AIP kind of picture. So I brought it over there and they liked it a lot and we did it." Dunas added that he "knew [James] Whiton . . . I didn't know Goldstein, I never met him, but I met the other guy."

An AIP kind of picture, their peculiarly Gothic script was: the studio, run by Samuel Z. Arkoff and James H. Nicholson, had famously had a long run of very lucrative horror films based on Edgar Allan Poe's short stories starring Vincent Price.

Dunas' career in film and television was, and remains, limited, including small acting roles in *Seconds* (1966) and *Shampoo* (1975). "Well," Dunas says, "I haven't done a hell of a lot. I did a couple of tv movies and [*Dr. Phibes*] was the biggest one that I did. And that's about it. I originally was at Fox when [Darryl] Zanuck was there and I did some stuff at that time. And then I got a hold of this picture and brought it to AIP . . ." In June, 1969, *Variety* reported that Dunas was scheduled to produce screenwriter Anne Edwards's script of her own Gothic potboiler *The Survivors*.

"As I recall, that was a long time ago, I knew one of the owners [James H. Nicholson]," Dunas explains. "And I had submitted another project to him. He liked it but didn't want to do it– it wasn't his thing. But he told me to keep him in mind. So my agent gave me the script and I brought it over there and they decided to do it … They loved it. So we decided to do it in London and we did it on the cheap. The whole picture cost $500,000." (Robert Fuest verified this figure; James Whiton says that on AIP statements that he received, the budget was $776,000.)

AIP's Head of Production in England, Louis "Deke" Heyward, was also brought on as a producer. Heyward, who had overseen Fuest's *Wuthering Heights*, backs up Dunas' story: "A fellow by the name of Ron Dunas found the script … and brought it to Jim."

"It caught on very quickly at AIP," William Goldstein recalled, "and within six months after they had the first look, they were in preproduction. They picked it up with the idea that there would be a series– we were told in the beginning perhaps five pictures."

As to Dunas' contributions to the film, Heyward said: "Ron was a very wealthy guy who fancied himself a patron of the arts. He may or may not have put some money into *Dr. Phibes*; they shipped him over to England and told me to treat him nicely. I found him a source of difficulty on the set." (What Heyward meant precisely by "source of difficulty," he didn't elaborate on.) In a later interview with Christopher Koetting, Heyward added, "Dunas and the other writers had nothing to do with [the script]. Dunas gave us so many problems that I requested he leave the set and he went back home."

In his later years, Fuest was dismissive of his producers. Of Dunas, Fuest said "All he wanted to do was play tennis." Fuest was far less sanguine in describing Heyward: "'Deke' Heyward was what we over here would call 'a wanker.'" Heyward had a history of mangling AIP's films, including *War-Gods of the Deep* (1965) and *Wuthering Heights*. Fuest and his colleagues also noted Heyward's incessant on-set boasting about his "war record," to the point where one of them remarked to Fuest, "If you think about all of the things that Deke did in the war, it must have lasted 25 years."

Patrick Tilley, screenwriter of Fuest's *Wuthering Heights*, recalls: "I wouldn't say Deke was a 'wanker' (e.g.: tosspot/jerkoff) but while he could summon up an imposing, all-powerful presence I felt he was essentially a lightweight who did as little work as possible - his main job was ringing up Sam and Jim at 2:30 a.m. in the morning London time to discuss progress on the various projects going through."

Heyward's accounts of *Dr. Phibes*' development were full of self-aggrandizing claims about his major contributions to the production, which should be taken with a gigantic block of salt, not just a grain. None of the film's other major contributors or any of the extent paperwork indicates that Heyward made any notable contributions to the film.

THE CREATORS

Most of *Dr. Phibes*' fabulously eccentric ideas, its "straight" dialogue, and its overarching structure originate with its creators and co-authors, James Whiton and William Goldstein. Born in Troy, New York, Goldstein earned a degree in Chemistry from Columbia University. Their script began life as *The Fingers of Dr. Pibe*, a 17-page treatment that they collaborated on. As of '64, Goldstein says, "The basic elements were there," but it would remain essentially unchanged for approximately the next four years.

"I'm a chemist," Goldstein says. "I worked as a chemist in the department of medicine at UC Medical Center at San Francisco. San Francisco, as you know, is a city of hills– Nob Hill, Telegraph Hill, and so forth. We lived on Mt. Parnassus, a half-block from the Medical Center, which was up on top, and that's where the original *Phibes* story was written."

Goldstein's co-writer was James Whiton, who he had known since they were boyhood "schoolmates together in Troy, New York," Goldstein continues. "We were in the same grade together and we pretty much stayed in touch. And then he went off to school– we went to different schools. But we did stay in touch, actually." In 1963, Whiton and Goldstein collaborated on a novel (under the pseudonyms "Dr. Boyd Boylan" and "Dr. Rex Lode") entitled *The Third Eye of America*, which was published by Lyle Stuart Press. (They are even pictured on the novel's dust jacket– Whiton as Boylan and Goldstein and Lode– with bogus mini-biographies underneath.) "It was a satire and it was MENSA's top selection for that year," notes Goldstein. At one point, the two authors got *The Third Eye of America* to Federico Fellini while he was visiting Los Angeles and he showed a passing interest in filming it. (In a 1981 letter to Whiton, Lyle Stuart himself wrote "From time to time we talk about 'The Third Eye' as the worse [sic] disaster we have ever experienced in book publishing!")

Prior to that, Goldstein says, "I don't know how to say this without being cliched-- I took a stab at writing things, but mostly for my own amusement... Jim and I also did a treatment, which started to get some traction, *The Great Big Fat Train Robbery*." Goldstein recalls Whiton as being "Very specific, very careful. Excellent in going over drafts and proofreading. Persistent with ideas. And we worked very well together, not only on the original script," but on the film's various abortive sequels. (Goldstein also received story credit, solo, on *The Amazing Dobermans* (1976).)

The idea for *Dr. Phibes*, Goldstein recalls, "Came to me in a dream. It was [called] *Dr. Pibe* at that time and the Dr. Pibe in my dream could fix things. And from that dream, I spent some time developing the story. I had the elements in the dream, but then I developed the story. And that was written pretty much whole-cloth from my office-bedroom on Hillway– that was the name of the street in San Francisco. We had a view from my room of the Golden Gate, which if you know anything about San Francisco, that's the channel under the Golden Gate Bridge: very deep and very cold, and at night the foghorns would blow. It was lovely." Whiton recalls them writing the treatment together between October and November, 1963. Goldstein, however, said on one occasion that the script was written between 1964 and 1965, and has produced a Writers Guild of America West statement that lists *The Fingers of Dr. Pibe* as having been registered on March 29, 1965 by Whiton. (The title was changed to *The Curses of Dr. Pibe* in 1969.) However, Goldstein has also said, "I was doing a lot of history reading at that time, 1963, which is when the original story was written." *Fingers* . . . was typed-up by Elinor Little, an editor of medical journals who had previously typed the manuscript of *The Third Eye of America*.

According to Goldstein, taking a campy approach didn't interest either him or Whiton: "The intent (to make light of Phibes' love for his Victoria) was never there. His was a sentimental 19th century love for a woman half his age. Played straight, it would come off as mawkish, so we used certain markers-- John Donne's poetry, for example-- and Vincent [Price] ran with them [in the film version]. The early reviews picked up on the campiness but no one has ever doubted the depth of Phibes' feelings for his Victoria."

The character Dr. Phibes has sometimes been erroneously reported to have been based on the life of Anton LaVey, the high priest of the Church of Satan, who did nothing to dismiss the rumors. Admittedly, there were certain superficial similarities between the two (LaVey was an organist, for openers, and built life-size tableaus in his house vaguely akin to Phibes' Casino de Monte Carlo set.), and LaVey later appeared in one of Robert Fuest's movies, *The Devil's Rain* (1975). And though LaVey lived in San Francisco at the same time as Goldstein, Goldstein is quick to quash any connection between the two Antons: "I never met nor spoke to Mr. LaVey. His claims are, to use your words, 'patently false'." Whiton adds, "That's total nonsense. I've never even heard of the guy [LaVey]." Interviewer Anthony Petkovich asked Fuest if LaVey was in any way an inspiration for Phibes, and Fuest—who struck up a friendship with LaVey while they were making *The Devil's Rain*—also said that LaVey in no way, shape, or form inspired or influenced the character. *Dr. Phibes* eventually wound up on the Church of Satan's Approved Movies List. And, no, the fact that the film was retitled *El Satanico Dr. Pibe*—*The Satanic Dr. Pibe*—in Mexico has nothing to do with LaVey, either!)

Aside from his background in medicine, other elements from Goldstein's life heavily shaped *Dr. Phibes*. The film has an obvious affection for English culture; when asked about this, Goldstein replies, "I read a lot, and English authors are among my favorite . . . I was doing a lot of history reading at that time, 1963, which is when the original story was written."

As for the film's religious themes, Goldstein explains, "I was a Sunday School teacher for a while in my teenage years, so I was fairly conversant with the Bible. And, of course, Exodus is a strong story to begin with and if you watch *The Ten Commandments*–

which had Vincent Price, by the way, in a cameo role– it's pretty well laid-out there."

Even Whiton's and Goldstein's friends crept into their fictional world. A major murder victim, Dr. Kitaj, was named after Ronald B. Kitaj, an exceptional fine artist and literally one of the 20th century's best draftsmen. "Ron, Jim Whiton, and I were high school buddies," Goldstein says. "He was an all-around man and a wonderful conversationalist. He settled in Westwood here [in Los Angeles] and we used to spend several hours once a week just catching up. So we were very close friends."

The authors not only paid homage to Kitaj, but to Kitaj's son, Lem. Born Anton Lemuel Kitaj, Lem was the namesake of Dr. Phibes himself, as well as Vesalius' son, Lem. "Ron Kitaj was a bit edgy when Phibes was released," Goldstein continues, "because his career was going full-bore in the '70s, but not so his teenage son, Lem, last seen on the O.R. gurney [in the film], who got huge bragging rights for his screen 'debut'." Lem was later revived in Goldstein's and Whiton's abortive *Dr. Phibes* sequel: "In *Phibes Resurrectus*, Lem, now a horribly-scarred young man in his 20's, is Phibes worthy adversary." Ironically, Lem Kitaj became a screenwriter himself under the *nom de plume* "Lem Dobbs." (A brief digression: One of the film's main characters, Tom Schenley, was apparently named by Robert Fuest: Elstree Studios, where both *Dr. Phibes* films were made, is on *Shenley* Road in Hertfordshire! Shenley is also a small village near Elstree.)

Goldstein also observes that "'Anton' has a Continental flair - [actor] Anton Walbrook, [composer] Anton Karras and, of course, Mr. Chekhov." In *The Curses of Dr. Pibe*, Pibe/Phibes' first name is never mentioned, and instead belonged to Dr. Anton Vesalius. Vesalius' name, by the way, is lifted from Andreas Vesalius, a pioneering 16th century anatomist and doctor. Though Pibe and Phibes are fictional, "Phibbs" is an actual name.

Lem Kitaj, who has since gone on to a very successful screenwriting career with films like *Dark City* (1998) and *The Limey* (1999) to his credit, offers his own memories of his appearance (of sorts) in the film and his father's relationship with Whiton and Goldstein:

I must have known beforehand that they were using our names as characters, but only because I don't remember that coming as a surprise when we saw the movie. We were living in LA the year it was released -- my dad a visiting professor of art that academic year, 1970/71, at UCLA-- so we went to see it at an LA theater when new. Don't recall which particular one it would have been at that time. I remember Jim/Bill going to the premiere -- which I think was a kitschy/campy Old Hollywood-style event in keeping with the film's style? I guess I was amused/excited to be connected to an actual movie in any way, even as an in-joke. In my whole life only one person ever noticed, though -- some other kid at the American School in London coming up to me after it had been shown on television the night before. Jim was my dad's closest friend from high school -- as recounted, they shipped out together in the Merchant Marine, lost virginity together, etc. Bill, though without that special bonding experience, virtually as close -- and more so once more at the end of my father's life, when living in LA again, after both had suffered loss-- widowers, etc.-- and enjoyed weekly visits, heart-to-hearts, two old guys with a lot of water under the bridge. But during that fun year in early '70s, we saw Jim and Bill, with his large extended family, and their other close pal from Troy High School (upstate NY), David Ward, who also ended up in Hollywood to try and make it in the movies, constantly. (See article in "Slate" online about my script "Edward Ford"). I'm sure my dad found use of my/his name equally amusing over the years. Was there some hint of slight discomfort or annoyance at first? I don't really think so, or remember any such thing, can't think why he'd have cared one way or another. When I briefly met Vincent Price on the set of *Theater of Blood*, I was probably too shy to mention that I was the "original" Anton -- if it even occurred to me I might.

But there was a single event in Goldstein's life– at the time, bitterly recent-- that most shaped *Dr. Phibes'* raw intensity: "I was a recent widower, and that was the background." Goldstein channeled his deep sadness at the tragic loss of his wife into poetic form– he created the ultimate grief-stricken widower. Dr. Phibes became, along with Boris Karloff's Im-Ho-Tep in *The Mummy* (1932), horror's great incurable romantic. (Interestingly, in the finished film, Phibes' adversary, Dr. Vesalius, has a son, but his wife is never seen or referred to, perhaps implying that he is a widower, as well.)

There are also obvious parallels between Dr. Phibes and several of Edgar Allan Poe's key works. James Whiton's father was a lawyer and his mother was a librarian, so he was frequently exposed to books as a boy. In his youth, one of Whiton's favorite works was a folio edition of Poe's "The Raven," as well as Poe's "Annabel Lee." Whiton concedes that these two poems' narrators and the dead lovers that they inconsolably pine for subconsciously influenced *Dr. Phibes*.

"What many have claimed to be– other than the love story– the key ingredient of the [first] Phibes film," Goldstein says, "is that it has a . . . death geometry . . . I just went over my material in my library– it was in the original script, which was written in 1967 and it was presented in a final draft to AIP in 1969. In that original story we had the G'Tach." (Whiton does not recall the script having been written in 1967.) The film's presentation of the G'Tach deviated from the original order: certain plagues were presented out of the original sequence, and others (the Plague of Pestilence, the Plague of Lice and Flies) were altered outright. This poses the question: How could someone as methodical– and with a degree in theology, no less- get the plagues out of order? Well, he *is* insane . . .

As has been previously noted, the film's plot bears similarities to certain literary works– Agatha Christie's *And Then There Were None*, Rohmer's Fu Manchu novels, etc.– and movies like *House of Wax*, Goldstein denies these being conscious. "I can't say that I had," he says. "Let me put [this in a] framework: I was a practicing chemist, and from a workaday point of view, my concentration was on that. I also had four kids to feed and I had recently remarried. Although I read and do read a lot, I can't pick out anything that influenced it, other than history . . . British military history." Goldstein and Whiton wrote few produced scripts after *Dr. Phibes*.

The Fingers Of Dr. Pibe varied wildly from subsequent versions of the story– it takes place in contemporary Manhattan, for starters-- but many of the basic elements were there. For openers, Dr. Pibe (no first name) commits a series of bizarre murders with his gorgeous accomplice, who is referred to simply as "Pibe's female assistant." (She is described as a gorgeous, blonde, "tall Amazon-type girl.") Pibe is obsessed with clockwork figures: his assistant is a complex wind-up figure, he has a clockwork orchestra, and his lair features a clockwork battle scene featuring groups of "horrible looking one-foot high mechanical soldiers of the 18th century variety" who gorily slaughter each other for his amusement. Pibe's waltz around his ballroom to the strains of his clockwork band are described very much like what would wind up (no pun intended) on-screen years later.

Even at this earliest stage in the script's development, Pibe/Phibes is hideously disfigured and at his dressing table applies false features (which, in this version, melt in high heat at inopportune moments)– the description of his face would remain almost verbatim through several versions of the story: "a surfaceless balloon of scar tissue." Pibe has a dead wife, Lady Pibe, and a portrait of her that he worships by candlelight. Another major character, Priscille Dakin, bears a strong resemblance to the late Lady Pibe, which figures into the storyline. Pibe's voice is described as "mechanically chilling and eerie as he talks through a throat box."

However, Pibe's/Phibes' murders have no overarching structure and there is no mention of the G'Tach, the ancient Egyptian plagues–Pibe's victims are many and seemingly random. He kills an old man, a garbage truck driver, blows up a jetplane, and burns down a theater. Oddest of all, Pibe's M.O. is mainly balloons adorned with images of his victims' faces, which he fills with irradiated seeds and then bursts over his targets! Pibe dispatches one of the protagonists, Dakin, with a sword cane. The film's finale finds Pibe wrecking his car in a lake, and the police finding no trace of his body. But in the *Dr. Caligari*-like climax, it turns out that the events of the story have all been a madman's delusions: living in an insane asylum, we see Pibe playing with a miniature theater full of dolls, and surrounded by doctors and nurses who resemble the story's various characters. (The 2018 British horror film *Ghost Stories* used a similar conceit.)

As for the titular fingers, Whiton explains that the inspiration came to him while he was working at Dow Chemicals in San Francisco: "One day after work on [a] streetcar going home and while seated in [the] rear seat by [the] window, a well-dressed businessman of about 45" sat down beside Whiton. "As [the] 1st stop approaches, he begins to furiously spin his fingers before his face. This [was] repeated on [the] 2nd and 3rd stops." Whiton said that he was "quite impressed" by the bizarre display. *Fingers* . . . opens with a similar incident involving Dakin on a train.

The next stage of the script's evolution, entitled *The Curses of Dr. Pibe*, was much closer to what was eventually filmed, but still drastically different, particularly in terms of its seriousness. The opening murder is by bees, not bats. Dr. Vesalius' son has died before the story begins, but, though horribly threatened, he survives the film. Having Pibe/Phibes be a child-killer– and right off the bat, to boot– would have been pushing the story's darkest overtones perhaps too far. Having several murders happen before the film begins was for reasons of "Budget efficiency," William Goldstein says. "Also, too much of a good thing really is too much of a good thing."

A character named Trout figured prominently in the script, but was a reporter dogging the Pibe investigation, not a detective as in Fuest's film. The Plague of Frogs victim is frightened to death by a bunch of frogs– a threat so utterly unthreatening that it was completely changed. (The Plague of Rats in this version also underwent a major shift– more about that, later.)

Phibes' assistant Vulnavia, whose face remains icy through most of the film, here is described as expressing "total tribal lust" when he literally winds her up. With no real explanation, as the film ends, Vulnavia is revealed to be a kind of living corpse, bald and hideously scarred, "her face . . . pocked with deep decaying sores." She lunges at the police, "only to collapse on the floor in a rush of gas."

One of the most notable omissions from later drafts is the array of arcane devices that Pibe has in his observatory, which is "Located on the back half of the top floor" of his home, the script reads, "and as such has a commanding view of London. In it are a large refractory telescope astrolabe, Foucault pendulum, astrological charts, plus a pair of giant gyroscopes mounted in tandem several feet apart." Clad in an "occult robe," Pibe makes the gyroscopes spin wildly and, later, makes things invisible using them. There are several scenes involving these devices, which seem intended perhaps for use in the fulfillment of the Curse of Darkness, but nothing is made of them.

In Dr. Anton Vesalius' first scene, he greets Trout at the Victoria and Albert Museum and gives him a tour of its Chamber of Horrors, whose figures include a Jack the Ripper-like fiend, which is actually Dr. Pibe in disguise, seen watching them. (Close-ups of Pibe's eyes figure heavily into *Dr. Pibe*, as they would in the actual film.) Later, a nun takes a group of schoolchildren on a tour of the Chamber of Horrors and a little girl catches an eerie glimpse of Pibe's maniacal eyes within his disguise. This scene also might have been struck from the script, like several others, because of the excessive ornateness (on an AIP budget, anyway) that building such a set would have required.

Budgetary considerations demanded that various scenes lose some of their grandeur, in particular, the Plague of Locusts: Pibe–disguised in drag (!) as a charlady squirts (not drips) a viscous substance into the nurses' (plural) room, unleashes "tens of thousands of locusts," preceded by a horde of army ants, *ascend* from a hole in the floor (not the ceiling) on and devour the two nurses. When the police discover their remains the next morning, the entire room has been stripped bare, leaving virtually only a "lone lightbulb ... swinging on half-chewed wires." When this scene was eventually shot, only a few dozen locusts attacked Nurse Allen, and seemingly only devoured her face, leaving the rest of the room untouched.

More is made of Pibe's background: he has degrees "in both music and bio-physics." Following Pibe's accident in Switzerland, the Detective on the case, Hill, explains, "A man did turn up several days later in that vicinity with nearly half his face and throat torn away." He is described as being born in Paris, the son of "British nationals" in the banking business. "He was from all reports a very inventive genius," Hill explains, "though somewhat of a recluse and eccentric." A Detective Doheny also reveals that "He apparently was very much a loner." Very nearly all of these details were later scrapped. (Note: At the time of *Dr. Phibes'* release, William Goldstein wrote a novelization that roughly follows the structure of the finished film. However, it is so extensively different from either Whiton and Goldstein's script and the later revised script that to cover it here in detail would require a pages-long synopsis. Originally printed in editions of 50,000 copies each, Goldstein's novelizations of *Dr. Phibes* and its sequel were reprinted in 2012.)

Astonishingly, the treatment and the screenplay that followed told the story of a lunatic killing off nine innocent people and, in spite of treading in this morally murky territory, it managed to make the audience root for the murderer. Viewers inadvertently want to see him pull it off, partly because of the character's tremendous charisma and intelligence and his scorching Phantom of the Opera-like romanticism. But this was nothing new in British cinema– films like *Kind Hearts and Coronets* (1949) had deftly crafted murderous anti-heroes without becoming nihilistic or losing audience identification.

"Whiton and Goldstein were good writers, very competent," "Deke" Heyward said, "but the script had that edge of nastiness. . . Here is a man on a vendetta, killing people. It could have been a gross piece of nastiness… There's a philosophical approach to making a picture of this kind. You're treading a funny middle ground between humor and murder. Precious few pictures have stayed on that tightrope." *Dr. Phibes* would be one of them.

Aside from his recent hit for AIP, Robert Fuest was a logical choice to direct *Dr. Phibes* in other respects. Though their visual styles and tone varied wildly, his *Wuthering Heights* and *Dr. Phibes* bore strong underlying thematic connections. Both were operatic stories about inseparable lovers descending into madness, of love beyond death, and dark, brooding protagonists with major scores to settle. The characters' vows of love and revenge in both films are, at times, almost interchangeable. In *Wuthering Heights*, Nellie the maid tells the vengeful Heathcliff "Let God take vengeance on the wicked!" "Why should he get all the satisfaction?" Heathcliff snarls back. Dr. Phibes would agree. "God," the film's Cathy tells Heathcliff, "I wish I could hold you until we were both dead." Earlier in the film, she wails "I don't just love Heathcliff, I am Heathcliff! All my thoughts, all my actions are for him. He's my only reason for living." Both *Wuthering Heights* and *Dr. Phibes* would conclude with men reunited in the Great Beyond with the women with their true loves.

Fuest had also directed an "Avengers" episode, "Game," starring *Dr. Phibes*' co-star Peter Jeffrey as a rich madman who orchestrates odd murders a la Phibes. And Fuest's *Just Like a Woman* had prominently featured a bizarre polymath, Graff Von Fischer, who is described in the film as "one of the great pre-War eccentrics–equestrian, swordsman, racing driver, architect"– a renaissance man *a la* Anton Phibes.

Though AIP had felt compelled to heavily truncate Fuest's *Wuthering Heights*, he was still very much in their good graces: "I may have done the wrong thing with the film, but it made money, and that is really all that AIP is concerned with. *Wuthering Heights* was a prestigious film for them; it was their first film to have a run at Radio City Music Hall in New York. They were planning to make Vincent Price's 100th film, and I think they liked the line 'From the director of *Wuthering Heights* comes Vincent Price's 100th film!'" (Though AIP eventually touted *Dr. Phibes* as Price's 100th film, it was actually only his 81st.)

In spring, 1970, Fuest said that he received *The Curses of Dr. Pibe* while vacationing in Crete. His first impression of it was "Unreadable." As he told Anthony Petkovich, the script "was something like 400 pages, the size of a phonebook, and made from paper which . . . Do you remember those cheap old pulp magazines which were made from light brown paper with little advertisements in the right-hand corner for diamond rings for five cents? You know what I mean? 'Your prayers answered or your money back, guaranteed'?

"Anyway, that's the kind of paper it was printed on, and it was a huge script and it was just. . . crap. I read it on the beach and thought, 'Oh, God . . .' But at the same time, it was a great idea. So I phoned [James] Nicholson about it." The reason for the script's excessive length was simple: Goldstein, being a novice screenwriter, was unfamiliar with standard script formatting and had typed it double-spaced! (In earlier interviews, Fuest described the script as being "275 pages long! The average script has only about 100!")

However, Fuest's then-wife, Gillian, recalls the script's arrival differently: as she remembers it, it reached Fuest at their home in Teddington. "I remember sitting up in bed with him," Gillian recalls, "and he said 'I've got this script, it's absolutely terrible, but have a read of it.' And we sat up [and read it] and we said, 'Yes, it is terrible,' and then we giggled ... It was like that ... It was just a bit of a joke."

Once he agreed to do the project, Fuest began rewriting it– paring it down to avoid *Wuthering Heights*-like trims. "Actually," Fuest observed, "I think that AIP understood that I had misunderstood what they wanted. This time, they told me they wanted a 90-minute film."

"I met the writers, James and William, once in L.A.," Fuest recalled, "and we went through the script. I don't remember the meeting in detail, but they must have given me a tacit agreement to set about working on a shooting script." Whiton says that he does not recall Goldstein having met Fuest: Goldstein was living in San Diego at the time. Whiton remembers meeting Fuest in L.A. once, however, when they joined AIP's story editor for lunch.

"I kept the basic idea but that's about all. Except for the scene with Hugh Griffith where he mentions 'the G'Tach,' which I lifted word-for-word. I have to admit I still don't know what it means." (Fuest exaggerated: considerably more of their initial script made it into the film.) On May 11, 1970, Whiton and Goldstein signed their contract with American International, which included an agreement that Whiton would rewrite the script according to AIP's and Fuest's notes. Whiton says that he rewrote and polished the script from June to August of that year.

As for his rewrites, Fuest said, "Well, I had to take the first *Dr. Phibes* script and make it appropriate for a normal audience, because Whiton and Goldstein's English was rather Victorian or Edwardian. . . very strange. They were Americans and I met them once, maybe twice, and we got on fine. But on the first *Dr. Phibes* movie, I give them all the credit because, although they didn't write many of the lines, they had the great idea, and for that alone, they deserve all the plaudits." Fuest heavily reshaped the script, particularly the dialogue, but though he would occasionally claim to have invented Phibes' clockwork orchestra and his organ-playing, these elements were all present in Goldstein and Whiton's original version.

"There was also that scene with the fellow up in the airplane being torn apart by rats in flight. Well, it was originally written with him being attacked by a horde of rats on a boat out on the sea, and Dr. Phibes is up on some nearby cliffs, looking at him with a telescope. But I thought, 'That's really dumb, because if the boat is infested with rats, all you really have to do is," Fuest laughed, "jump over the side.' I mean, a guy running up and down the boat shouting 'Rats! Rats!' is ridiculous. But if you have the guy go up in the air being attacked by an army of rats ... Well, where is he going to go?"

Fuest was also unsatisfied with the script's original ending: "In the script, [Phibes] goes up a tower and throws Vulnavia off, and then sets fire to it, and then runs away to a big sports arena, where he's surrounded by police cars, and I think gets away in a balloon or just vanishes or something ... But the whole ending ... it was insane." Goldstein (and contributor Brian Clemens) had no recollection of ever having seen this "balloon" ending because it was written by James Whiton without their involvement, Whiton says.

By the time his revised version was finished, Fuest's instantly recognizable style was apparent throughout the script. Vincent Price perfectly described Fuest's immense talent for off-the-wall humor: "He was one of the funniest men in the world, with a wild, mad sense of the ridiculous ... Bob was really a wickedly funny man and as inventive as they come." Therein came Fuest's first major contribution to *Dr. Phibes*, and one of his most important: "It was dynamite, but totally serious. Wow! I mean, it had it all. . . It was just a trip. I decided that it would work much better as a send-up."

It was Brian Clemens who concocted the wildly inventive, "Avengers"-like climax: "That was happening in A.B.P.C. [Elstree]," Clemens recalled, "where I was stationed, as it were– I had offices there permanently for many years, and Bob is a very close, personal friend. And we got talking over lunch and he said, 'I've got problems with this script,' he said. 'I don't think the ending is right.' So I said, 'Well, let me have a look at the script.' And he did and I studied it and about half an hour later, I went back to him and said, 'Look, Bob, you can do this, this, and this.' And he did, and that solved his problem. He's often told that story," Clemens laughed. Fuest remembered Clemens taking longer than a half-hour, but, either way, he had done an exceptional job. "The operation, the key, the acid. . . was ALL Brian Clemens," Fuest said.

Clemens' partner, Albert Fennell, who had co-produced Fuest's *And Soon the Darkness,* was less sanguine when he read an early version of the script. "...When I got [Fennell] to [read] *Phibes* in Italy," Fuest said, "he said, 'It's rubbish, Bob. It's crap. You can't make a fool out of a [villain]' and he came up with a lot of great cliches about how it would ruin you and all this rubbish." Fuest laughed. "And I said, 'Listen to me, I think we can do it.'"

Almost all of the film's funniest moments emerged from Fuest's alterations, such as the subtly comic interplay between Trout and the Goldsmith, among others. As originally written, for instance, Dr. Lonsgstreet's role is *silent,* and there is no intro to the scene with Mrs. Frawley or her intrusion into his stag film-viewing. Fuest had contributed to a hilarious absurdist comedy series, Peter Cook and Dudley Moore's "Not Only But Also," though to what extent is uncertain. The series' standard bill-of-fair essentially resembled *Dr. Phibes*': quietly bizarre characters dealing with ludicrous situations unflappably. Case in point: the batshit crazy Sir Arthur Streeb-Greebling calmly describing his unstinting efforts to teach ravens to fly underwater.

Fuest's revisions, dated November 17, 1970, feature two excised pages of dialogue and business for Terry-Thomas' randy Dr. Longstreet. In them, Longstreet pours himself a drink and reads his stag movie's title aloud-- "Sin, the Serpent, and Sexy Sara- Part Three"; thoroughly aroused, "he increases the size of his drink in anticipation." Having forgotten her purse, his housekeeper Mrs. Frawley surprises him and asks about the projector. Longstreet stumblingly tells her it's a "Barrel organ"—"One of the dying arts. Relic of a bygone age and all that. . ." She asks him what it plays. "Jolly little roundelays," he replies. She asks to hear one and he nervously begins to crank it: "He cranks the handle and a la Terry-Thomas with teeth and mouth he mimics a musical instrument."

Totally abashed, he notices her purse and goes for it, unwittingly unblocking the projector's lens. He realizes it, contorts his body into a weird position to cover the lens, and begins doing some ludicrous exercises. "Now exercise," he says, "awfully good for the kidneys!" As Frawley leaves, Longstreet, "in a state of near-collapse," reaches for his drink. He finishes eating a chicken and snaps its wishbone, making a wish. "His wish comes true," in the form of Vulnavia. In this version, she actively embraces and kisses him.

Fuest and his cast also loaded the film with classically British asides: "Darkness?" "Yes, Darkness." "Coffee." (Author's Note: Screenwriter Robert Blees, who was soon to be AIP's Story Editor, reportedly had no hand in writing *Dr. Phibes*. William Goldstein says that Blees was not involved and none of the film's major contributors that were interviewed for this article ever mentioned Blees' name.)

The shooting script, titled *The Curses of Dr. Phibes*, is dated October 30, 1970. The pink pages with what appear to be Fuest's rewrites are dated November 4th and 11th, just as shooting was beginning on Monday, November 9th at Elstree. (It wrapped on Wednesday, December 23rd with some pick-up shots.)

Fuest restructured the story and characters, as well as retooling the dialogue. He created classic lines like "Because when the acid reaches him, he will have a face like mine." (The climactic revelation of Phibes' face wasn't in the initial shooting script, which Vincent Price wrote a concerned note about in his personal copy of it. In *The Curses of Dr. Pibe*, Phibes' actual visage is revealed within the first ten minutes!) He also wrote Phibes' speech: "I have no faith in doctors. After my crash I was told that I would never speak. But as you can see I have used my knowledge of music and acoustics to recreate my voice. But I digress. After the last few days I'm sure you've become only too aware of my ingenuity. Now you shall see your son under circumstances which may bring back memories to you." This was later divided into an exchange between Phibes and Vesalius.

Shots and gags were dropped and reworked. For instance, Phibes was originally supposed to be *shown* firing a unicorn head from a catapult. In the scene where Phibes prepares a "black, treacly distillation" that will drip onto Nurse Allan's face, he races into the shrine room, switches the lights fully on, and falls to his knees, "hissing wildly." He then delivers his speech about rejoining her in "a secluded corner of the great Elysian Field of the beautiful beyond. . ." But the scene would have ended with an out-of-place gag that might have worked well at some other point in the story: "He rises swiftly and starts to move away, but is rudely jerked back.

He remembers to unplug himself." Probably the most successful gag in the film became the death-by-unicorn: having lulled the audience into expecting a pattern where each murder is built-up to, the impalement's unexpected suddenness and utter absurdity helped make the gag extremely effective.

The spirit of the film became increasingly apparent in the text over time. In scene 105, Vulnavia assembles the infernal device used in the Curse of Hail, which is described as being composed of "certain pieces of compact machinery, rather exotic in appearance and used for God knows what." (This description was Whiton and Goldstein's.) A scene involving headlines in the papers about Phibes' murders— "LONDON SURGEON IMPALED." "ANCIENT CURSES REENACTED." "ELEPHANT TUSK VICTIM."– and Waverly ranting about them was nixed. So was a close-up of Phibes' tear-streaked face as he walked away from his altar to Victoria. (And the reason that Phibes recites John Donne's "The Good Morrow's" stanzas out of order is because they were simply written that way in the script. Several preceding lines from that poem were originally scripted-in, but removed.)

Hackneyed material was excised, like a "dark and stormy night" opening, and Phibes reciting Elizabeth Barrett Browning's Sonnet 43 ("How do I love thee? Let me count the ways."). Numerous tiny bits of business were jettisoned, like Phibes drinking from a flask as he watches Kitaj's plane plummet. The Rabbi was given one of Phibes' lines about the Curse of Darkness: "To move the earth its final step."

Viewing Fuest's personal script reveals a stream of hand-written notes and revisions where he continually retouched it. This exchange, for instance, was heavily reworked for the film:

Vesalius: "Because of Phibes' familiarity with the G'tach, I presume he's of the Jewish faith."
Trout: "As a matter of fact, he's not. The G'tach is part of the Old Testament. Anyone with a religious background would know about the curses."

Vesalius: "Theology... Hmmmm. That rather nicely explains the curses of the G'Tach." [Which became the line "That rather nicely explains his knowledge of the Old Testament."]

Not only was Fuest's signature askew sense of humor apparent throughout, but his tendency to "wrong foot" the audience deliberately, as he put it. "I suppose I love to present ironical situations that would never happen in real life," Fuest said. Early in the film, Vulnavia moves to Phibes' garage in a white gown and headdress and, seconds later, is dressed in cossack-like outfit, and it was no continuity error. Goldstein and Whiton had already laid the groundwork with their own off-the-wall inventions, like a doctor's impalement by a unicorn's head, but Fuest pushed the gag several steps further by having the detectives unscrew his corpse-- an unforgettable, and hysterically funny, moment.

John Cater vividly remembered Fuest tweaking the film's dialogue virtually till he called "Action": "I didn't even know that [Clemens] was responsible for any part of the script, but he was around a lot and that is entirely possible. I think, though, that it was Bob Fuest who did most of the rewriting, for me anyway. He is a marvelously imaginative man and, believe me, he is never bound to what the script says– he is always open for spur-of-the-moment changes. I can remember several times where Peter Jeffrey and I would rehearse our next scene over lunch and then return to the set, only to find that Bob had spent his entire lunch break rewriting the scene that we had just futilely prepared. And because we all got along so well together, and because Peter and I are really old pros when it comes right down to it, we were able to do these new scenes perfectly, as if we had practiced them over and over. Bob knew exactly what he was doing, and I think he liked the spontaneous freshness of unrehearsed lines."

The characters names are only one of the film's many singular elements: Anton Phibes and Vulnavia, along with Vesalius, Harley Augustus Crow, Schenley, Hedgepath, and Kitaj. And the actors who portrayed these characters matched them– what *Dr. Phibes* lacks in standard leading men, it makes up for with memorable oddballs. (These names can be attributed mainly to Whiton and

Goldstein. Their book *The Third Eye of America* is full of similarly bizarre creations, such as Dr. Fritz Womber, Dalgor Suchecki, Dr. Rasper Papsjon, and Dr. Chaserow Rigney.)

Dr. Phibes' overall bizarreness is heightened by the huge gaps in its characters' back stories (particularly how the pre-disfigurement Phibes is never shown). The unanswered questions that it raises about them are plentiful. Who is the mute Vulnavia and where did she come from? Why is Phibes so obsessed with automata and toys (the images of his face on his car windows, like a vintage tin toy car; the windup figure during the Curse of Hail, etc.)? What's inside all of those curtained rooms in Phibes' ballroom? What happened to that dog that Vulnavia was walking– did she *rent* it? And, as Dave Tompkins wrote, "How did Phibes not short himself out when taking slugs of Moet through the speaker jack in his neck?"

(The film's pre-release ad art and even its one sheet presented doctored--no pun intended-- images of Phibes which indicate that he is almost a steampunk cyborg. In *The Curses of Dr. Pibe*, when Pibe is wounded, he bleeds machine oil. The film's half-sheet poster continued this line of thought: "Behind every successful man is a woman. . . Behind Anton Phibes was the lovely Vulnavia, winding him up, plugging him in, cleaning his electrodes, and changing his oil.")

Phibes' origins are also obscure. Of what nationality is the name Phibes? Who healed Phibes' wounds after his wreck? All that we see of Phibes' body in the film is his forearms and disfigured face. Is the audience to assume that the rest of his body was as badly damaged as his face, and that he makes up his forearms, too? Is more of him mechanical than just his throat jack? Why does Scotland Yard never seem to have any photos of Phibes? (Goldstein and Whiton's script included a scene where Dr. Vesalius explains that Pibe's nerve damage would be so severe that he would require multiple daily doses of cocaine or another opiate. In another scene, an "old Oriental Man" visits Pibe and delivers cocaine, which Pibe then injects, partly off-camera.)

To ask such questions is to detract from the film's mysteriousness and glorious irrationality, and why try to explain away the mysterious? Many movies' plots are equally ludicrous and improbable, but conventionally so. *Dr. Phibes* is anything but conventional– one of its most winning attributes. (Author's Note: William Goldstein's novelizations of the two *Dr. Phibes* films go into far more detail about Phibes' background, including his recovery from his car crash, than the films do.)

```
"THE CURSES OF DOCTOR PIBE"


        Story and Screenplay


                 by

         Hyman   Rappaport
```

THE MALEFACTORS

At some point during *Dr. Phibes'* pre-production process, the name "Hyman Rappaport" appeared on *The Curses of Dr. Pibe* script. The problem was that, not only was Hyman Rappaport not involved in writing the film, he didn't *exist*. Unbeknownst to Whiton and Goldstein, their names had been removed from the script by underhanded parties (who shall remain nameless) and replaced with the fictitious Rappaport in a direct attempt at theft of their property. (For evidence, refer to the copy of *The Curses of Dr. Pibe* among Vincent Price's papers in the Library of Congress... Whiton and Goldstein's names are nowhere to be seen on it, only Rappaport's.)

In 1970, Whiton was hired by AIP to rewrite a script called *Barracuda 2000 AD* (which was announced in AIP's 1971 preview book along with *Dr. Phibes* and listed elsewhere as having been initially written by Robert Bloch). At one point, Whiton says, he was called in for a further polish on that script, which he was typing up on a card table in a room that AIP used as a script library. He perused the scripts, he says, and happened upon *The Curses of Dr. Pibe* with only Rappaport credited on its cover. Whiton contacted an old friend with the Writers Guild of America West (WGAW) and took the matter up with them for arbitration. "The Writers Guild called it an act of felonious misrepresentation, as did the Los Angeles DA's office," Whiton writes.

No lawsuits were filed. In a letter dated February 16, 1971, Mary Dorfman, the Credits Administrator of the WGAW wrote to Goldstein: "The Writers Guild Credit Arbitration Committee, after carefully considering all the material submitted to it in the case of DR. PHIBES has decided the writing credits shall read as follows: Written by James Whiton and William Goldstein."

Robert Fuest (top of head visible beyond camera) and his crew filming The Abominable Dr. Phibes.

THE PROTAGONISTS

It is uncertain at what point *Dr. Phibes* became a vehicle for Vincent Price, but the casting was flawless. The film was the eighth film that he had shot in the UK since 1964; it was his nineteenth film for AIP. American unions had driven the cost of production in Hol-

```
                                                                27.

83.   CONTINUED:

      in horrible detail.   TROUT and the RABBI's VOICES CONTINUE
      OVER INTO SCENE.

                     TROUT (V.O.)
              ...To forever end the sleep
              of man?

                     RABBI (V.O.)
              Yes, the hand of death and
              darkness upon the land.  The
              last of the ten curses.

      PHIBES takes the gold 'rat' amulet from its appropriate
      place on the G'TACH plaque and places it around his neck.

84.   INT.  STAIRCASE OF PHIBES' MANSION.  DAY.

      PHIBES descends the great oval staircase which extends the
      depth of the building -- five floors.  It is quite formal
      what with its snaking ebony and white balustrade, crystal
      lamps, carved alabaster wainscoting and pictures (mostly
      portraits) bunched in the manner of the 18th Century.
      His cane and heels CLICK on the marble stairs and he
      becomes almost a figure out of some remote past; of
      tragic dignity and of immeasurable suffering.  On the
      main floor he pauses, inconsolably, at the doorway to
      the Shrine Room before entering it.

85.   INT.  SHRINE ROOM.  DAY.

      We OPEN TIGHT ON the portrait of Lady Phibes.  Candlelight
      flickers about the canvas and WE HEAR the strangely metallic
      SOUNDS of PHIBES' MOANING.

86.   WIDER ANGLE

      REVEALS DR. PHIBES kneeling, head upturned, before her
      shrine.  His eyes have a haunted look of incalculable
      sadness.
```

From Robert Fuest's personal shooting script: "Bollox" to rococo. Phibes's signature Art Deco interior décor was born. (Courtesy of the Robert Fuest estate. Reproduced with their permission. Reproduction in any form is strictly prohibited.)

```
                    SERGEANT
            He worked it off the motor ...

 ANT positions the spout on the machine so that it
  the open side door.

                    SERGEANT (cont)
            ... brought the internal
            temperature down to at least
            one hundred degrees below zero.

  the 'hail' machine on and hundreds of hailstones
  upon the ground.

                    SERGEANT (cont)
                    (points to corpse)
            Mercifully, he didn't feel much.

                    TROUT
                (turns, walks away)
            Like HELL he didn't!
                                        CUT TO:
 ESALIUS HOUSE      NIGHT.

 VESALIUS sitting on a couch - shirt sleeves - waistcoat -
 htly undone. HE drains a scotch and looks across at
  sits opposite him, dressed in pajamas and dressing
  chess board on the table between them.

  s up, pauses and then makes a triumphant move -

                    LEM
            Check.

                    VESALIUS
                (deep in thought)
            Hm ...?
                                Continued Page 36A.
```

'chess piece from 'hail victim'

Fuest's drawing of the closeup of a chessman that segues into Vesalius's pivotal conversation with his son. . (Courtesy of the Robert Fuest estate. Reproduced with their permission. Reproduction in any form is strictly prohibited.)

P

My work is nearly finished Vulnavia – go now – start to destroy all I have created.

Work faster Doctor – the acid is descending – my wife existed only six ~~weeks~~ minutes on the operating table – and then she was dead – you murdered her –

V

No

P

Murdered her – but you have what she did not – a second chance. You must operate and remove the key – the key that will unlock the band around his neck – perhaps your hands will shake and he too will die under your knife – a few remaining minutes only you have – because when the acid reaches him – he will have a face like mine.

From Fuest's shooting script: Fuest's handwritten version of Phibes's climactic speech. (Courtesy of the Robert Fuest estate. Reproduced with their permission. Reproduction in any form is strictly prohibited.)

lywood so high that AIP's horror films (and others, like *Wuthering Heights*) were mostly being shot in England.

Dr. Phibes was a major improvement on the caliber of films that Price had recently appeared in– forgettable AIP fare like *The Oblong Box* (1969) and *Cry of the Banshee* (1970). He manfully gave strong performances in all of them, but outside of *Witchfinder General* (1968) and *Scream and Scream Again* (1970), the scripts were sub-par. *Dr. Phibes* wound up being among Price's handful of final important starring roles; until his death in 1993, he would almost exclusively be cast in support.

Though Goldstein and Whiton originally pictured Joseph Wiseman (*Dr. No*) as Dr. Pibe, going so far as to indicate Wiseman in their initial treatment. Though they didn't write the role of Phibes with Price in mind, it could easily seem that they did, judging by its intense similarities to Price's standard characters. Price had a long-standing tradition of "dead wife movies" throughout his career– tales of men obsessed with– guess what? Beginning with *Dragonwyck* (1946), all the way through his Poe adaptations at AIP, and on to *Madhouse* (1974), tormented widowers were Price's stock-in-trade. And, like Price's archetypal character in *House of Wax* (1953), Phibes was a scarred artistic genius seeking murderous revenge, whose hideously burned face is unmasked during the film's climax. Phibes' torched wax effigies of his victims are also reminiscent of the melting wax statues in *House of Wax*'s fiery opening scene.

Price's enthusiasm for his part and his appreciation for *Dr. Phibes'* high quality was always clear in interviews. Fuest dealt well with actors– even the notoriously bitchy Robert Quarry spoke well of him– and few appreciated him more than Price did. During a break on *Dr. Phibes'* ballroom set, Price told journalist Iain McAsh: "It's a wonderful part for me, with a super script. Robert Fuest, who made the new version of *Wuthering Heights*, is the best young director I've ever worked with, he's so creative and brilliant. It's also the first time that I've acted with Joseph Cotten in thirty-two years. We're great pals and see quite a lot of each other at home in Hollywood.

"I think that *Dr. Phibes* is going to be a marvelous film. I'm sure it will be a memorable one. We have some wonderful sets designed by Brian Eatwell, he's turned this film into a visual masterpiece. This

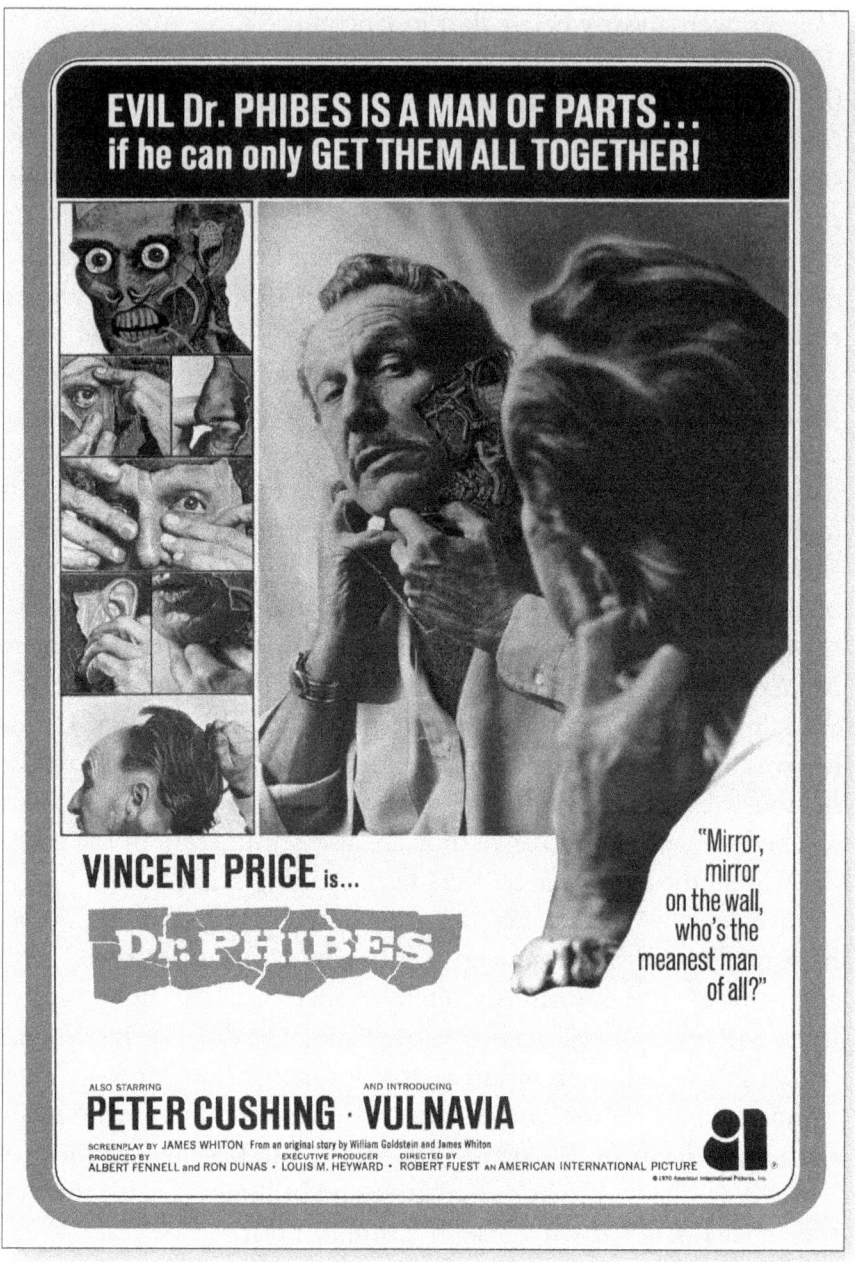

A pre-release ad, published prior to Peter Cushing's departure from the project.

Phibes with his mechanical voice-replication system.

puts it into a class above the average horror film where they use a lot of fog and dreary Gothic sets. Bob Fuest, who was a set designer before he turned director, realized at once that to make *Dr. Phibes* different, and give it integrity as a *Grand Guignol* horror picture, it had to have a difference. The 1920s was a great period and it hasn't been used in this type of film

before. It's much more terrifying to set the story in a period which many people can still remember rather than in a creepy mansion in some ancient time and country unknown to them." [Author's note: The 1920s was used *infrequently* in horror, anyway.]

In subsequent years, Price severed his ties with AIP and became weary of horror. But at that point, he stated that he found horror stardom very satisfying: "It is. But, you see, I love to act. Making these horror films is a marvelous experience for me, especially when they're so different like *Dr. Phibes*. I've never done anything quite like it before. It is made with a kind of imagination which is not expensive, but has great artistic taste."

Fuest directs Price in his orderly disguise. (From the John Jay estate. Courtesy of Mark Ferelli.)

Price and Fuest had a mutual admiration society at work. The director warmly recalled how the gentlemanly Price would wait in line for coffee like any other crewman instead of flaunting his star status to get ahead in line. Twenty years later, Price still praised Fuest as effusively as ever-- "Working with Bob Fuest... was inspirational," he told Michael Orlando Yaccarino— and just as impressed by his excellent sense of humor: "Bob was quite different from Roger [Corman] in that respect. Roger's sense of humor was like a guillotine." When asked about *Dr. Phibes* and its sequel at a 1990 *Fangoria* convention, Price called them "Two of the funniest pictures ever made... [Fuest] was a madman— and wonderful. He would say, 'Do this,' and you did it, because there was nothing else to do!"

With his face nearly frozen in a deadened scowl, most of Price's performance as Dr. Phibes is built on pantomime and eye movements. His eyes beautifully express in turn Phibes' cold meticulousness, infinite grief, hellish wrath, and utter delight at having successfully exterminated another victim, made all the grimmer because of his virtual inability to smile. His earlier Gothic horror films "had to be larger than life," Price said. "It's tremendous fun to play, it's so wild. Now, Phibes is an entirely different thing. Phibes is all inside, seething and boiling, and you can't do too much of that because movies are too facial, so it all has to be sublimated. I have to do a lot with my eyes and hands." Price's performance is, without a doubt, the backbone of *Dr. Phibes*. He made the role utterly his.

Since Price's mellifluous voice was such an integral part of his screen persona, Phibes' long silences were a major departure for the actor. He doesn't speak to another character until the film's final reel. "All he did was talk to himself," Fuest remarked.

When it came time to shoot the climactic confrontation between Phibes and Vesalius, Price's lines were read aloud off-camera. Though Fuest can't remember who read them, "I have a feeling that Jo [Cotten] did it," he said. As for shooting Price's scenes with his face stilled by makeup, Fuest said, "It wasn't a problem"– they were well-prepared for them in advance.

Price and his co-star Joseph Cotten were both veterans of Orson Welles' Mercury Theatre, where they had last appeared together in Thomas Dekker's "The Shoemaker's Holiday" in 1938. According to Ron Dunas, Cotten wound up appearing in the film as Dr. Vesalius because of a chance encounter that they had in London. "I was lucky just to find him," Dunas says, "and I don't know why he happened to be in London, but it sure worked out well. . . He's a classy guy."

Peter Cushing had initially been announced as Vesalius in ads, but he bowed out early because of the illness and death of his wife, Helen, who he adored with a Phibes-like passion. Cushing had to drop out of several other films at the time, including *Blood From the Mummy's Tomb* (1971). When asked if he knew anything about Cushing's initial involvement with *Dr. Phibes*, Fuest couldn't recall ever having heard about it. However, Cushing appeared in *Dr. Phibes*' sequel.

Cotten became the film's rudder, in certain respects—he greatly helped the film maintain its seriousness during shifts away from comedy—he's its perpetual straight man, lending the story sobriety and gravitas amidst a sea of quirky performances. Fuest said that

"But you can't kill me, doctor . . . I am already . . . dead."

Cotten "was very nervous" about appearing in a horror film, but still treated the material seriously and professionally. Like the rest of the cast, he delivers an 'A'-movie performance in this relatively low-budget film.

Fuest fondly remembered Cotten's consideration for technical matters. "The couch behind Jo [in Vesalius' living room] had a squeaky spring," says Fuest, "but Jo (ever the professional) timed his sitting so the squeak didn't coincide with his dialogue, and so we didn't have to post-sync." "Deke" Heyward also praised Cotten, who he said was always prepared, showing up "knowing his lines letter-perfect, attempting to contribute, using every one of the tricks that he had acquired over years in the business to enhance the picture. He was a big plus." Cotten and Fuest remained friends and Gillian Fuest recalls that, a year or two later, Cotten and Sterling Hayden came over to their house for dinner.

[Author's note: Actor/director Mel Welles, who directed Cotten in *Lady Frankenstein* (1971), told me that Cotten told him that Price specifically recommended that he (Cotten) begin taking roles in horror films. They offered steady work to once-major stars with

Joseph Cotten as Vesalius with the toy train Fuest said he would killed for as a kid.

waning careers whose recognizable marquee names and sizable talents would lend those films greater legitimacy. Cotten was 65 and, like Price, was ever-increasingly cast in supporting roles, usually as authority figures. Horror films afforded him a decent cash cow, which he accepted. Over the next decade, he would appear in others like Mario Bava's *Baron Blood* (1972), Welles' film, and *The Hearse* (1980). Notably, *Dr. Phibes* is the only one of these latter-day horror films listed in Cotten's filmography in the actor's autobiography, *Vanity Will Get You Somewhere*.]

MAKEUP/COSTUMES

The script indicated that Phibes' burns have rendered his face unrecognizable, his nose and ears melted away, leaving "An expressionless balloon of scar tissue," as the script described it. Maskmaker and *Dr. Phibes* aficionado David Lady has aptly compared this very unusual make-up to Tom Savini's equally different "Cropsy," the mad killer in the slasher film *The Burning* (1981)– a

Cotten poses with the fake Kees Van Dongen painting.

Fuest (right) directs Peter Jeffrey (as Trout, at left) and Cotten (center).

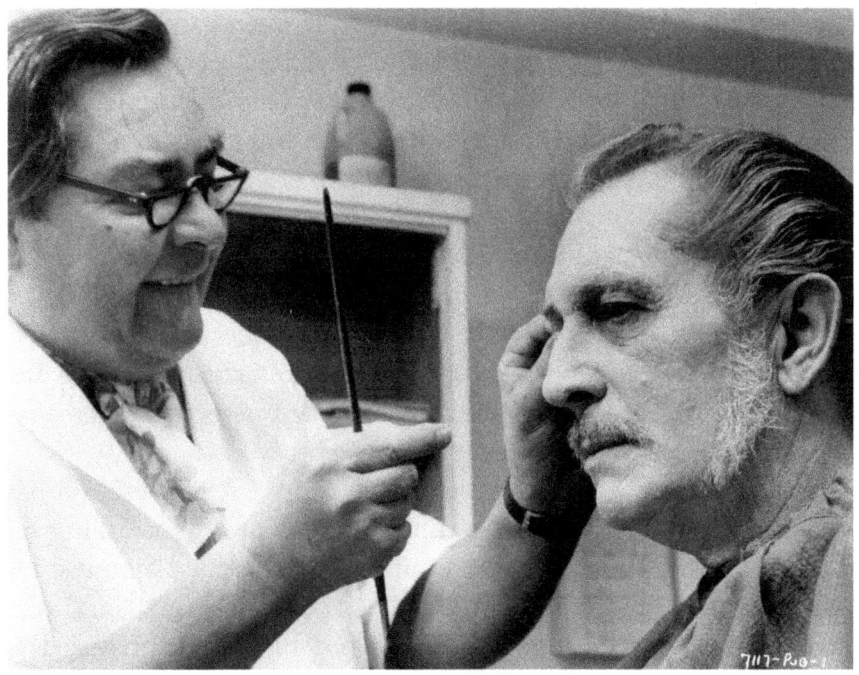

Trevor Crole-Rees makes up Price.

face reduced to near-featurelessness. Few other horror movie burn makeups– even Price's previous ones-- have presented damage so extensive. There are several visual cues that seem to allude to Phibes' disfigurement: when Vulnavia hacks up Phibes' ballroom's backdrop, she aims directly for the faces of the painting's subjects; when Nurse Allen's face is the target of Phibes' Plague of Locusts (though it's also just the handiest target); and when Phibes melts full-size wax effigies of his victims' faces.

Phibes' shattered face is eerily appropriate for the era in which the film is set. In Post-World War I Europe, disfigured veterans were not uncommon. Unintentionally, one of *Dr. Phibes*' distant cinematic cousins is a 1918 newsreel of Red Cross workers rebuilding the faces of hideously scarred soldiers. Images of a noseless soldier getting fitted for a new proboscis are uncannily reminiscent of Phibes' makeup ritual.

The film's makeup artist, Trevor Crole-Rees, specialized in scars and mutilated faces--specifically, collodion scars. Collodion is a substance that has been used in films since Lon Chaney's day– its two popular varieties immobilize and pucker the skin, respectively, creating phony scars. Crole-Rees provided such scars for the "acid tears" in *Unearthly Stranger* (1962) and various disfigurements in *Circus of Horrors* (1965). For *The Naked Prey* (also '65), he sculpted a nasty scar running down the forehead, eye, and cheek of a disgusting slaver, who is gorily impaled. Shortly after *Dr. Phibes*, Crole-Rees grafted a half-mask of actor Ralph Bates' face onto Martine Beswick's lovely features for the climax of *Dr. Jekyll and Sister Hyde* (1971), a film that involved many other members of *Dr. Phibes*' crew. He also returned for Dr. Phibes' sole sequel, *Dr. Phibes Rises Again*. Crole-Rees reportedly retired from films in the 1970s and opened a pub. *Dr. Phibes* is arguably his magnum opus, with makeups that are positively his most recognizable works.

In *Dr. Phibes*, Crole-Rees was called upon to devise Phibes' shattered face, the immobilized mask that hides it (including his removable ears and nose), Dr. Dunwoody's shredded features, Dr. Longstreet's deep pallor, and Dr. Kitaj's rat bite wounds. (Crole-Rees may have also done the lifecasts of Phibes' victims used to make the wax effigies that the Doctor melts.) Crole-Rees mainly worked with Price, maintaining his face's rictus.

"Phibes was something I had to take very seriously when I was doing it so that it would come out funny," Price told *The Guardian* in 1973. "All the same, it was just agony for me because my face was covered with plastic, and I giggled and laughed the whole time, day and night, and the makeup man and I were practically married because the makeup kept dissolving and he had to patch me up every five minutes." Ron Dunas remembered Price having little or no difficulty acting with a stultified face: "No, not really. He was very adjustable and he had a lot of flexibility and he could just do about anything." Phibes' "actual" skull-like face was a rubber mask that could fairly easily be pulled on and off.

Academy Award-winning makeup artist Dave Elsey (*The Wolf Man* [2010]) is a major admirer of the *Dr. Phibes* films. He offers some fascinating insights into the clever and well-thought-out design of Phibes' makeup:

Ah, now... I'm sort of in love with the makeup. It's very clever. For a start, it's boldly different to how we usually see Vincent Price. The signature widow's peak is gone, and the perfect arching eyebrows have been replaced by caterpillar-like ones. It shows a real understanding of how someone might reconstruct their own face using rudimentary makeup skills. Look closely because the devil is in the detail here.

For a start, the wig, which is a graying Beatles-'like' creation, (think Justin Beiber, kids) is all swept forward so that wig lace isn't a problem. Wig lace takes skill to hide, you see, which is why very few commercial wigs bother with it. Phibes' wig shows that he isn't troubled by detail and is just trying to 'approximate' his old looks.

Likewise, the long sideburns that frame his face. They seem to be hiding the edge of his mask around his jaw line. This is well-observed stuff!

There is a marked color difference between his face and where it would blend around what remains of his eyes. Phibes is only trying to make something that can pass for himself!

His face is a crude flesh color as you would expect from the theatricality of Phibes' mask. The good Doctor is no makeup man ... No, he's someone who has just overcome his disfigurement as best he can.

Then there is the weird sheen and plastic-looking skin. All perfectly judged by Trevor Crole-Rees. It all builds to create a very crude and haunting, yet iconic, look.

I think its truly brilliant, and I missed its detail in the sequel, when for whatever reason they chose to pull back from it. His Skull mask is less good, but no less iconic. [Makeup artist] Rick Baker and I argue over the skull mask all the time...

One angle that is never explored in the various scripts or the film is having Phibes use a variety of faces for his masks rather than just his own, a la *The List of Adrian Messenger* (1963). When producer "Deke" Heyward attempted to launch an animated series, "The Sinister Dr. Phibes," such an idea was on the drawing board. In Jack Kirby's conceptual drawings for the show, Phibes is shown using a variety of disguises. (The scripts never indicated any disguises for Phibes and, even if they had, the budget probably wouldn't have allowed for it.)

Phibes' hooded robes indicate the tension between his dual fascinations with religion and his perversely monastic life and his epicurean tastes: they are almost like a monk's robes, but monks' aren't silky and don't glisten. Phibes' wardrobe has an austere palette— mainly whites and blacks. Price himself wrote on his script that Phibes should wear "No red or crimson," in keeping with this.

Vulnavia's costumes vary wildly, from almost Indian saris with bizarre headdresses, to fairy tale-like gowns, to Russian-style outfits. The majority of the cast wears conservatively elegant 1920s three-piece suits. Brian Eatwell's widow writes that "Brian was very disappointed in the costume designer on *Dr Phibes*' work, as he felt that he never got the wit of the film and his costumes were dull." Though Elsa Fennell is credited as costume designer, she very possibly didn't design Vulnavia's outfits. (Note: Elsa Fennell was associate producer Albert Fennell's sister.)

Phibes always wears gloves, perhaps to hide some disfigurement. His forearms and his disfigured face are the only parts of his anatomy that are shown in the film. Like so much of *Dr. Phibes*, this raises all sorts of questions: Does Phibes have to make-up his forearms, like his face? Is the rest of his body hideously scarred? Is he, as the film's early ads indicate, semi-mechanical– a sort of steampunk cyborg?

And, as is so often the case in the film, all of these questions and their answers are left to the viewer's imagination.

[Author's note: This may be heresy, but has anyone else ever noticed how much Dr. Phibes' basic hair, sideburns, and mustache resemble Captain Kangaroo's? Or as Dave Tompkins described him, Phibes looks like "Captain Kangaroo with a hangover."

Trout (Peter Jeffrey), looking characteristically frustrated.

Hugh Griffith (right) as the Rabbi with an unidentified man.

INTERESTED PARTIES

Dr. Phibes' supporting cast was filled-out with an ensemble of classically bizarre British character actors. Their eccentric and distinctive delivery and mannerisms produced a long string of lines and moments that the film's admirers hold dear. To name only a few: Aubrey Woods' Goldsmith drawling "Fash-ion-able!" and then asking Trout, "Aren't you going to write down 'fashionable'?"; Terry-Thomas' abashed Dr. Longstreet hastily explaining that his movie set-up "keeps out drafts"; and Peter Jeffrey's Trout exclaiming "Bees in his library?"

Since British actors were paid considerably less than their American counterparts, AIP could affordably assemble an outstanding cast. "All those guys, all those character actors really worked on the cheap," Ronald Dunas explains. "They were very inexpensive and we got a lot of 'em... And we got them for very little money. All the character actors we got were good, though, I thought."

By 1970, gap-toothed comedian had become the British cinema's crown prince of oily, leering lechery. Excelling in craven and morally deficient roles, Thomas shines as the randy Dr. Longstreet. Doing his patented shtick, the actor's every line, leer, and gulp of brandy are hilarious. According to the shooting schedule, his scenes were shot on Wednesday and Thursday, November 18th and 19th. But Price nearly one-ups Thomas in their scene together with Phibes' reaction to the nude paintings adorning Longstreet's wall, his glass of brandy, and the general air of lechery. After murdering Longstreet, Phibes still can't help but give his lascivious victim an eloquent parting gaze of disgust and reproach. (Fuest used a similar gag where a character walks offscreen and peeks back on-camera to comic effect in one scene in his *The Final Programme*.)

"As far as Terry-Thomas goes," Fuest told Anthony Petkovich, "I specifically picked him for his part in *Dr. Phibes*, and made sure he came back for the sequel. Had to be good news, you know. I worked with him on the first *Dr. Phibes* for a day and on the second *Dr. Phibes* for a day, and we really laughed most of the time."

As hilarious as the scene turned out, Fuest expressed dissatisfaction with it in an interview with Tony Earnshaw: "I was unhappy in the first film about the bleeding of Terry-Thomas. There's too much silence there. Terry was having a bit of a bad day. Two or three lines came and went, and he didn't actually do them. So I was unhappy about that. It works, but it isn't as funny as it could have been. If you remember, Vulnavia comes in and he says "I'm Dr. . ." and she puts the needle in him. Then Phibes comes in and tears his shirt. There were two or three lines which are a bit lost. Well, they're not there!"

Several members of what could be called Fuest's stock company appear in *Dr. Phibes*, including the bulbous-nosed Peter Jeffrey, an "Avengers" veteran who had recently played the Headmaster in Lindsay Anderson's *If...* (1968), Aubrey Woods (who, in 1971, sang "The Candy Man" in *Willy Wonka and the Chocolate Factory*), and Hugh Griffith. The latter two had both also recently appeared in Fuest's *Wuthering Heights*. The Graveyard Attendant, John Franklyn, had a much more sizable role in Fuest's *And Soon the Darkness*. Edward Burnham (Dr. Dunwoody) and Alex Scott (Dr. Hargreaves) were both "Avengers" alumni, with the latter having appeared in Fuest's

The lascivious Dr. Longstreet (the great Terry-Thomas) gets a the surprise of his life: Vulnavia (Virginia North).

"It's a new thing on a market... It keeps out drafts!" Longstreet (Terry-Thomas) confronted by his housekeeper, Mrs. Frawley (Barbara Keogh).

Longstreet, about to meet his maker at Phibes's hands.

Schenley (Norman Jones) pensively watches Vesalius gaze at a portrait of his son, Lem (Sean Bury).

episode, "Game" alongside Peter Jeffrey. Yet another "Avengers" connection was prolific character actor John Laurie, who briefly cameos as the aged Mr. Darrow; at that time, Laurie was also co-starring on the hit British comedy series "Dad's Army."

Aubrey Woods "was a theatrical actor," Fuest said. "He played the Jeweler, he was in a film called *Just Like a Woman*, which is the first film I made. He was basically a theatrical actor who was a friend of the first producer and I thought he'd be very good– and he was very good– as that rather camp and silly jeweler, whom he played beautifully . . . beautifully judged. Lovely performance. Sweet guy, very nice man. He's got a cottage in the Lake District here . . . Lovely man, very theatrical– [He says] 'Old boy,' and all that sort of thing."

Griffith, who was scheduled to appear in the film for a single day, was the only actor who the filmmakers remembered creating anything vaguely resembling a difficulty. Deke Heyward recalled that he "desperately wanted" to use Griffith in his films, but, by that time in Griffith's career, the actor's alcoholism had eroded his employability. Heyward said that he made Griffith swear to never drink during production of any film he hired him for. "Well, I did five, six pictures with him," Heyward said, "and he adhered to that promise."

According to Ron Dunas, "Hugh Griffith had a drinking problem. He loved to play gin rummy. And I didn't really like to play gin rummy, but I kept him busy all morning so he wouldn't drink, so in the afternoon we could shoot him. That's how we did it. He's a wonderful character actor." Griffith later appeared opposite Price in AIP's *Cry of the Banshee* (1970), and two more Fuest films, *Dr. Phibes Rises Again* (1972) and *The Final Programme* (1974).

Actor John Cater was cast as the hectoring, officious Superintendent Waverly, whose voice matches his name. In conversation with Sam Irvin, Cater vividly recalled how being unprepared inadvertently shaped his uncannily good performance. "Everything was so fast," Cater said. "I really have the feeling that someone else was supposed to play my part or something. I will never really discover what did happen. I came to shoot my part, one day at the studio, and had not really prepared myself at all. I had been working on a television show up until the day before, and I had sort of let all caution go with the wind. I knew my lines but had not really practiced them to decide on all the little nuances and everything that polishes up speeches. Well, I got up there before the camera and let my lines rip like a bull at the gate. It just so happened that that was the sort of performance it needed, because it was that sort of man. So, they were so pleased by my performance that they wrote me in for the rest of the picture, which was quite an honor. I wish everything went quite as well." Cater's machine-gun delivery and sour manner perfectly suited this "pompous little runty man," as Fuest described the character.

The supporting cast also included Norman Jones as Trout's partner, Detective Tom Schenley, and Derek Godfrey as Harley Augustus Crow. Jones was yet another "Avengers" vet, having appeared in the Fuest-directed "They Keep Killing Steed," and Godfrey had originated the role of Jack, the mad 14th Earl of Gurney, in the first stage production of "The Ruling Class." Dr. Phibes' sole female victim, Nurse Allan, was played by the lovely Susan Travers, whose previous horror film credits included a brief but unforgettable cameo in *Peeping Tom* (1960) as a disfigured model and *The Snake Woman* (1961) in the title role. (Oddly enough, Travers would play another woman murdered in a bed shortly thereafter in Alfred Hitchcock's *Frenzy* (1972).) Charles Farrell, Dr. Hedgepath's stunned chauffeur, had appeared as the derelict mercilessly beaten by the droogs in *A Clockwork Orange* (1971). A young Brightonian, Sean Bury, was cast as Vesalius' son, Lem– one of the boy's few film roles. (As with "The Avengers," for budgetary reasons, *Dr. Phibes* has precious few extras milling about or driving around in vintage cars.)

Horror starlet Caroline Munro appears in the all-important role of Phibes' dead wife, Victoria Regina Phibes, which was essentially a modeling job rather than a performance. Munro was under contract at Hammer Films, who insisted that her name not appear in the credits. Victoria's image on Phibes' altar was central to the film and Munro, who was never lovelier, was well-chosen. Her showiest scene comes when Phibes watches a slideshow of vintage photographs of her. They were shot, Munro told *Cinema Retro* magazine, at "a beautiful mansion... We did a lot of shots over a two-day period."

Victoria Regina Phibes (Caroline Munro).

"I had no dialogue," she continued, "so most of [Fuest's] directorial instructions to me consisted of 'Don't breathe on this take!' I had to be careful not to show the slightest expression because I was 'dead..' As easy as it sounds, these scenes were actually rather difficult to do especially when you had to strictly control your breathing. I recall it was very difficult to concentrate with all of the commotion going on around me…

"The most challenging scenes involved lying in the coffin with Vincent. You see, I'm allergic to feathers and I was attired in this beautiful negligee- but it was covered with feathers! It took a great deal of willpower not to sneeze or sniffle. On occasion, I would simply have to sneeze and this would result in having to do another take."

The belly dancer in Dr. Longstreet's stag reel was played by professional belly dancer Julie Mendez. Reportedly, Mendez actually owned her own snakes and performed with them frequently. She can be seen doing an almost identical version of the snake dance from *Dr. Phibes*, and in the very same costume, in an episode of the popular British tv comedy "On the Buses" entitled "The Snake."

Snake dancer Julie Mendez and her partner, in Longstreet's stag movie.

In it, Mendez plays an Indian dancer who performs for the series' main characters. She and her snake have fairly sizable roles and her titillating dance is presented in full color and with as many adoring close-ups as the tv censors would allow. Prior to *Dr. Phibes*, Mendez had gyrated and shimmied alongside Peter Cushing in the opening scene of Hammer's *She* (1964), and did another snake dance in *Devils of Darkness* (1965). Fuest told Marcus Hearn, "Brian [Eatwell] found this particular snake act lady on the back of a stage magazine."

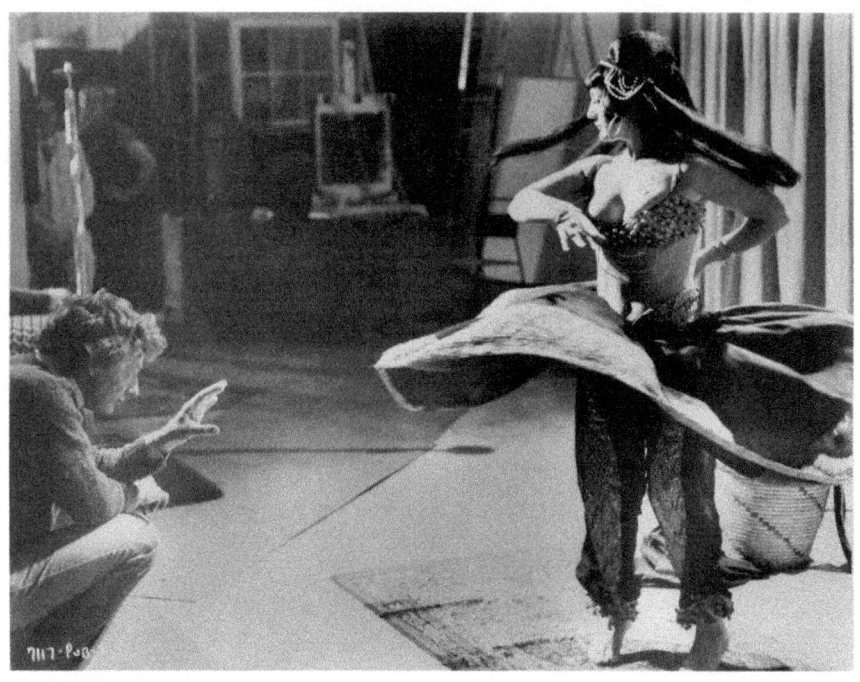

Fuest directs the film-within-a-film as crew members look on.

Mendez and her snake.

Virginia North and a co-star in the play "Council of Love."

But who played the Clockwork Wizards?

THE GIRL

On Thursday, November 26th at 11:30 am in Room 102 at Elstree, the girl who would play Dr. Phibes' assistant Vulnavia, model-turned-actress Virginia North, was "presented to the press at a

PHOTOCALL." According to a press release, AIP sought "a comparatively unknown actress" to play Vulnavia, and, that, she was, having only appeared in a few films, like the James Bond film *On Her Majesty's Secret Service* (1969) and, before that, in the Bond knock-off, *Deadlier Than the Male* (1966). (Just as deceptively as AIP would market *Dr. Phibes* as Price's 100th film, they wrote "Presenting Virginia North..." on the film's posters.) Fuest was quoted as saying that they wanted an actress "with the quality of 'spiritual sex.'" If anyone can be said to exude that quality, North could, along with being almost supernaturally photogenic. Seldom has an actress who appeared in only one horror film left a greater imprint on the genre.

Enigmatic, inscrutable, mute, Vulnavia is the inversion of the horror movie cliche that a mad doctor's devoted assistant must be hideous, malformed, insane, and almost invariably male. She's none of those things, nor is she clad in rags or excitable— she's the anti-Dwight Frye. "The reasoning behind it is obvious," North said. "It's nice to see a pretty girl in a movie." She's a looker with impeccable (if, at times, bizarre) fashion sense who, even in moments of seeming delight or duress, remains completely placid. She is the icy Helen of Troy of horror cinema.

Though silent, Vulnavia communicates through her graceful body language, like the sublime way that she weightlessly lowers her arms while descending Phibes' ballroom steps one last time. Nothing fazes her— not bloody murder, not working for a masked lunatic who drinks from a socket in his throat... nothing. She remains mute throughout the film— the closest she comes to speaking is her final agonized scream in the closing reel. ("It would have been terrible if she had spoken," Fuest told Marcus Hearn. "Quite wrong.")

Since Vulnavia is easily the film's most beautiful character, it's appropriate that she should steal some of its most beautiful scenes, beginning with her grand entrance, heralded by a musical fanfare and a flare of heavenly light that surreally whites-out the image (spiritual sex, indeed). The non-sequiturs of Vulnavia gliding ethereally through Phibes' ballroom with flowers or dancing with Price are *Dr. Phibes'* most dreamlike scenes, and when Vulnavia enters Dr. Longstreet's living room, his stag movie projected onto her, dream and (movie) reality merge.

Vulnavia (Virginia North). (From the John Jay estate. Courtesy of Mark Ferelli.

Dr. Phibes is at its most unforgettably beautiful and low-key when Vulnavia leisurely sweeps up Phibes' ballroom as the Clockwork Wizards play "One For My Baby and One for the Road." Resting, perched contemplatively atop a riser beside the band, in glorious close-up, she coolly, languidly takes a deep drag on her cigarette and exhales with otherworldly poise.

Throughout the film, Vulnavia is deliberately posed in the manner of Art Deco statuary and paintings, most obviously in the lakeside

Vulnavia in her red and gold sari and quilled headdress; the costume seems to have been patterned after one worn by silent film actress Barbara La Marr in The Brass Bottle (1923).

scene where she walks a greyhound. Women elegantly posed with greyhounds are very common in Art Deco, like in the statues of the sculptor Chiparus. Vulnavia is something like Phibes' Galatea.

The stylish designs of the French artist Erte also seem to have influenced Vulnavia's presentation. When asked if Fuest admired Erte's work, his widow replied, "Of course. . . But then who isn't a fan of Erte? He is part of all our European DNA, really, in a way." Brian Eatwell, however, was not enamored of Erte's work– he found it "too effeminate," Eatwell's widow says.

Hers is an enigmatic presence. Who is Vulnavia? Where the hell did Phibes find her? Did he create her? Is she an automaton or other type of synthetic being– the next evolutionary step from his Clockwork Wizards? Why is she in his thrall? Of what nationality is her name? Why is she so stoic? Why is she so devoted to Phibes– is she just well-paid or what? The absence of ANY kind of answers to these questions or any back-story for her adds immensely to her allure.

Most of North's few comments to the press were typically insubstantial P.R., but several remarks tantalizingly indicate that Vulnavia was conceived as another of Phibes' creations. "Vincent and I are both baddies," she said. "I play this super-efficient humanoid he manufactures. I act as his girlfriend, dancing partner, and assistant destroyer. And, although I'm on the screen with him nearly all the time, I don't speak a single word from beginning to end. Neither do I smile." Ironically, shortly before she played Vulnavia, North had appeared in a mute role as the Devil's daughter in the play "Council of Love" at London's Criterion Theatre. "The people who made the movie saw me in the play," North said, "and decided I was what they wanted. Though she never speaks aloud, North can clearly be seen mouthing the words "Come on" or "Come, boy" in a low-angle shot of her and her greyhound.

"I don't know why they don't let me speak," North said. "Not speaking is more sinister, I supposed. But, then, I do get to scream."

Was Vulnavia meant to be an android-- synthetic or a living beauty? "I have no idea," said Fuest. "It's one of those things: [she's] whatever you want. . . She's a good prop. . . [Phibes] couldn't do it alone." Vulnavia's name, by the way, was "Sheer invention," Goldstein laughs. "It just fit." Whiton says that he invented the name, and that her full name was originally Vulnavia Matlock, though Goldstein doesn't remember it this way. (Author's note: A friend of mine remarked that "Vulnavia" sounds like an obscene combination of "vulva", "navel", and "volcano".)

Shortly after writing his first Phibes novel in four decades, William Goldstein stated that Vulnavia is, according to his take on the Phibes mythos, clockwork: "The new book goes into that in some detail. She is a creation of Phibes, an early creation, as are the [Clockwork] Wizards. . . She is the penultimate creation of Phibes preparatory to his finally bringing Victoria Regina back to life. . . I'll keep it simple: he uses the existing science of the time to accomplish that. His whole goal, of course. . . is to restore the Eden that they once knew. It goes to a larger question: can we go beyond death? Every lover understands that. And watching Phibes, we're going to see one man's attempt to do that." (In Goldstein and Whiton's *The Curses of Dr. Pibe*, Vulnavia is blatantly a clockwork girl: she sits deadly still until Phibes winds a key on the back of her neck– then, she dances lustily with a him– light years away from North's Vulnavia.)

Of her role, North said, "It's genuine anti-type casting. I'm really a very talkative, very friendly girl." Fuest agreed, referring to North as a "Terribly nice girl. So innocent." Ronald Dunas called her a "very sweet and beautiful girl."

While Fuest was filming the shot where Vulnavia follows Phibes and his wheelbarrow full of brussels sprouts and cabbages up his ballroom stairs, North turned toward the camera and stared silently. It happened accidentally– her look seemed to say, "What the hell am I doing in this world?" Fuest said. "It was as if she were commenting on the absurdity of the goings-on around her." It delighted him so much that he kept it in.

Fuest said that North was very easy to work with and that she was barely involved in the film's press coverage. She apparently attended the Hollywood premiere, about which she remarked "The Americans have gone crazy over [the film]. It's become the 'in' film of the moment there." During that period, North was interviewed by the South American press and said she was set to appear in two films that never came to fruition: the Italian *Dracula's Last Will*, to be directed by Vitaliano Girella, and *Collective Ceremony*, costarring Mark Spitz.

Not long after filming wrapped, North married rich and retired from acting. She took the title Virginia, Lady White and apparently never gave interviews about her show business past and aged gracefully. She died in 2004, aged 58.

THE DESIGNERS

In Scene 84 of *The Curses of Dr. Phibes*, Phibes' home most resembled an English manor house. First, it reads, "PHIBES takes the gold 'rat' amulet from its appropriate place on the G'TACH plaque

Women posed with greyhounds are a common motif in Art Deco statuary and painting, echoed here by Virginia North.

In a rare behind-the-scenes image, Vulnavia's greyhound keeps warm. (From the John Jay Estate. Courtesy of Mark Ferelli.

and places it around his neck." Then, he "descends the great oval staircase which extends the depth of the building – five floors. It is quite formal what with its snaking ebony and white balustrade, crystal lamps, carved alabaster wainscoting and pictures (mostly portraits) bunched in the manner of the 18th Century. His cane and heels CLICK on the marble stairs... On the main floor he pauses, inconsolably, at the doorway to the shrine room before entering it."

Wisely, Fuest crossed out that description in his shooting script and wrote a single word over it: "BOLLOX." In hindsight, the script's initial vision of Phibes' mansion seems almost inconceivable:

Art and Art Nouveau styles are inextricably linked with the film's look and appeal. Of the decision to go Deco, Fuest said, "That was mine, really... It's so vague and strange, the original script... It's like [set in the] Sherlock Holmes period."

"In the original script, there were seventeen flights of stairs to Dr. Phibes' dungeon under the ballroom," Fuest quipped to Sam Irvin. "Well, that blew the art department's budget right there, so I knew that there was going to have to be major rewriting."

Goldstein was delighted with this shift away from his initial vision: "Loved it. It just fit well– it fit much better, first of all, with that era. That's the era of the time between the wars– there was an experiment in style. Architecture changed radically– some wonderful stuff came out of that very difficult time, ending in tragedy, of course. But in that ten-year period, just some wonderful stuff [appeared]– architecture and art and so forth. And the film captures it perfectly."

As his art director, Fuest enlisted his dear friend Brian Eatwell. They had worked side-by-side as art directors on television– "Brian and I worked for a TV network here in the UK and I was responsible for tempting him away from TV into the wicked world of movies," Fuest wrote. The two of them worked almost uncannily well together. Fuest once described their relationship as "Art directors on heat!" Eatwell's widow, May Routh, explains that when Eatwell bonded with a director, it was as if they were married– a sentiment that Fuest seconded. Fuest and Eatwell also lived close by each other in Teddington, about forty-five minutes away from Elstree.

Simultaneously, Eatwell was forging an equally warm and fruitful relationship with director Nicolas Roeg on his films *Walkabout* (1971), *Don't Look Now* (1973), and *The Man Who Fell to Earth* (1976). The hallmark of Eatwell's work was wild, unfettered imagination, and directors of a similar bent like Fuest and Roeg adored him for it. Eatwell was also ambidextrous: his work in the desert wastes of *Walkabout* couldn't be further removed from *Dr. Phibes*.

Eatwell's enthusiasm and natural charisma aided him in leading his crews to new levels of creativity. "He had such talent and commitment and involvement," Routh says. "He had such passion that he could command an army." (Though Eatwell's credit reads "Sets Designed

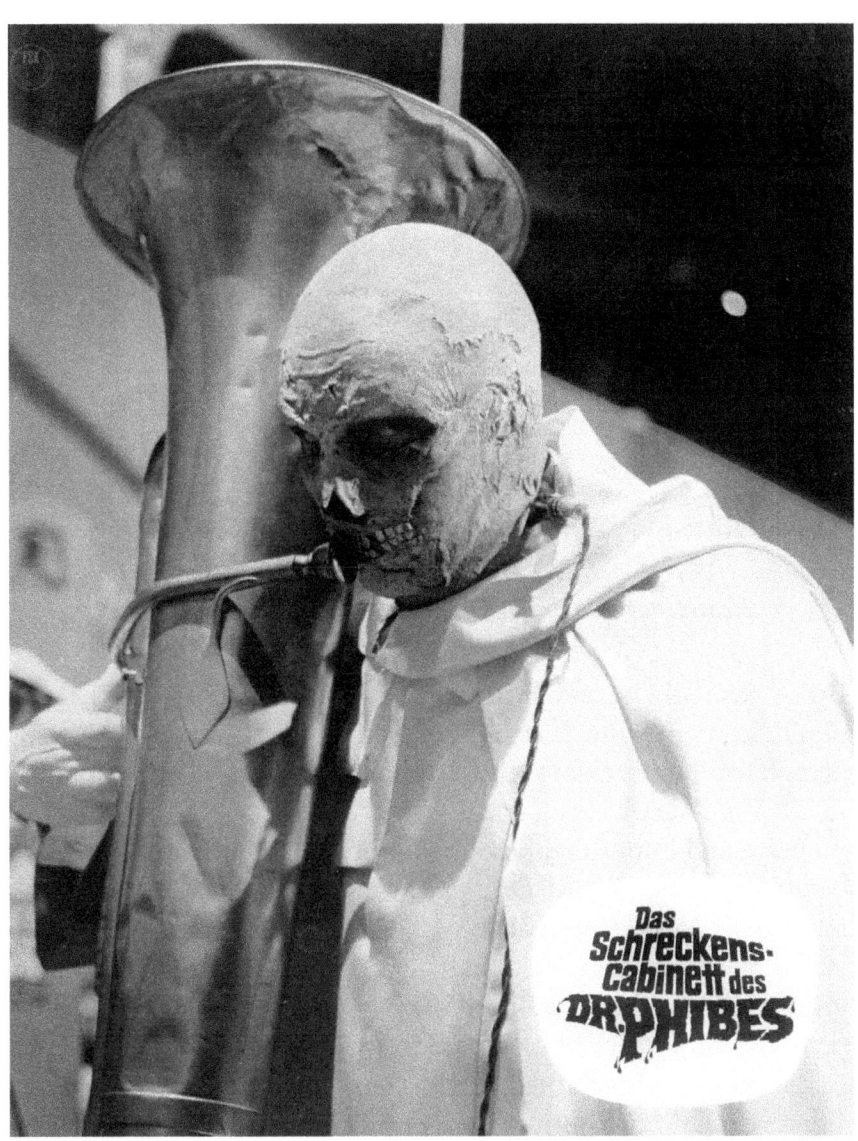

A gag photo, used in the film's German lobby card set. Question: Is this Vincent Price or a double?

Fuest (far right) directs his gasping, sweating crew while filming on-location at the "Aeroplane" Club. (From the John Jay estate. Courtesy of Mark Ferelli.)

By...," it should be noted that the term "set designer" in the English film industry in those days signified a kind of draftsman who drew up plans based on the chief art director's designs. Eatwell's contributions to *Dr. Phibes* far exceeded that.)

Fuest's and Eatwell's thorough grounding in and shared love of art would carry the look of *Dr. Phibes* to transcendent heights. "Brian loved both Art Nouveau and Art Deco," May Routh says. "He collected books on the period, but I don't think Le Corbusier was of great interest to him. He loved the decor, design and objects of the period. I know he loved Lalique glass wear, and streamline statuettes. . . The whole image of the Deco movement." [Author's note: When I first visited May Routh at their home, I noticed a book of designs by pioneering Art Nouveau designer Charles Rennie Mackintosh. When I later asked if the book had belonged to Eatwell, she replied that it had, and that he had greatly admired Mackintosh's work. Mackintosh, the leading proponent of the arts and crafts movement

Fuest and an unknown man with one of the film's vintage cars.

A deleted gag. (Does this footage exist?)

of the early 20th century, probably most influenced *Dr. Phibes* in the Nouveau designs adorning Phibes' ballroom floor and walls.

The film's 1920s ambiance wasn't an isolated cultural phenomenon, either. In the late 1960s and early '70s, a wave of '20s nostalgia had struck, particularly in the UK, somewhat like the revival of 1940s swing culture in 1990s America. The '20s influence was felt in fashion (miniskirts included), decor, and most prominently in music. Paul McCartney has said that he and John Lennon were heavily influenced by the music of their fathers' era, which manifested itself most clearly in '30s-style tunes like "Honey Pie" and "When I'm 64." It was as if kids were obeying the Beatles' song "Your Mother Should Know," and dancing to songs that were hits before their mothers were born.

In 1966, The Kinks scored an enormous hit in England with their semi-'30s throwback, "Summer Afternoon." Other UK pop groups like The Bonzo Dog Doo Dah Band, The Temperance Seven, and The Alberts recorded similarly antiquarian songs. Peter, Paul, and Mary's "1700 Album" (1967) featured the trio decked out, respectively, in pin stripe suits and a flapper dress standing in front of a vintage car. That same year, The Left Banke's hit debut album "Walk Away Renee/Pretty Ballerina" featured a cover decorated with an Art Nouveau motif that could easily have adorned any of Phibes' doorways. In the US, Tiny Tim's askew cover of the highly antiquated "Tiptoe Through the Tulips" was a smash in 1968, and the Mamas and the Papas' "Dream a Little Dream of Me" also took off. Not long before *Dr. Phibes* was shot, The Pipkins placed high in the charts with their retro one-hit-wonder, "Gimme Dat Ding."

In 1966, The New Vaudeville Band's "Winchester Cathedral," with its Rudy Vallee-like muffled tenor vocals, had climbed to #1 on the US charts and to #10 in the UK. (On the group photo on the back of their "Winchester Cathedral" album jacket, the band is shown in '30s garb, posed alongside period knickknacks including a little Deco bust that strongly resembles one of Dr. Phibes' Clockwork Wizards, as do the 20s-style characters on that same sleeve's front.) The greatest irony of all was that "Winchester Cathedral" won a Grammy as "Best Contemporary Song." The 1920s styles had become so old they were new.

And that same year— 1966— Art Deco design began a major revival with an exposition in Paris, which aimed to celebrate the 1925 International Exhibition of Modern Decorative and Industrial Arts... The year that *Dr. Phibes* takes place. Formerly termed art moderne, that exposition officially renamed the form "Art Deco." Though the style had fallen out of vogue, Art Deco's adventurous discarding of past design forms suited the tenor of the tumultuous '60s well. English art historian Bevis Hillier, among many others, helped fan the flames.

Nostalgia in general and the 1920s in particular were experiencing a renaissance. In January, 1971, the year that *Dr. Phibes* debuted, the thoroughly '20s musical "No, No Nanette" (which had premiered in 1925—again, that fateful year) was making a smash comeback on Broadway. Choreographed by the iconic Busby Berkeley and starring '30s icon Ruby Keeler, it was the height of nostalgia. The show ran for over 900 performances and won several Tonys and Drama Desk Awards. The connection with *Dr. Phibes* wasn't lost on Vincent Price, either. "Vincent Price described [*Dr. Phibes*] to me as the 'No, No, Nanette' of horror films," said horror author Robert Bloch. Meanwhile, that year, director Ken Russell was crafting his own typically manic vision of Jazz Age musicals with *The Boy Friend*, a gorgeous paean to Art Deco brilliantly designed by Tony Walton (a friend of Brian Eatwell's) that also happened to have been shot at Elstree around the same time as *Dr. Phibes*. Walton created a Deco universe that Phibes would have thrived in. Case in point: Russell's "I Could Be Happy With You" number, where dancers Christopher Gable and Twiggy (posing like a Deco statue) whirl atop a gigantic, gleaming, spinning 78 record, complete with a Phibesian horn fanfare and waltz.

The 1970s would see a deluge of escapist nostalgia movies, often set in the '30s, and though *Dr. Phibes* isn't escapist in that sense, it did arise partly from the public's fascination with the stylish, seemingly more romantic past. There were other cultural connections between the 1920s and early 1970, as Fuest pointed that year: "Fuest... says the 1920's decor heightens the tensions 'because it was so similar to our own, a tense age attempting to wipe away the past.'" The few Art Deco horror films that preceded *Dr. Phibes*, such as *The Black*

Prepping the Plague of Bats. (From the John Jay estate. Courtesy of Mark Ferelli.)

Cat (1934), seem to have in no way affected its look. (*The Black Cat*'s set pieces, including a black-clad organist playing in an Art Deco palace and an embalmed wife preserved in a basement, do bear a peculiar resemblance to *Dr. Phibes*, albeit not deliberately.)

English scholar Laurie Ede covered *Dr. Phibes*, Fuest, and Eatwell exquisitely in her neglected book, *British Film Design*, and her prose is so flawless that it deserves quotation at length. "Of course," she wrote, "...[Art Deco was] highly modish in 1972 [sic]. According to Bevis Hillier, the nostalgia craze would not peak until the following year, with the opening of the Biba store in Kensington. So *Phibes* was hip. The Nouveau and Deco motifs within the sets echoed similar decorations to be found in modern clothes, home

The Curse of Blood. The large painting beside Price can also be seen in The Legend of Hell House *(1972).*

furnishings, and- potently- in the lettering on album covers and rock festival posters.

"Fuest and Eatwell's rendering of Deco would not have satisfied the purist... The sets were eclectic and impressionistic. *Phibes* showed some of the links between Nouveau and Deco; the former elements were seen in the filigree detail around the proscenium archway and also the organic elements in Phibes' home. Otherwise, the film conflated periods to create a commonsense world of Deco. Dr. Vesalius (Joseph Cotten)'s house and the hospital interior had streamline moderne windows and decorative chrome features drawn from the 1930s; but the doctor's house also featured earlier elements, including a familiar woman and hound figurine, modeled after the work of Otto Poertzel or Louis Icart." The *Casino de Monte Carlo* backdrop in Phibes' ballroom seems to be patterned after the drawings of Georges Barbier.

AIP's press releases indicate that the studio was well aware of the intense attraction that the film's lavish sets held for audiences and critics. "[*Dr. Phibes*] is an elaborate production," one such release ran, "in which particular attention has been given to designing sets that emphasize the period - tubular steel furniture, first attempts to streamline, frosted lighting, etc., - a period that seemed to wish to obliterate itself of all save that which was functional." True, but it was also elegant as hell.

Arguably the film's most important piece of design– and also the first prop that the audience would see during Phibes' electrifying entrance– was Phibes' pipe organ. In the style of the cinema organs of the time, it rises from his ballroom floor. The organ's basic design clearly seems patterned along the lines of the 1920s Art Deco Compton Organs, akin to the ones in London's State Cinema and Odeon Theater, Leicester Square. Eatwell recalled that it was "a rented carcass of a Wurlitzer, with appendages in fluorescent acrylic designed by yours truly."

Journalist Denis Meikle visited the set and was startled by "the anachronistic sight of a Plexiglas-shrouded organ hovering high off the studio floor and being cranked into shaky hydraulic life by" two uninterested crewmen.

(A digression: Donald MacKenzie, a British cinema organ historian, graciously relates the history of the actual rented organ used in *Dr. Phibes*: "The organ console used in the *Dr Phibes* films was originally installed in the the Tivoli Theater, Strand, London. It was a Wurlitzer organ (Opus 1978) of two manuals and nine ranks (sets) of pipes - a model 200 which was built in 1928.

"The organ was sold by auction to a scrap metal dealer who put the console on a barrow and wheeled it away. On this journey Robin Richmond (the famous broadcasting organist) spotted it and bought it from the scrap dealer. He put it in his garage, I believe when he lived in Bathurst Mews. When Robin moved from there, he sold it to David Pawlyn, an organ-builder who specialized in the restoration and repair of old cinema organs. David hired it to the film company who added the surround, which I think is designed to give the illusion of organ pipes sprouting upwards from the console. Although this is very much in the Art Deco image of the cinema organ, there was not an original cinema organ which had this type of surround fitted - so this was unique and therefore specially created for the film.

"Incidentally, a good number of the glass surrounds installed on British cinema organs were manufactured by the Holophane Company. The console was used in other productions including a TV advertisement for 'Boost' (a Cadbury's Chocolate Product)." The organ reportedly still exists—sadly, in terrible condition.

Eatwell had a hand in the production of the other major props constructed expressly for the film, including Dr. Hargreaves' fatal frog mask, the Clockwork Wizards' masks, and the brass unicorn heads. "There was a model shop on the lot that manufactured said items from my drawings," Eatwell said. "At the wrap, specially designed props would be stored in a secure lock up, where they would languish for a reasonable length of time in case of re-shoots before being stolen. That was the system." Decades later, makeup artist Dave Elsey ran across the frog mask in bad disrepair at an effects artist's shop, stashed under a desk. (Photos of one of the prop storage areas at Elstree taken during the production of Hammer's *To the Devil. . . A Daughter* (1976) clearly show Dr. Phibes' unicorn heads sitting on shelves near the frog mask. Two unicorn heads were built, one with a shortened horn to complete the desired impalement effect, and one with a full-length horn for the unscrewing and the brief shot of the head resting on a table.)

The Art Nouveau Aubrey Beardsley-esque designs that Eatwell chose to decorate Phibes' walls became emblematic of the film. "I recall I came across this motif as a black and white image in some obscure reference book and was taken by it," Eatwell said. "I scaled it up as necessary, applied my choice of colors and passed it on to the sign shop at the studio. They made individual silk screens, and there you go. On reflection, it was an economical and effective way of giving character to a large and mainly plain set, much of which is composed of drapes. The budget was very tight on this production!"

Eatwell wasn't exaggerating: Dr. Phibes' immense ballroom was constructed almost entirely of arches and curtains. Since a couple of the curtained areas are actually revealed, the audience assumes that each one contains a room. Journalist Iain McAsh, who visited the set, described this "splendidly baroque setting" as "a haunted ballroom... Painted in garish shades of pink and mauve, it was a light, gay, colorful interior of the 1920s 'flapper' period." Purple dominates Phibes' walls, as well as in Nurse Allan's room and the gentleman's club walls, which almost subliminally touches upon two of the film's central themes: in Christianity, purple can signify mourning and penitence. (In Fuest's *Just Like a Woman*, there had been a restaurant set that was almost a dry-run for Phibes' ballroom, decorated in a similar Art Nouveau style in shades of mauve, blue, and gold.)

Fuest laughed when discussing the smoke and mirrors used to create the ballroom on Elstree's Stage 1: "If you actually analyze it very carefully, it's really rather like a fairground. It's a grand set, but it's sort of cutouts and paint... It was a big studio, so we had a lot of depth." Decades after visiting the set, Denis Meikle wrote that "The ballroom itself was little more than an array of 'flats,' the likes of which I had last seen adorning the end-of-term plays at my alma mater. Even Phibes' organ was a rickety affair in close-up..."

"[Eatwell] would go to work... without actually doing any drawings," Fuest laughed. "I remember I walked him to a producer's office one day and the producer– this was at Thames Television– he turned to me and he said, 'Can't Brian Eatwell draw?' And I said, 'I don't know, I've never seen any of his drawings.' I said, 'We don't work like that. I just sort of wave my hands about and say 'Wouldn't it be good if we could do this and that thing' 'You don't do storyboards or impressions?' And I said, 'Well, we don't need to.'" (The reality of this was that Eatwell was an excellent painter and illustrator when it was required of him.)

However, as huge as the ballroom set was, its size proved inadequate for one major shot. For the "*High Noon* shot," as Fuest later called it, of Phibes and Vesalius confronting each other from opposite ends of Phibes' ballroom, Fuest couldn't achieve the widescreen composition that he wanted without revealing the studio lights above the set. "I wanted to shoot like a western... We were so far back, I took my script and put it across the lens of the camera... The top maybe 1/8th of the screen is black– it looks like the ceiling... Take it away and all the lights come in!"

Fuest would kid about the effect's simplicity and jokingly say that he had held the script down on it "with a coffee cup."

For Phibes' basement, Eatwell cleverly recycled and redressed various elements from the ballroom– parts of the bandstand and walls, etc. Cinematographer Norman Warwick judiciously disguised the minimal set dressing by masking large portions of the basement in darkness. Since this set, containing Phibes' altar to his Victoria, required a funereal feel, this dismal lighting suited it well.

The sets of the various characters' homes were loaded with period art, statuary, and furniture rented from various prop houses, and sometimes furnished by the filmmakers themselves. "A lot of it was from Brian and my house[s]," Fuest said. "And there are what we call prop houses here, where you hire stuff, that do specialize in that kind of 1930s, 1920s stuff, you know. At the same time, we have people who specialize in 1920s Cadillacs– that sort of thing… And they all have this kind of specialty and if you want to choose the best place to go, it's there… and designers [go there]. And that's how they make their bread."

Dr. Vesalius' opulent living room was the epitome of Eatwell and Fuest's Deco style. On the main floor, Vesalius is first glimpsed working on a toy train set, which, in a way, was wish fulfillment for Fuest: "Growing up during the war years, there were no toy trains like this and I would have killed for this model. (L.M.S., by the way, stands for London-Midland-Scotland.)" (A toy train also figured prominently in Fuest's final feature film, *Aphrodite* [1982].) As for "The basic elements of the set" itself, Eatwell, said, "the curved metal and fiberglass screens, I recycled in the hospital complex."

Much of the fine art and antiques decorating Vesalius' home made their way into the film (and others) through a symbiotic relationship that Eatwell was cultivating at the time. Eatwell became close with Aubrey Newman, a prop house owner, who was essentially a "Cockney street trader" who knew little about art, according to May Routh. Newman relied on Eatwell's rarified artistic sensibilities when purchasing outstanding *objets d'art* at auctions, which Eatwell later

incorporated into his sets. "Aubrey bought an amazing amount of things under Brian's suggestions," May Routh explains, "that made his prop house then very important because so many people were coming to rent the wonderful objects that he had. His prop house became, I think, the most important in London." Overall, the film's period props are exceptionally accurate and carefully-chosen for a low-budget horror film, right down to the copy of the British magazine *The Bookman* resting on his "Bat" victim's dresser and the vintage tin of Crowe's Cremine makeup remover on Phibes' dressing table. (The painting of a busty nude in a gold frame hanging on Dr. Longstreet's wall can clearly be seen decorating a home in the 1972 comedy, *The Adventures of Barry McKenzie*. The main painting in Longstreet's drawing room can also be seen in *The Legend of Hell House* (1973).)

About Vesalius' living room, Eatwell said, "I seem to remember that the set developed around some of the better props I accumulated and thought were relevant. I did commission an artist chum to produce the phony Kees Van Dongen painting behind the piano. Certain props in a movie tend to 'find a good home' after the shoot. I sometimes wonder what happened to that. For the record, Vincent certainly did not contribute anything. He was far too smart to risk that." (African and Oceanic art also made their way into Vesalius' home, and a print of Sir Frederic Leighton's "Flaming June" can be seen on Dr. Longstreet's wall.)

Fuest, bemused, recalled one such incident where a member of the film's production staff, who will remain nameless, attempted to abscond with some of the *objets d'art*: "Brian Eatwell, the art director, told me— he said, 'You know, I've just seen [anonymous] come out of the set with some pictures under his arm.'" Fuest confronted this person: "And I said, 'Where are you going with those, [anonymous]?' or whatever. And [anonymous] said, 'Well, the picture's over.' And Brian said, 'They're not our pictures. We hired them. They have to go back to the company that we hired from them, the dressing company.' And [this person] said, 'Oh, really?' So he obviously got away with two that we didn't know about! [Laughs hard] He was genuinely plundering the set. He didn't realize that once the thing was over, that he couldn't park his car outside and stuff it back in the motor. He was such a rascal! Nevermind, nevermind..."

When asked about this incident, the party in question 'fessed up to this bit of naughtiness: "There were some photographs that we used– they were so great that I stole some of them and they found out about it and they charged me and I paid them. And I've still got them... They were old art photographs. They were wonderful." Are they still hanging in this interested party's home? "Absolutely," the person replied.

As elegant and lavish as *Dr. Phibes* looks, Fuest and Eatwell's sets were designed and executed astonishingly economically. For instance, the first floor of the Hospital set was recycled as its second *and* third floors. To differentiate the three, the "third floor" was redressed to make the corridors look as if they were being repainted– large areas are unpainted and brooms and other tools are scattered about. The angle that the "second floor" is shot from obscures the chrome railings on the left side of the screen– plainly visible on the "first floor"-- and, again, the railing is obscured on the "third floor" by large objects. Nurse Allan and Vesalius enter an elevator door on the "first" floor and exit the same door on the "second." Since Fuest and Eatwell were dealing with a uniformly designed building– a hospital– their decision made perfect sense. (Furthermore, as Eatwell indicated, they reused portions of Vesalius' living room for the hospital's waiting room, including the curved metal and frosted glass screen/window. Other sets wound up being reused in later films: the Goldsmith's shop from *Dr. Phibes* was transformed into a Victorian morgue for Brian Clemens' *Dr. Jekyll and Sister Hyde* the next year)

Fuest considered the mansion set from the Curse of Frogs scene the "least successful" one in the film. "It was a bit sparse," he remarked to Marcus Hearn. With that said, he duly noted "It's amazing how much value you can get from half a dozen huge chandeliers."

Eatwell's gift for theatricality was most apparent in the cleverly spare set of the Rabbi's office, which is basically composed of a wrought-iron door and a ring of columns. The area beyond the columns, like Phibes' basement, is swathed in black– possibly duvatine curtains-- giving the peculiar sense of the office existing in a virtual netherworld or void.

But the film's finest design inspiration was the operating theater underneath Phibes' ballroom floor, which remains hidden until the film's final reel. "He was wonderful," Fuest said of Eatwell. "In the *Phibes* film, where Jo Cotten operates on his son, that was... on the stage that we had. I don't know how Brian got a hold of some early plans, but we realized that there was a sort of tank in the middle of the studio, like a waterproof tank [for]... when they needed a pond or a brook, when the script called for an extremely corny farmyard scene or something. And he found that they've got this fantastic tank. We had lit the floor-- I mean, that was brilliant... What a wonderful move. When the floor lights up, there's this guy underneath." Fuest said that, for the film, the water tank was redressed and "Painted. Nobody in the studio knew it was there. And Brian said, 'There's a tank under here, like a cellar.' Of course it was completely dry because nobody had used it for like forty years."

Fuest had Phibes' ballroom built over the pool, which he topped with a glass floor with an Art Nouveau motif. The pool was dressed with various props like Phibes' speaker system, but the tiles lining its walls were left up. As the floor lit up underneath Price and Cotten's feet, Eatwell's inspired concept cleverly gave the film one of its most startling– and startlingly beautiful– revelations. (That same pool at Elstree was reused in Fuest's *Dr. Phibes* sequel, *Dr. Phibes Rises Again*, as an actual pool during the film's climactic confrontation between Phibes and his enemy, Biederbeck.)

The film's design climaxes with the Curse of Darkness, when Phibes entombs himself with Victoria's exquisite corpse. The tomb's lid closes, revealing relief images of an eclipse. Despite the plot's various elements tying off symmetrically, the eclipse seems to imply that Phibes' darkness isn't eternal. After all, unlike Phibes' love for Victoria, eclipses are brief. But the ending also includes a wonderful visual stroke that is lost on viewers seeing the film outside of an actual darkened movie theater. With the screen virtually black, the credits roll, closing with blackness and Dr. Phibes' laugh. For that brief time, the audience shares the experience of the Curse of Darkness with Phibes.

As for the film's actual locations, Rosary Priory (formerly known as Caldecote Towers, currently Immanuel College) stood in for

Phibes' mansion in the fictitious Maldine Square. (The building, located at 87-91 Elstree Road, had previously been used in the "Master Minds" episode of "The Avengers.") "The Phibes vault was designed by yours truly and built on the stage," Eatwell noted, scenes of which were cut together with several shots taken on location at London's Highgate Cemetery.

"The choice of locations is a fairly straightforward process," Eatwell said. "We employ a location manager, thoroughly brief him as to the style of the movie and let him loose. He does the legwork and returns with a stack of stills of several choices for Bob and myself. So as not to waste our time with mere possibilities, he will have already determined the parking for the crew, a place to feed them and in the case of night shooting, somewhere to park the generator that won't infuriate the local residents. A week or so before shooting, Bob will go out with the cameraman, determine the main angles so the necessary equipment can be ordered. Since I was totally occupied with construction and dressing back at the studio and there were no alterations to be made, I doubt very much if I was even there on the night [that Fuest shot at Caldecote Towers]."

"We had a very good location manager," Ronald Dunas said. "He found us some really close-in locations that were inexpensive. It really worked out well." Most of the locations were "Close by" Elstree, Dunas says. The picturesque lakeside road where Hedgepath's car breaks down "was close to London," he adds. "It was just outside, a few miles." Several Elstree locations included Tykes Water Lake and Bridge on Aldenham Road. According to the shooting schedule, Dr. Hargreaves' final "masked affair" was shot on location, though it has the look of one of Eatwell's studio-bound netherworlds. (A brief digression: Uncredited crew members on the film include assistant art director Christopher Burke, who later worked with Eatwell on *The Man Who Fell to Earth* (1976); focus-puller Steve Clayton; clapper/loader David Worrley; and property buyer Davis Lusby. Interestingly, in my conversations with Robert Fuest, he never mentioned credited art director Bernard Reeves.)

The film's period automobiles were a kind of continuation of the vintage cars that Steed and Peel drove in "The Avengers." Phibes' is a 1926 Rolls-Royce 20-horsepower touring car and, as of 2012, was repainted and belongs to an English car collector. (According to the film's publicity materials, the other main cars used are a 1927 Vauxhall, a 1925 Bullnose Morris, a 1927 Sunbeam, and a 1924 Austin Saloon.) Dr. Kitaj's plane, a 1936 DeHavilland Hornet Moth (registration code G-ADUR), has changed hands numerous times, was also repainted, and, as of 2011, is in private hands.

THE CAMERAMAN

Along with Eatwell, one of Fuest's key collaborators on *Dr. Phibes* was lighting cameraman Norman Warwick (pronounced "Warrick"). He and Fuest had almost certainly first met while working together on "The Avengers." Of Warwick, Brian Clemens says, "I'm pretty sure he was on 'The Avengers' or another of my series like 'The Professionals' or something. He was married to an actress– I think her name was Hannah Gordon.

"... He was very efficient, of course. You had to be, in television—that sorted things out because we made an 'Avengers' every ten days, and to a quite high standard. And it has to be, where you've got a woman, particularly, because you can't just light women without taking a great deal of care. Otherwise, they come out looking ugly or old," Clemens laughs.

"We had several lighting cameramen, including Gil Taylor who won an Academy Award or maybe two . . . We had very high-quality cameramen because our film industry was at a very low ebb and they couldn't work on big movies, but they came to work on 'The Avengers.'"

By 1970, Warwick had distinguished himself as a camera operator (sometimes on the second unit) on films like Michael Anderson's *1984* (1956) and *The Dam Busters* (1955), Michael Powell's *The Queen's Guards* (1961), *The Collector* (1965) and *The Italian Job* (1969). (Though the imdb erroneously credits Warwick with having worked on John Huston's *Moulin Rouge* (1952), the film's cinematographer, O swald Morris, recently said that Warwick was not on its crew.)

Warwick shot numerous horror films, including productions from both of England's premiere horror film companies, Hammer and Amicus. As a lighting cameraman, he photographed the intermittently very stylish *They Came From Beyond Space*, *Torture Garden* (both 1967), *Dr. Jekyll and Sister Hyde* (1971), *Tales From the Crypt* (1972), *The Creeping Flesh* (1973), *Tales That Witness Madness* (also '73), *Son of Dracula* (1974), *The Godsend* (1980), and several episodes of the "Hammer House of Horror" tv series. His non-horror credits include James Clavell's adventure, *The Last Valley* (1971), and *The Kids are Alright* (1979), a rockumentary on The Who.

The Creeping Flesh and *Dr. Phibes* represent two of the best examples of the horror film work that Warwick was 'typed' with– they both showcase his deft, artful lighting. He excelled at subtle, painterly shadings within wax museum-like pools of light, and lighting actors expressively from the side or below. *Dr. Phibes* abounds with gorgeously lit and composed images. Case in point: the first clear shot of Phibes' masked face in the film, with its beautiful, gently shifting tones, sometimes soft, sometimes harsh.

An outstanding bit of Warwick's lighting is the striking close-up of Price's face lit from below as he piteously speaks to his portrait of Victoria. American horror hostess Vampira referred to this vivid style of facial shading as "Jack-o-Lantern lighting." However, while shooting the medium profile shots of Phibes, Warwick photographed his face fully-lit. But the scene is so well-photographed, well-acted, and affecting that minor shot-mismatching like that is hardly perceptible. The film's sheer lack of technical errors is a testament to Warwick's technical skill, especially considering its relatively low budget and the sheer number of reflective surfaces– mirrors, glass, polished metal, etc.-- that the crew could have shown up in. And, besides, in a movie this good, what difference do minor technical errors make, anyway?

Director Michael Anderson, who used Warwick on some of his best films' camera crews, spoke glowingly of him recently: "I remember Norman Warwick very well. I only worked with him as an operator and he was one of the best in the industry. He had an exceptional eye for detail and composition and was in every sense a perfectionist. No wonder that he later became a great cameraman. He was not afraid to speak up or to share his vast knowledge with others ... He felt the scene with you and the actors instead of just watching the scene through the camera. He would sometimes say 'It looked good, but it didn't feel right ' and I would take the scene again– a rare quality that I am privileged to have shared."

Fuest found one of his initial encounters with Warwick endearing: he took the time to explain a camera's inner workings to Fuest. "I think, in the nicest possible way, [Warwick] could see that I was going to direct and I had my heart on directing," Fuest said. "So he took me and I think he might have thought, 'Perhaps if I tell him how a camera works, he might remember me when he starts shooting again!' [Laughs] We were talking over lunch or on the set and he opened the [camera's] gate and explained the various basic machinery. I've never forgotten. I've forgotten what he said, but I've never forgotten the moment, if you know what I mean! And also he had a great sense of humor, which is absolutely essential, really."

According to Fuest, like with Brian Eatwell, he and Warwick, were almost psychically attuned to each other: "He would watch me and we knew each other. And I think we probably hardly exchanged a word because I could see he was very quick. And then when he was finished, he would sit on a little stepladder with a notebook and take notes, and we'd do it again, you know. A very gentle [man] and a wonderful raconteur, too."

Fuest had very definite ideas about photographing a film unpretentiously. "I hate the zoom lens," he told Sam Irvin. "If you are going to move in on something, for God's sake, move in. If you take the lazy way out, the effect is going to be lazy ... I also don't believe in overdoing the camerawork. If a scene is really absurd, like Vincent Price putting the locusts down a tube, let the camera just capture what's going on. Absurd angles are not going to help a scene like this. The audience just wants to sit back and take it all in; wild camerawork during something like this only draws attention to itself. I always like each angle I use to be nice enough to frame as a still. I suppose this comes from my background as an artist." However, Fuest did allow one very showy shot, which memorably sets the film's tone of weirdness from the beginning: when Phibes is photographed emerging *sideways* playing his organ during his grand entrance.

For the shot where Vesalius knocks Trout out with his phone, Fuest had a piece of stone (or something resembling it) placed on a raised platform in Vesalius' living room set. The camera was placed almost at floor level, and Peter Jeffrey toppled over toward the camera onto a cushion mounted on the fake floor. While the camera was still very low, it was used for an extreme close-up of Jeffrey's face as he regains consciousness. Low-angle shots appear throughout the film, like when Vulnavia's boots walk step past the prone Chauffeur, or when she yanks Phibes' golden axe out of his ballroom floor. Also notable are Fuest's clever visual and aural segues: the cut from Phibes' Rolls' headlight to a table lamp; the cut from Vesalius setting down sheet music to his hand finishing the movement with the posters at Mr. Darrow's; or Inspector Trout asking his underling to cover a victim's face up—"What's left of it"—to Phibes literally covering up what's left of his face.

Fuest's highly recognizable style of shot composition had already been apparent in "The Avengers" and *Wuthering Heights*: objects looming large in the foreground or middle-ground with the actors artfully posed around them, usually with all of them in focus, with deep, sharp depth-of-field. Regardless of who Fuest's cinematographer was, it was his signature technique. Take for example Fuest's gorgeous composition of Phibes' telescope dominating the frame, with his two figures carefully arranged around it: Phibes on the right gazing through the telescope at Dr. Kitaj's off-camera plane, and Vulnavia playing her violin on the left. This level of conscious- and successful-- artistry was very rare in early '70s American International movies.

As for this tendency to compose his actors in the back of the frame around objects in the foreground, Fuest thoughtfully said, "It's just a kind of way that I . . . I can't say I worked it out [because] it's kind of intuitive, I guess. But it's a kind of visual orchestration, if you know what I mean– you need a hook and then behind it, you can build something and see something happening . . . So that the whole thing is just not a static two-shot with a bottle of champagne in the front." When an example of Fuest's style was presented to him, Fuest, as usual, laughed and said, "Yes, there's 'a lot of typical Bob Fuest,' as somebody might say."

THE BAND

Phibes has created an artificial world for himself to match his artificial voice and face. A painted facade of a casino is his nightlife; a mechanical orchestra is his entertainment. He even has an ersatz profile on his touring car's windows. He has a companion who could very well herself be synthetic. Phibes is a recluse's recluse: he interacts with almost no one except Vulnavia for the majority of the film, and is seldom seen talking to anyone except photos of his dead wife. It seems only logical that he would create the company he keeps. As the witty Ed Naha quipped, after Phibes's disfiguring accident, he "goes into hiding, broods a bit, and creates a mechanical world that makes Disneyland look like Muncie, Indiana."

Further compounding Dr. Phibes' glorious absurdity, the centerpiece of Phibes' ballroom is his mechanical band, the Clockwork Wizards. Cleverly, these figures were specifically designed to look like vintage tin toys with printed features and even a seam down the center of their utterly 1920s faces. These automatons resemble, for example, the Lehmann Company's wind-up figures, which were popular in the period in which the film is set. (Note: Mechanical bands were nothing new in films: there is a similar– but hand-cranked– one in John Ford's *Steamboat Round the Bend* (1935).) Like Phibes and Vulnavia, the Clockwork Wizards remain perpetually elegantly-attired and stone-faced. Phibes' fondness for clockwork figures carries over into the Curse of Hail, when he sets a wind-up figure playing "Elmer's Tune" in his victim's backseat.

Though it wasn't apparently even remotely the filmmakers' intention, *Dr. Phibes* resonates eerily with the world of automatons and their creators. Like Phibes, several of the finest automaton-makers in history experienced profound losses in their lives that fed their creative drives– for instance, Jaquet-Droz, the creator of any number of incredibly complex automatons, suffered through the premature deaths of his wife and daughter. This partly drove him to

Phibes's basement sanctum sanctorum—a brilliant example of Brian Eatwell's economic set design, using curtains, set pieces recycled from the ballroom set, and dark lighting to overcome the film's budgetary limitations.

Unmasked!

invent formidable clockwork creations. Perhaps to these automaton-makers, creating artificial life, of sorts, helped them understand and come to terms with death.

Pibe's/Phibes' clockwork orchestra can be traced all the way back to *The Fingers of Dr. Pibe*. James Whiton says that he further explored clockwork figures in a teleplay for "The Wild, Wild West." Whiton's first contract in Hollywood was at CBS Studios in 1965 for producers Dick Landau and Fred Freiberger. For their "The Wild, Wild West," the producers gave Whiton material on master magician Robert-Houdin to help inspire one of the show's wild, wild villains. "Robert-Houdin is the father of modern magic and Houdini took that name," Whiton says. "When he was 13, his father sent him off from Paris to Switzerland as an apprentice watchmaker. And by the time he was in his early 20s, he was a master of doing that, a master of legerdemain, and a master of hidden things that were all done with clockwork. And he had clockwork figures that would move and what have you ... That's what inspired me. I had pitched that [episode], too: [the villain] would have been [played by] Burt Lahr." That episode, sadly, was never produced.

Various clockwork elements had been winnowed out of *The Curses of Dr. Pibe* script as Fuest had developed it, primarily a 10-foot-tall Etruscan warrior figure that the eager Pibe has fling a huge sword at a set of life-size cardboard figures of his victims. (This element metamorphosed into the wax effigies of his victims.) A mechanical harpist was dropped from Pibe's/Phibes' orchestra, as well. During Pibe's/Phibes' "night on the town" with Vulnavia in his ballroom, he enacts a programmed drama where "The Girl" (as she was referred to at that point, is stolen from his arms and waltzed away by his mechanical drummer, who he proceeds to shoot multiple times.

The delightful touch of having Dr. Phibes' profile and the back of his head printed on the back windows of his Rolls-Royce came to Fuest while he was in Tunisia in the late 1960s. He was there scouting a movie that was to star Orson Welles and Terry-Thomas. Fuest was reminded of tin toy cars with images of artificial passengers printed on their sides: "I remember looking at a bus full of tourists. And all of their faces looked like they were painted on the sides, like toys, you know?" He made a mental note of doing this full-sized, discussed it with Brian Eatwell, and worked it into Phibes' Rolls-Royce touring car. Fuest and Eatwell were only limited by their budget and imaginations. "In *Phibes*," Fuest said, "you could use anything you could think of!"

THE FILMING

"For a man who wasn't very experienced," Ronald Dunas says, "Fuest was very, very together and very well-organized and he had very good people underneath him. The production manager was exceptional and the art director was good. So he was very good at picking people to work with ... He was very good with actors and he was exceptionally well-prepared for a man who hadn't done a hell of a lot of directing."

Phibes prepares for an (artificial) night on the town. The cyclorama was likely the work of production painter Bill Beavis and his crew.

He may be a hideously disfigured murderer and madman, but he has class.

"Deke" Heyward was equally pleased with Fuest and his work, particularly the director's spontaneity. "The creativity was flowing like crazy," Heyward said in Vincent Price's daughter, Victoria's, biography of her father. "Everybody contributed because Fuest encouraged that. You'd do a funny little shtick during the walk-through, and he'd say, 'Keep that in!'"

Part of the smoothness of the *Dr. Phibes'* 33-day shoot is attributable to high Fuest's comfort level at Elstree Studios. "I found it wonderful," Fuest said. "We have Pinewood and Elstree here– those are the main two studios and I preferred Elstree, I think because I did my first 'Avengers' there and I did everything that I really rated there until around '71, '72 . . . But, I mean, every time I worked there, it was terrific.

"And when I did work again in a studio, I did 'The New Avengers' at Pinewood and that was not nearly so much fun. It's one of these things-- if you spend six, seven years in a place, people get to know you, the crew, the people in the restaurant know you, the bar people, and they're all very nice, charming. I don't know– it's just like home. It was a really a very nice atmosphere there [at Elstree]. And, of course, you know an awful lot of producers and directors that work there. It was nice. 'Nice' is a silly word– but it was very pleasant. Great atmosphere."

Gillian Fuest has similar recollections of the shoot being drama-free. "It was fun, actually," she says. "There was one of the 'Carry On' films [actually, *Up Pompeii*] being made on another set and people kept on wanting to come and do a bit in the *Dr. Phibes* thing! I remember [comedian] Frankie Howerd wanting to have a bit of space in it . . . He wanted to do something in it, he wanted to be part of the fun." The only actor who appeared in both films was *Dr. Phibes'* Jeweler, Aubrey Woods.

Fuest also recalled that film's cast watching his crew film Dr. Phibes. As he told Marcus Hearn, "On the other stage, they were shooting a comedy . . . [It] wasn't going terribly well . . . And they used to come onto our set and I would look up and see all these white Romans in their togas standing against the wall, watching Vincent walking about trying not to laugh. It was a great moment."

Comedian Frankie Howerd shares a laugh with Price during a visit to the set. Howerd was filming Up Pompeii! *(1971) in a nearby soundstage.*

Dance rehearsal: (L-R) Price, unknown, choreographer Suzanne France, and Virginia North.

Various members of the press visited the *Dr. Phibes* set, which led to an ironic incident. "I was told to go and interview Vincent Price," says Jane Fuest, "to get an interview with him for a chat show for BBC Television. And I had to go to the set of *Dr. Phibes* and Vincent arranged to meet me [off the set]. He was just fantastic.

"But they told me at the office that I must try and get an interview with this wonderful director who was directing *Dr. Phibes*. And so I tried to do that, but he was much too busy, much too grand to see me." Seven years later, Jane and Robert Fuest met, fell in love, and were married within several years. "Of course I told him!" she laughs. "I think he thought it was funny."

For Dr. Hargreaves' fall down the staircase, actor Alex Scott had a stunt double. Fuest told Marcus Hearn that he double asked if he could take the fall twice-- "It was Christmastime," Fuest said, and the stuntman was paid by the fall. He was looking to earn a little extra holiday money.

Fuest recalled the production moving seamlessly, even potentially trying scenes like the Curse of Rats. That sequence, Fuest said, was "No problem. They were all right. The actor [Peter Gilmore] said, 'You know I hate rats.' I don't know whether he was kidding me or not, but he was ok." When Marcus Hearn later asked Fuest about the locusts, Fuest replied "You can get them at the Old Testament shop on Charing Cross Road."

Very few scenes or shots seem to have been cut. There is an extant still of a missing portion of the Curse of Rats scene of a man bound and gagged in a truck with a bunch of wicker baskets in the back, with Norman Jones peering in at him. "The corpse in the car was an 'ad lib' piece of nonsense that Brian [Eatwell] and I thought up," Fuest said, "but [it] just didn't work in the final scheme of things."

A rumor has circulated that a scene from the shooting script where Dr. Kitaj bids his assistant, Audrey, farewell was shot with Hammer horror vet Joanna Lumley playing her. As clearly as he remembered the rest of the shoot, even into his eighties, Robert Fuest had no recollection of having shot any such scene. The scene is crossed out diagonally in his personal script, like all of the other deleted, unfilmed scenes. "Maybe it was there once . . . I can't remember it," Fuest laughed. The scene was listed on the shooting

One of Vulnavia's glorious interludes. (From the John Jay estate. Courtesy of Mark Ferelli.)

schedule and when Fuest was told this, he replied, laughing, "Oh, well, no wonder we got ahead!"

Fuest definitively said that *Dr. Phibes* ran ahead of schedule: "Oh, yes. Absolutely, yes. Let's say, Jesus . . . If a thing goes two or three days over, that constitutes going in on-schedule. We never went a week over. I've never been a week over. We might have gone a bit over. Certainly not on the *Phibes* [films]. Albert [Fennell] was the [line producer]– he was brilliant. Everything was realistic– that was the main thing. We didn't get that terrible thing where you know you have to shoot three days in two and all this crap."

Fuest's creativity and economy contributed heavily to the film's success, along with his affection for and gentleness with his company. "Deke" Heyward told Tom Weaver that Fuest, "For the most

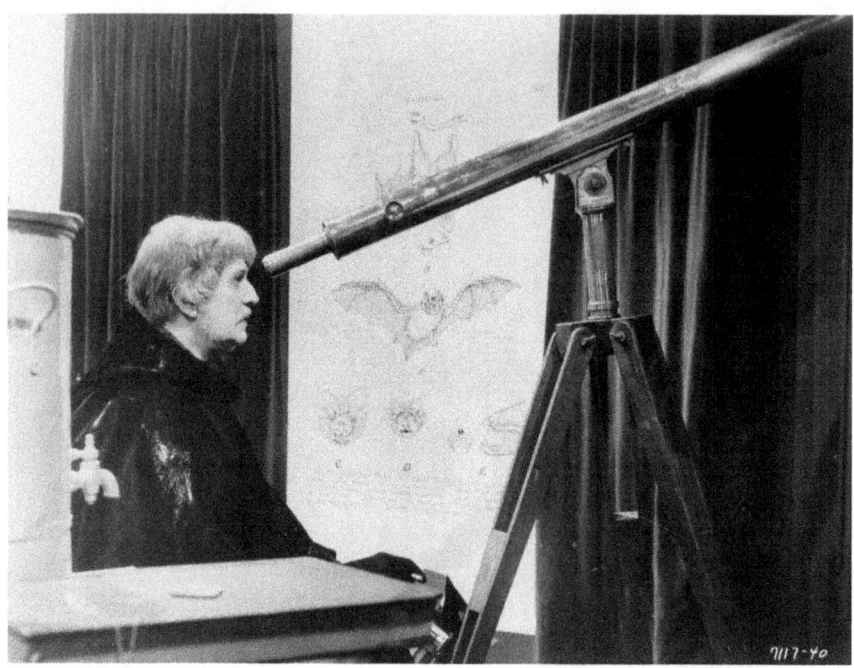

Phibes in repose with his telescope and the film's little-used Observatory set. Note the cigarette in Price's hand and the studio light below him!

part," deserved the credit for the finished film. "Bob Fuest had a great sense of style and flair," Heyward said. "He struck up a very good rapport with all of the actors; being an ex-scenic designer himself, he knew how to guide Eatwell, and I think that was a very strong key to the picture. He conceptualized a lot, and he also had a very sly English sense of humor. I would say, 'Hey, wouldn't it be funny if . . .,' and he'd ponder; he was a very serious young man. I was always expecting him to say no, and he'd say, 'Yes, but I think it would be funnier if . . .,' and he extrapolated on any thought I had . . . Also, he was very conscious of budget, which I'm sure doesn't mean diddly-squat to your readers, but it means a lot to a producer."

Despite his initial dislike of the script, Fennell guided the film very professionally. "Albert was good news," Fuest recalled. "Albert Fennell worked as a line producer— he did all the heavy math and budget and that kind of thing. He did it on *Phibes* and 'The Avengers' and he was Brian Clemens' partner, and he never took a credit . . . He very rarely took a credit . . ."

Fuest was unsure as to why Fennell was uncredited: "I have no idea. No idea at all. When I first met him, he was doing 'The Avengers,' which was his– he did get credit on [it], Brian Clemens and Albert Fennell . . . [Fennell] was the English producer and was responsible for giving AIP all the budget and the breakdown and organizing the film negative . . . All the crap that goes with sending stuff to America. And he was there on *Phibes* 1 and *Phibes* 2, and then also on 'The Avengers.' Very nice . . . Every now and then he got very cross. Basically, he was terrific."

Fuest gave every indication that making *Dr. Phibes* was one of the single most pleasant and satisfying experiences of his filmmaking career. "He loved *Dr. Phibes*," Jane Fuest says. "I think he remembered it with such fondness– he remembered the music and 'Over the Rainbow'– he remembered details about it and all the people that were in it with SUCH fondness that they obviously had a wonderful time doing it."

Phibes's ballroom floor was based on a stained glass design by Charles Rennie MacKintosh.

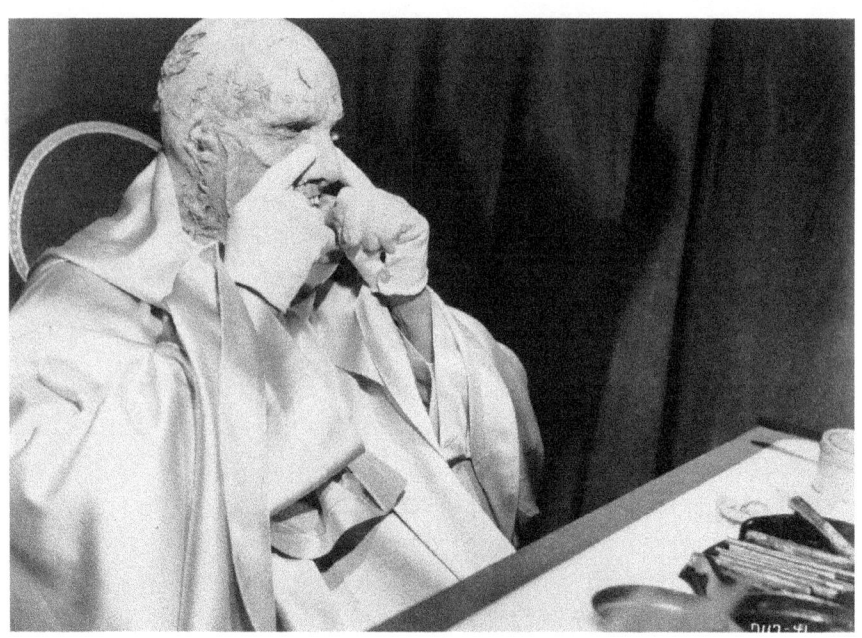

Phibes puts his face on, literally.

Love means never having to say you're ugly.

Another one for the road.

Vulnavia assists with Phibes's blood drive.

THE MUSIC

During filming, Fuest recalled, he recorded "stuff at home" from his vast personal record collection. He would then supply his soundman with these tapes for playback on-set to create the desired atmosphere. (He may have even intended to use those specific pieces in the film, but couldn't because of rights issues or some other complication, but that is pure supposition.) The crew was delighted. Once, while Fuest was eating lunch, an intrigued electrician came over and not only asked him about what music they were playing that day, but where he could get a copy.

"Perhaps cinema history was made when I would announce the piece on the daily call sheet," Fuest wrote. "At the bottom, it might read: 'Sc. 47, 49- Ballroom Int- Phibes alone in the ballroom (playback the last movement of Sibelius' Fifth Symphony).'" Sweeping, moody, and brooding as Sibelius' Fifth is, it accurately represented the Anton Phibes that Fuest was shaping.

For one of the scenes where Vulnavia is "wandering around and drifting in the breeze and everything," Fuest said, he played Joaquin Rodrigo's "Concerto de Aranjuez." Journalist Iain McAsh watched that scene being shot and noted: "Vulnavia waltzed across the ballroom to the playback strains of a haunting Spanish concerto and presented a magnificent bouquet of flowers to her master." (If you play or hum the Adagio from "Concerto de Aranjuez" during this scene, Virginia North's movements are visibly choreographed directly to that tune and out-of-synch with the similar piece on the film's soundtrack.) Ironically, Joaquim Rodrigo wrote the "Concerto de Aranjuez" when he was told that his pregnant wife, Victoria, was going to die; the piece was a means of purging his grief. Unlike Anton Phibes, Rodrigo's Victoria survived, but their unborn child didn't.

For another of Vulnavia's interludes, Fuest used one of Heitor Villa-Lobos' "Bachianas Brasilieras"– probably Number 5-- featuring a soprano backed by eight cellos. For whatever reason, these actual haunting pieces weren't incorporated into the film and very similar-sounding new compositions by John Gale, which seem directly patterned after them, replaced them in those scenes. (Author's note: "Seem" is the operative word here. When I asked John Gale whether or not Fuest had asked him to pattern his compositions after Villa-Lobos or Rodrigo, he replied "No, that's all news to me.")

"When the titles come and Phibes is playing [Felix] Mendelssohn ["War March of the Priests"]", Fuest said, "In those days, I had this record, a long-playing record" of the piece. Phibes returns and continues the piece immediately after committing the "Bat" murder. The album is EMI's Classics for Pleasure (CFP 153) "Great Organ Works" performed by Nicolas Kynaston at the Royal Albert Hall . . . where Anton Phibes once performed, according to Mr. Darrow's poster in the film.

Fuest "took the recording" and "We did it to playback on this organ." The version that he shot the scene to, and which it was cut to, was from his own commercial lp. When he got the recording from the record company to use in the film's sound recording, it was sped up in order to fit more music on the album. It was about 45 seconds short, which destroyed the continuity, drove the editor crazy, and necessitated their recutting the scene."

Kynaston, still under thirty at the time, recalled the recording and Dr. Phibes several years ago: "I made two recordings at the Royal Albert Hall in 1970 and in 1972 for Classics for Pleasure (part of EMI) and entitled *Great Organ Works*. Originally produced on LP, they were later transferred to CD and were bestsellers. I received an award for sales of over 100,000 in one year and over the full time they were on sale that number reached a million.

"The agreement for the Mendelssohn 'War March of the Priests' to be used in the *Dr. Phibes* film was made without reference to me, but I was paid! It was also used in a commercial advertisement. I only saw *Dr. Phibes* once but now can't remember it, it was so long ago! I don't own a DVD copy and have never seen it on sale. Other films in which I played were *Tales From the Crypt* and Ken Russell's *Lady Chatterley*.

"The organ in the Royal Albert Hall is the largest in Britain and was built by Henry Willis in the 19th century, but has been considerably altered over time." On the same *Classics for Pleasure* LP with the Mendelssohn piece was Kynaston's recording of Bach's "Toccata and Fugue in D Minor" which, as he mentioned, opens Amicus's horror anthology *Tales From the Crypt* (1972).

For the majority of the film's score, Albert Fennell brought on composer Basil Kirchin, an experimental composer with a background in pop jazz dating from the 1950s. Kirchin had already scored several films, such as *Primitive London* (1967); *The Strange Affair* (1968), which was designed by Brian Eatwell; and Peter Medak's first film, *Negatives* (1969). Kirchin's film career was short, ending with *The Mutations* (1974). As Fuest recalled, "The director, David Greene, and I shared the same musical taste, and I liked the music that Basil had done for two of his films, *The Shuttered Room* and *I Start Counting*. I much enjoyed working with him, but in truth was a bit disappointed by some of the results. The themes worked. The themes worked, but the orchestration was too austere and too understated. Not the Anton Phibes I knew."

Fuest owned a copy of this hit Nicolas Kynaston organ LP and drew Dr. Phibes's *unforgettable opening theme from it.*

Dissatisfied with Kirchin's work, Fuest called composer John Gale, who he "had known from my days of working on commercials," Fuest said. "He had never done a film. I paid him $500 to write some additional music for the first *Phibes* film. He did thirty minutes worth of music for that film, and we were so pleased that we hired him to do all of the music for the second one."

"John Gale came to the rescue with the lovely Vulnavia theme," Fuest said decades later, "and with a bit of help from the library, we got there in the end." Gale said recently that Fuest left him to his own devices composing Vulnavia's theme: "He just showed me the clip, explained what was going on, as it were, and said, 'I want this Thursday.'"

Fuest discussed his dissatisfiaction with Kirchin's score with him, as Gale recalls: "Bob came to me and said, 'We're just unhappy with one bit of the music,' which was 'Vulnavia's Theme.' He said, 'Do you think you can do something about it?' So, I was shown the clip—not with the music. And of course she's a speechless, mute girl–very pretty. And I think he said, 'Do it by Thursday.' So I got down to it. I thought I would use a 'song without words'–use a soprano. So that was the piece I used and he was very pleased with it."

For Vulnavia's Theme, Gale says that he was not going for a Spanish concerto sound: "Apart from the 'song without words' idea because of Vulnavia being a mute, I just used a technical phrase called a 'turn' in music, which is used in Baroque music mainly. If you take a crotchet anywhere and above the crotchet is the letter 'S' on its side–that means that you convert that crotchet into semiquavers by playing the note, the note above it, then the note, then the note below it, and return to a note that follows the crotchet."

After over forty years, Gale couldn't remember the name of the soprano he hired: "Oh, dear. I've been trying to think about that. I was very friendly with an operatic agent–she's dead now–and I think got her [through] her, and for the life of me I can't remember her name."

When asked how many musicians he had to record Vulnavia's theme, Gale exclaimed, "What a question!" and laughed. "In her theme? I think it was a string orchestra–I used a sort of organ piece because Phibes played the organ. It was mainly a string orchestra. I think they used the original *Abominable Dr. Phibes* track in *Phibes Rises Again*, but I think I re-recorded it."

This unforgettable track was Gale's sole contribution to the soundtrack, and it was recorded at CTS Studios in Kensington Gardens Square in London: "And that's where the main music of *Dr. Phibes Rises Again* was done, too. And I used a BIG orchestra for that and a big choir." (Fuest used Gilbert Vinter's tense library music cut "Voodoo Victim" to accompany Phibes observing Vesalius's operation. That same track appears in Monty Python's Flying Circus's sketch "The Day Nothing Happened," to ironically counterpoint the life of the utterly dull Ralph Mellish. That same library needle-drop cut can be heard in the psychedelic vampire oddity *Alabama's Ghost* (1973) and on the animated series "Ren and Stimpy.")

After scoring the film, Kirchin said, "They took out a lot of my serious music and spoofed it up with other pieces. That hurt at the time. I was in Switzerland when that happened and came to deal with it as only being a movie after all." Ironically, Beaver and Krause's score to Fuest's *The Final Programme* (1974) sounds uncannily like Kirchin's *Dr. Phibes* score. Perhaps in the latter film, the sound worked much more to Fuest's satisfaction.

Dissatisfied Fuest might have been, but Kirchin's score worked. Alternating between lush, sweeping numbers and bizarre and experimental jazz, Kirchin captured the story's demented, mordant elegance, poignance, and grandiosity eloquently. Johnny Trunk, whose Trunk Records released several of Kirchin's albums, describes the *Dr. Phibes* score as "Typical Kirchin, complex yet oddly simple and distinctive." Kirchin's musicians were Stan Roderick, Peter Hughes, Daryl Runswick, and Chris Karan. Kirchin "had a number of 'Praetorian Guards' he relied on," Trunk says. "These were some of his regulars—classic and dependable UK jazzmen." In hindsight, many of Kirchin's pre-*Phibes* albums, like *Abstractions of the Industrial North* (1966), sound eerily similar to the film's score. Kirchin's post-*Phibes* music became much more experimental, but echoes of it can be heard in his bizarre 1974 *Worlds Within Worlds* album.

Part of the film's score—mainly the music building up to the Plague of Bats—was built around a Kirchin composition titled "Plaques and Tangles." It had originally been composed for a film on mental illness to be screened at an international psychiatric conference in 1968, according to Jonny Trunk. The musicians who played on it were Evan Parker, Kenny Wheeler, Chris Karan, Peter McGurk, and Harry Stoneham. The film is apparently lost, but the entire soundtrack was released as *States of Mind* on Trunk Records. In hindsight, "Plaques and Tangles" suited Fuest's tale of an unbalanced mind perfectly.

The film's soundtrack features some notable trumpet passages, which may have been Fuest's doing. "Bob loved Jazz and he loved Brass Bands," says Fuest's widow. "He really loved music of all kinds and, yes, he did have a fondness for the trumpet." Trumpet solos herald some of *Dr. Phibes*' high points– during "You Stepped Out of a Dream" as Vulnavia and Phibes cut a rug, and, poignantly, with "Somewhere Over the Rainbow" at the film's close. As a younger man, Fuest had even played drums in a jazz band, and later played jazz piano well. (Fuest's love of trumpets subtly slipped into *Dr. Phibes*' sequel, *Dr. Phibes Rises Again*, where he named several characters after famous trumpeters.)

The core of the film's score, though, was its string of 1920s and '30s standards, used with a combination of affection and delicious irony. The tension between elegance and grue peaks when Phibes'

Clockwork Wizards click and whir into "What Can I Say (After I Say I'm Sorry)?" or "Charmaine" played delicately on a violin as green goo dribbles onto Nurse Allan's face. Scoring Dr. Longstreet's exsanguination with "Close Your Eyes" was a deliciously ironic choice. Perhaps the film's musical *piece de resistance* is "You Stepped Out of a Dream" performed as a siren's song behind Phibes and Vulnavia's evening "on the town." *Dr. Phibes* is a musical film on many levels and, despite Fuest's reservations, it was scored impeccably.

THE VOICE

Dr. Phibes' synthetic voice is a hollow, tinny croak echoing from his speaker, with his halting speech accentuated wildly by his eyes and gestures. He speaks jaggedly, his words fractured: "Out-let," "in-ex-or-ably," "att-rib-u-ted." In the script, his voice is described as "harsh, metallic, rattling, and thoroughly ominous." That Phibes must plug a cable into his neck creates a visual pun: a "vocal *cord*." (This Vocoder-like effect prefigured the electronic voices of the Phantom in *Phantom of the Paradise* (1974) and the architect Varelli in Dario Argento's *Inferno* (1980). William Finley, who portrayed the Phantom in the former film, stated that Dr. Phibes' synthetic voice definitely influenced the Phantom's overall design.)

The unforgettable mechanical-sounding effect applied to Price's own mellifluous voice for the film was the work of dubbing editor Peter Lennard. Co-producer Albert Fennell had given Lennard his first break as a sound editor on "The Avengers," and would subsequently hire him on every one of his productions until Fennell's death. Fuest told Marcus Hearn that he considered Lennard "an absolute master" of his craft. As Lennard recalls:

Having completed the final dub [of *Dr. Phibes*], the film was sent to the U.S. for approval by the gods [AIP]. They loved the film but wanted to change some lines from Vincent Price for clarification for the American audience. As you may know, Phibes talked by inserting a jack plug into his neck. These lines were pre-recorded and played back on the set so that Vincent could wobble his head and throat while delivering the dialogue. His lips remained shut.

We therefore had to treat all Vincent Price's dialogue throughout the film as if coming through a speaker. After a lot of experiments with eq. etc., on the first film the Powers agreed on the British format. (Eq. means equalization, adding bass, treble or middle. We used a lot of eq. on Phibes' voice to sound as if it came out of a box.) In those days, our dubbing theatres did not have the fantastic synths that they have today (We were way behind the music industry) so it was not that complicated. We sent the final dubs and picture to the U.S. as the altered lines were to be shot there where Vincent Price was situated. The Americans also had to redub these lines into the final film. It should not have been too complicated since only the length had to be roughly the same as the original and sync. was no problem as he spoke from a jack plug, nodding his head up and down.

The film came back and Albert Fennell (Producer), the director, and myself ran the new dub in the theatre. To our horror when the new lines played, they hardly sounded like Vincent. To make it worse, to my recollection, some of the lines were inserted directly between other lines that had been treated in our theatre. Albert and the director went mad and said that they would have to be redone. The gods at A.I.P. in the U.S. said they were not to be redone so the film went out as it was.

Vincent Price was very popular in the U.K. (A.B.P.C) Studio. I remember him many times poking his head through the hatch in the studio bar and ordering a drink from the bar lady in a kind of Phibes voice, which made the whole bar laugh. All the sound effects were either shot in the theatre [or] provided by my extensive library, which was about the 3rd biggest in the U.K at that time. I brought the library with me to Spain, but have hardly used it since.

In the decades since *Dr. Phibes*' initial release, Phibes' electronic voice was hailed by hip-hop pioneers like Grandmixer DXT, Afrika Bambaataa, and Rammellzee as an ancestor of the Vocoder, a hip-hop staple. "[Phibes] had MIDI before anybody," Grandmixer DXT told Dave Tompkins. "Dr. Phibes' organ skills were ridiculous." Also within that urban milieu, a Bronx-based graffiti artist, Teebag 170, used "Dr. Phibes" as one of his many pseudonyms.

Fuest told Marcus Hearn that AIP was unhappy with one of Joseph Cotton's lines, where Vesalius said that Victoria died in the "recovery room." This forced Lennard to "get 'operating' out of going through all of Jo's words," stitching together scattered syllables. The results were seamless.

Lennard's sound effects gave the film subtle, deliciously weird undertones— sounds like the eerie hiss of Phibes inhaling as he tests his false nose; the sizzling drip of wax from the doctors' melting effigies; Phibes' unnatural slurping when he eats or drinks; the click of the frog mask's catch; the tick-tick-tick of the Clockwork Wizards' mechanism coming to life; the horrible, distorted first-person sounds of Dr. Hargreaves' head squashing; and the dry sucking noise as Phibes finishes draining Dr. Longstreet.

THE GODS

During production, Fuest had played it safe, sending only one side of *Dr. Phibes to* Sam Arkoff and Jim Nicholson back in Hollywood. "I knew the film was going to be quite different than anything AIP had done before," Fuest told Sam Irvin. "I also knew that they did not particularly like change. So when they demanded to see rushes, I showed them stuff which was right up their alley like the rat attack scene, the scene where the locusts eat the nurse. They liked it, but had no idea I was making a funny film. Had they known, I think they might have stopped me. I wanted to finish it, and show them the complete thing, and hope they liked it."

"Nicholson and Arkoff thought we were making a straightforward film," Fuest later told Anthony Petkovich, "not the kind of sendup which we ultimately presented; and that was because all of the rushes which we sent to the States were totally straight, without any kind of tongue-in-cheek humor or wit or wisdom in them."

As James Whiton remembers it, a rough, music-less cut of *Dr. Phibes* was held in early February, 1971 at the lavish Beverly Hills Hotel. The morning of the screening, Whiton was literally thrown out of his bed: an earthquake hit Los Angeles. It was appropriate— a film about biblical wrath being met with a natural disaster.

"It was quite extraordinary that day," Fuest said. "The screening was in Beverly Hills at ten in the morning. Five hours earlier, there had been an earthquake in Los Angeles. How beautiful it would have been if the quake had hit during our screening! Projector wobbling, lights swinging, and all. It would have been smashing. We just missed it by hours. Such is fate."

Whiton remembers around twenty-five people attending the screening, including himself, Fuest, James Nicholson, and Samuel Z. Arkoff, along with various other executives and probably William Goldstein, as well. "We finally had the screening and they came out of the screening room smiling from ear to ear," Fuest said. "It was so freshly different from anything Vincent Price had made at AIP since the beginning of the Corman films. They knew it was different, but they really liked it."

THE TITLE

Though *Dr. Phibes* appears to have been filmed as *The Curses of Dr. Phibes*– the title on the shooting scripts– AIP eventually changed it. (Many stills from the film feature the title "Dr. Phibes"– no Curses, no Abominable-- as does the film's trailer.) "There were two titles," William Goldstein recalls. "One of them was *The Curses of Dr. Pibe* and the other was *The Fingers of Dr. Pibe*. Now, if you're asking how Pibe became Phibes– those were our original titles, by the way– how the difference [came to be], and I've told this story many times– how true it is, I don't know. I knew [AIP Vice President] Sam Arkoff. But for some reason, [Arkoff] had a slight lisp, and he couldn't get 'Pibe' out, so it became Phibes." As for the appellation "The Abominable," "That came at AIP," Goldstein says. "It's a wonderful fit." Fuest told Marcus Hearn, "Abominable" has "got to be one of the most curious words that's ever been used in a film's title." (In Whiton and Goldstein's contract with AIP, dated May 11, 1970, the film is listed as "The Incredible Dr. Pibes" aka: "The Curses of Dr. Pibe." In the film's theatrical and tv trailers and on its still photos, the title was simply *Dr. Phibes*.)

One of the film's most endearing touches is its singularly antiquarian closing credits sequence, *a la* vintage movies like *Gone With the Wind*, where each separate echelon of the cast is given its own subheading– among them, "THE PROTAGONISTS," "THE LAW," and "INTERESTED PARTIES." It was the last nail in this beautifully wrought coffin.

Dr. Phibes's *grand world premiere at LA's Pantages Theater. Vincent Price and interviewer Army Archerd can be seen near the theater's entrance.*

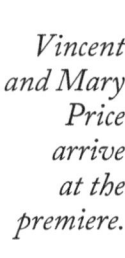

Vincent and Mary Price arrive at the premiere.

(L-R) Army Archerd, Vincent Price, and Mr. and Mrs. Sammy Davis, Jr.

James Whiton arrives at the premiere.

Whiton at the Pantages.

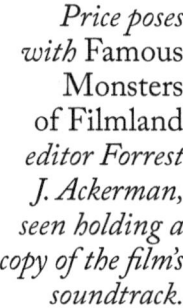

Price poses with Famous Monsters of Filmland *editor Forrest J. Ackerman, seen holding a copy of the film's soundtrack.*

James Whiton at the Pantages. (Photo by John Ward. Courtesy of James Whiton.)

(L-R) James Whiton, Barbara Grupe, and David Ward. (Photograph by John Ward. Courtesy of Whiton)

James Whiton and Barbara Grupe pose with the Pantages' awesome lobby display. (Photograph by John Ward. Courtesy of Whiton)

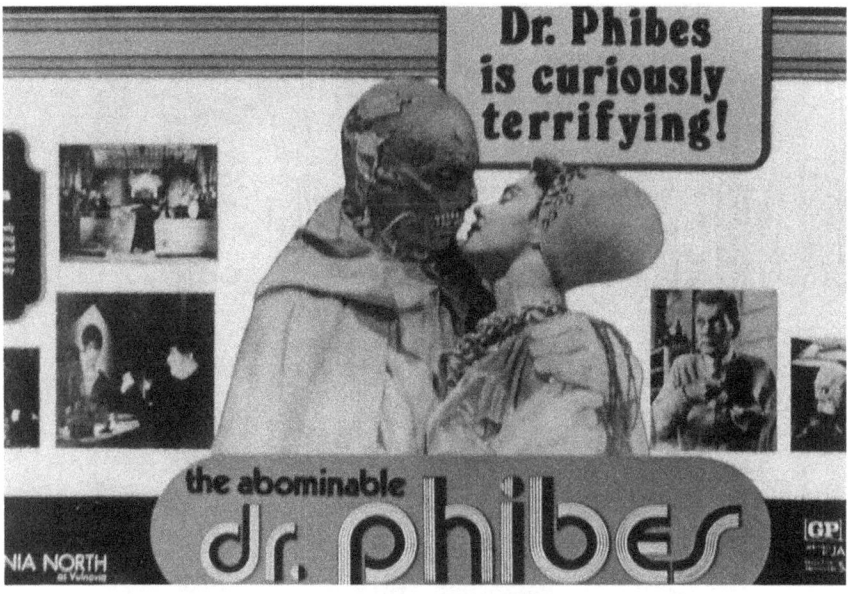

A closer view of the Pantages' lobby display. (Photograph by John Ward. Courtesy of Whiton)

An AIP promotional gimmick.

THE PUBLIC

AIP erroneously touted *Dr. Phibes* as Vincent Price's 100th or 101st film– it sounded nice. On May 20, 1971 at 8:15 pm, a "COLOSSAL OLD-FASHIONED HOLLYWOOD PREMIERE" was held at the Pacific's Pantages Theatre in Hollywood, "TO HONOR MR. VINCENT PRICE FOR HIS 100th PICTURE." The evening was telecast nationally on "The Steve Allen Show." AIP pulled out all the stops (no pun intended), splurging on bleachers, spotlights, antique costumes, and antique cars, all designed to complement the film's milieu. Stars like Sammy Davis, Jr. attended, as did *Famous Monsters of Filmland* Editor Forrest J. Ackerman. Voice actor Paul Frees, who had impersonated Al Jolson on the film's soundtrack on "Darktown Strutter's Ball," reportedly escorted Virginia North. Steve Allen interviewed Dead End Kid Huntz Hall, who was in attendance. Jim Nicholson came, but Sam Arkoff was apparently in London at the time and couldn't make it.

The guest list for the *Dr. Phibes* premiere included many AIP alums like Florence (*Queen of Blood*) Marly, Claudia Jennings, and the stars of their recent hit *Count Yorga, Vampire*, Michael Macready and Robert Quarry. Other guests included Russ Meyer, Price's former co-star Agnes Moorehead, L.Q. Jones and Alvy Moore, and "Peter Lorre, Jr." (An unrelated imposter).

According to *Boxoffice* magazine, the film's soundtrack LP was "given to every couple... Hundreds of guests appeared in costumes of the 1920s, including 200 winners of the KGBS 'Dr. Phibes' premiere contest." They further reported that Arkoff was in London prepping "The Return of Dr. Phibes."

AIP touted the premiere as having "a large display of the latest far-out inventions of the seventies." (Whatever that meant.) "[The premiere's] Theme is 'Stars and Vehicles of the 30's/Stars and Miracles of the 70's." (Why it was the '30s and not more appropriately the '20s is anyone's guess.) The proceeds from the event went to Los Angeles' Variety Clubs International's Boys Clubs.

AIP executive Milt Moritz felt that scoring the Pantages was a kind of coup, and that the setting itself somehow mirrored Phibes' ballroom's lonely period elegance: "That was probably the highlight of the film, when we had the premiere there. You went into that big cavernous theater and it was something out of the 20s and it lent itself so beautifully to the film. It really captured the mood of it... In its day, it seated close to 3,000 people... And you would have, say, a hundred people in the auditorium watching the film–it's pretty lonely because [it's gigantic]. We used to do promotions on 'How much can you stand seeing a film all by yourself at one of these big theaters at the stroke of midnight?'"

A stunned William Goldstein was present. (He had previously seen the film with several other people at AIP's offices, where they watched it on a moviola.) The event, Goldstein says, "Was a black-tie affair, red carpet, searchlights piercing the sky, and vintage cars moving up and down Sunset Boulevard. And as a kid from the country, my eyes filled with stardust," he laughs. "It was wonderful. I had my new wife with me. It was everything you read about."

As for the finished film, Goldstein was elated: "Filmmaking is a collaborative art, but the original package– everything worked beautifully– the art direction, the opener was spellbinding, and for that, you must give credit to Bob Fuest. Vincent nailed it as only he could and the deaths were clear and logical and have left a cultural imprint."

(Milt Moritz of AIP vividly recalls the Pantages' massive lobby display for *Dr. Phibes*: "On the outer lobby of the theater, there used to be a big wall–whatever the picture was playing there or coming, you'd do an oversize display. But that was in the outer lobby. The outer lobby of the Pantages today is totally different from what it was. In those days, you had the boxoffice almost in the center of the lobby. You would have those two big walls on the right and left of the outer lobby–I think it was as you walked in on the right side you would do a big cutout wall. And it was Dr. Phibes holding Virginia North in his arms.")

Reports vary as to when the film was released nationally– some say it was May 24th, 1971, others May 18th. According to Samuel Z. Arkoff, it was his partner Jim Nicholson who concocted *Dr. Phibes'* note-perfect tagline: "Love means never having to say you're ugly," a parody of Ali MacGraw's focal line in the hit *Love Story* (1970). This witty phrase perfectly fused *Dr. Phibes'* morbidly comic tone and intense romanticism. But, oddly enough, that catchphrase became a barrier for audiences.

As Arkoff recalled in his autobiography: "We previewed *The Abominable Dr. Phibes* widely, which was not our usual course. And everyone in Hollywood loved the movie and the ad. But when the picture opened in 1971 for a trial run it died at the box office. We were puzzled as to why audiences were treating the movie as though it were the black plague– until we took a closer look at our ad campaign. The public just didn't know what to make of the ad and the trailer. Was this a horror movie? Or was it a comedy? In Hollywood, the line was an inside joke; everywhere else, people were confused." AIP had gotten too smart for its own good.

"We reshaped the ad," Arkoff continued, "put a serious horror-style tagline on the campaign and sent the picture out again. This time, it attracted the usual horror fans, and with word of mouth, it also drew a more stylish, campy audience." The new, bland, conventional tagline for *Dr. Phibes* was also ridiculously hyperbolic: "Probably the most terrifying motion picture you will ever see." (Variations on this tagline were common in the late '60s-early '70s. AIP touted *Wild in the Streets* as "Perhaps the most unusual motion picture you'll ever see." *Walkabout* (1971) was advertised as "Just about the most different film you'll ever see.") The film's newspaper ad mats replaced the original "Mod"/Deco clinch between the unmasked Phibes and Vulnavia with Phibes' disfigured face in a "death's head" design, complete with crossed severed limbs. It may have been blunt, but, as Arkoff said, it paid off. (The American *Dr. Phibes* ad campaign killed the surprise reveal of Phibes' disfigured face during the film's climax by clearly picturing it in the one-sheet art, newspaper ads, and even the trailer. The British ad campaign was cannier, hiding Phibes' features behind this warning: "The authorities will not permit this photo to be shown on advertisements." There was also a set of three all-text British double crown posters with taglines like "There's a lot of people dying to tell you about 'Dr. Phibes' (unfortunately they're all dead.)" and "Dr. Phibes. . . Not so much a person—more a way of death [. . .] thanks to a great deal of painful research.")

Dr. Phibes' trailer opens with some simplistic "limited" animation, equal parts *Yellow Submarine* and Terry Gilliam's *Monty Python* cutouts. (Price narrated the theatrical trailer and Paul Frees narrated the tv version using the same script.) Shot in vivid, shifting, almost psychedelic colors, this prelude features Phibes and Vulnavia dancing, followed by a close-up of Phibes kissing Vulnavia. Phibes' face colorfully alternates between his masked and unmasked visages, and climaxes with his head cracking open, *a la* Gilliam. Since AIP followed entertainment trends religiously, they were no doubt aware of *Monty Python*'s popularity and very possibly hired someone to deliberately ape Gilliam's style. Gilliam himself recently said that he wasn't involved in this particular trailer (though he did animate the opening titles of AIP's other Price vehicle, *Cry of the Banshee*, around that time). The animation in the *Dr. Phibes* trailer is enjoyable, but lacks Gilliam's imagination and panache. Meanwhile, host Elliot Mintz spoke with Vincent Price about *Dr. Phibes* on the local L.A. TV series "Head Shop," aimed squarely (no pun intended) at a "with-it" audience.

AIP "did a huge amount of business" with *Dr. Phibes*, Ronald Dunas recalls. "I don't know what the total value of it was, but I think it's somewhere in excess of $40 million– something like that. It really was a very successful picture. And after I made that, I had some studios call me and ask me if I had anything like that to give them, which I didn't!" he laughs.

AIP's Milt Moritz had a wildly different take on the film's gross: "[*Dr. Phibes*] should have done better. In fact, we used to blow the grosses so out-of-proportion that I don't even remember what the heck the true numbers were, to tell you the truth. In those days, you basically had ... The only paper that would publish the grosses was *Variety* and they were so phony. You could call in any number you want. You could down $100,000, then $50,000, then ... Nobody was tracking your grosses so no one ever knew. Any numbers that were published in those years–believe me, how accurate they are is questionable." Moritz recalls this being true of other studios, too: "Absolutely. Everybody wanted to be number one or whatever."

THE CRITICS

After having gotten AIP into Radio City Music Hall, Fuest took them one step further: *Dr. Phibes* was screened at the Museum of Modern Art in early June, 1971, and again at the museum's 1979 AIP retrospective. Willard Van Dyke, then-head of MoMA's film department, told *Newsweek* that he had invited AIP to screen the film there because he had been impressed "that somebody would take the time and trouble to re-create so perfectly the '30s type of horror picture." "The film was a big success," Fuest told Irvin. "It ran six months in Paris in one cinema alone. AIP immediately approached me to do a sequel."

The *Fort Lauderdale News*' critic wrote: "John Wayne recently won an Academy Award for putting himself on in *True Grit*. Price's portrayal here makes Wayne look like a beginner at the art. For Price is doing the same thing– laughing at films which have made him famous."

The New York Times voiced the most common complaint about the film: "The tone of steamroller camp flattens the fun." Accusations of being merely weird for weirdness' sake have been leveled at it, and Speaking for the film's detractors, one commentator observed that it's "Too clever by half."

But notices were generally very good:

Evening Standard (UK). August 19, 1971.
"He sets a new style that Hammer will find hard to rival with a self-service sarcophagus and an automat embalmer. "Progress, progress . . ."

The Sun (UK). August 19, 1971.
"It is the Everest of high camp."

Jewish Chronicle (UK). August 20, 1971.
"The film exudes a bizarre fascination . . ."

Kinematograph Weekly. August, 21, 1971.
Edited by Graham Clarke.

"This is a first-class, cod horror, exciting in its absurdity and very funny. Excellent X attraction . . . Vincent Price as Dr. Phibes, of course, strides through this phantasmagoria of witty burlesque with an enjoyment that is bound to be shared by audiences, and the nonsense is ably supported by some deadpan funny performances."

Evening Mail. August 20, 1971.
"On Film." Neil Stevens.
"Price makes it a real comedy of terrors."
"With not a word to say, Virginia North conveys the essence of everything this film is about."

Harpers Queen. September, 1971.
"Queen's Counsel." June Stockwood.
"*The Abominable Dr. Phibes* is a horror film not to be missed."

ABC Film Review. October, 1971.
"Joining Phibes in Phear and Phun." Peter Haigh.
"*The Abominable Dr. Phibes* is one of the most stylish macabre thrillers in many a moon, raising the genre to a new level."
But there were exceptions to the generally praiseful tone:

Daily Express. August 20, 1971.
Michael Walsh.
"All you need for the complete appreciation of the abominable doctor is a strong stomach and weak head."

Critics' descriptions of *Dr. Phibes* were often as colorful as the film itself, like Bridget Byrnes in the *Herald Examiner*: "Outwardly mute, he stethescopes his voice in eulogies to his dead lady and threats of doom to his victims: His subtle sense of superior menace is displayed to advantage." Future director Joe Dante (*Gremlins, The Howling*)—then, a critic—gave the film a glowing write-up in the *Film Bulletin*: "Successful horror spoofs are as rare as werewolf tusks, but *Phibes* manages to serve up enough style, wit and—yes— even subtlety, along with some pretty horrific horrors, to entertain a broad range of audiences." Youngsters, of course, adored the film. A young fan named Lee wrote to Vincent Price in 1971: "My mom was scared. I was scared a little. I think the sick part was when the locusts ate that gooky stuff on that lady's head and they ate that gooky stuff up and her skin with it . . . All the movie was good. Much Love, Lee." Price kept the letter for his files.

The film's sternest critic was the outstanding British horror film historian David Pirie. Pirie called *Dr. Phibes* "Perhaps the worst horror film made in England since 1945." Pirie recently said in hindsight: "I was too scathing before but my bottom line is, cross horror and comedy and you always get comedy, not horror. So I don't really put those kinds of camp extravaganzas in the field."

But the naysayers were, and are, in the minority. Among the film's fans are directors Frank (*The Shawshank Redemption*) Darabont, screenwriter Stanley (*Wall Street*) Weiser, and Vincent Price aficionado Tim Burton. In 2010, Burton wrote: "Vincent Price played so many great tragic characters. The most fun to watch is Dr. Anton Phibes in *The Abominable Dr. Phibes*." (Conversely, Brian Eatwell thought very little of Burton's *Edward Scissorhands*, calling it "atrocious and naïve).”

Logically, the great Ken Russell, whose films were as wild and bizarre in their own way as Fuest's, was a big fan of the Dr. Phibes series. Russell's widow, Lisi Tribble, recalls: "Ken loved *Dr. Phibes* and consequently Fuest. We watched it and he talked about how compatible his and Fuest's worldview were. He especially loved that band! He loved the acid meandering down in the tube. He loved the river journey with his dead wife. Each person dying through their own misdeeds-- tailor-made deaths - he loved that. He loved Vincent Price playing the organ . . . He loved that his mask's lips wouldn't move. He chortled all the way through Phibes, delighted in it; and in what he thought was a good sequel, going to Egypt and the desert. He liked the idea of someone made monstrous through injustice and undying love."

The film has occasionally been wrongly accused of various errors, which deserve to be cleared up, while others have been largely overlooked. Robert Fuest confirmed that actor Sean Bury wasn't dubbed in post. (Author's note: In my earlier version of this essay,

I noted that the scene where Vulnavia plays her violin at around two in the morning appeared to have been shot "day-for-night" and was meant to be timed-down (darkened during printing) later, and that these timing directions were probably lost at some point or ignored by whoever made the print that was used for the film's video releases– a common problem seen in video transfers. However, after having seen a 35mm print of the film where that scene was as well-lit as the video versions, I cannot say this for sure.)

One problem that rankled Fuest but that generally goes undetected is that the sepia slides Phibes watches of Victoria are "in completely the wrong aspect ratio," Fuest told Marcus Hearn. He had a "back-projectionist from Pinewood" who was "supposedly brilliant" in to do the job. And though this technician "made such a fuss with all this equipment" he had brought, his work was "totally inept." To remedy this, the scene features cuts to insert shots of black and white images of Victoria that are correctly projected.

Though it looks strange, the reason that Phibes' hand movements don't match the music emitting from his organ is that pipe organists' hand movements rarely match their fingering: there is a delay between the keys actually being hit and the notes issuing from the organ. This odd phenomenon has also been incorrectly regarded as a mistake in reference to Candace Hilligoss' organ-playing in *Carnival of Souls* (1962). Actual errors include the fact that Dr. Longstreet has a movie projector with anachronistic built-in musical accompaniment, circa 1925, and there is a briefly-visible crew/equipment shadow in the foreground while Schenley chases after Dr. Kitaj's plane.

THE SEQUEL

Briefly glimpsed within Phibes' tomb-for-two in the film is a telephone. When asked about it, Vincent Price reportedly insisted: "How [else] would the outside world contact me – for a sequel?" *Dr. Phibes* proved so popular that AIP frantically cranked out a follow-up, *Dr. Phibes Rises Again* (1972). Written by Fuest and AIP's story editor Robert Blees, the film opens with Phibes' revivification by a timed mechanism within his crypt. He's pitted against the brilliant Biederbeck, who, unlike the police in the first film, was actually a worthy adversary. The two compete for the key to the secret Egyptian river of eternal life, where Phibes hopes to revive his Victoria and, Biederbeck, to prolong his epically long life. Phibes triumphs, naturally. Playing on audiences' obvious affection for Phibes, in the sequel, the good doctor loosened up a bit, becoming a shade funnier, lighter, sympathetic, and all-around likable. At the film's climax, Biederbeck screams "What kind of fiend are you, Phibes?" "The kind that WINS, my friend," he replies– easily the film's finest line, and the series' coda. But *Dr. Phibes* really didn't need a sequel: Phibes' embalmment gave the story symmetry as it stood, bringing the story neatly full-circle. [Note: For full coverage of the making of *Dr. Phibes Rises Again*, see the next chapter. –JH]

Phibes Resurrectus, based on a script by Whiton and Goldstein, was announced in the coming attractions sections of magazines like *Famous Monsters* and *Boxoffice* during the '70s. An AIP press release ran: "American International expects to have a DR. PHIBES series [sic] with Vincent Price every year through 1975." Ironically, various sequel ideas involved resurrection– something that Dr. Phibes has yet to achieve on the big screen.

EPILOGUE

With its raging romanticism, wit, deft sense of the macabre, and its boundless style, *The Abominable Dr. Phibes* has won generation upon generation of fans. The good doctor lives on as model kits and toys, in comic books, musical tributes by a variety of bands, and in companion novels by his creator, William Goldstein. And since, along with Whiton, Fuest and Price, Goldstein really is one of Phibes' papas, he deserves the last word on their offspring.

"We all need a little affirmation and this one has been more of a forty-year love affair," Goldstein says. "It's nice to get the comments... It's nice to meet and speak with people like Justin Humphreys. And it's nice to get every now and then serious offers with the financial positives that go with them. Mainly, the fact that, if I may say so, here's my baby who has gotten legs of his own and it's still attracting attention– that's a good thing, that's a good feeling."

Somewhere, Anton Phibes is chuckling fiendishly.

He's won.

Vulnavia Interlude

In the spirit of the marvelous non-sequitur interludes in both Dr. Phibes films where Vulnavia wafts around ethereally, here are several pages of her in all her mysterious glory—text-free and "silent," naturally.

Chapter 2
The Coffin Hasn't Been Built That Can Hold Him: The Making of *Dr. Phibes Rises Again*

By Justin Humphreys

"[Producers James] Nicholson and [Samuel Z.] Arkoff just wanted to do it, make their money, and to hell with everything else. The movie does have its moments, though. But it was rearranged and chopped and changed and, well, it's just not the same as my originally planned version." —Robert Fuest

> *"The wisdom of the heavens now be shown...*
> *Where in this place where Pharoahs once reside*
> *A palace I have built beneath the stone.*
>
> *And filled with thoughts of our eternal ride*
> *We'll watch the darkest waters ebb and flow*
> *To wait*
> *<u>UNTIL THE GREAT APPOINTED TIDE</u>."*
> *Dr. Phibes, from the script to* Dr. Phibes Rises Again.

THE CHAPTER:

American International Pictures never passed up an opportunity to make a sequel or milk a franchise if they stood to profit by it. Whether it was their '50s teen monster movies or the '60s Beach Party movies, they would ride any horse that paid off until it died. AIP had had a lucky streak with Vincent Price's series of Edgar Allan Poe vehicles, so a Dr. Phibes series seemed like a potentially equally rich vein to mine.

But making a follow-up to *The Abominable Dr. Phibes* posed several immediate problems. For openers, the original was a beautifully self-contained work: Phibes appeared, got revenge, and then seamlessly embalmed and interred himself—The End. Where—and why—do you carry that story any further? Secondly, Dr. Phibes' plot was structured around the Egyptian Plagues theme-killings. What similar overarching structure would take their place? And, lastly, how do you maintain audiences' perverse sympathy and affection for this most inventive of murderers?

Fortunately for AIP, they had a bottomless font of imagination at their disposal in the form of director Robert Fuest. If anyone could map out Dr. Phibes' criminal adventures with style and wit, it was him.

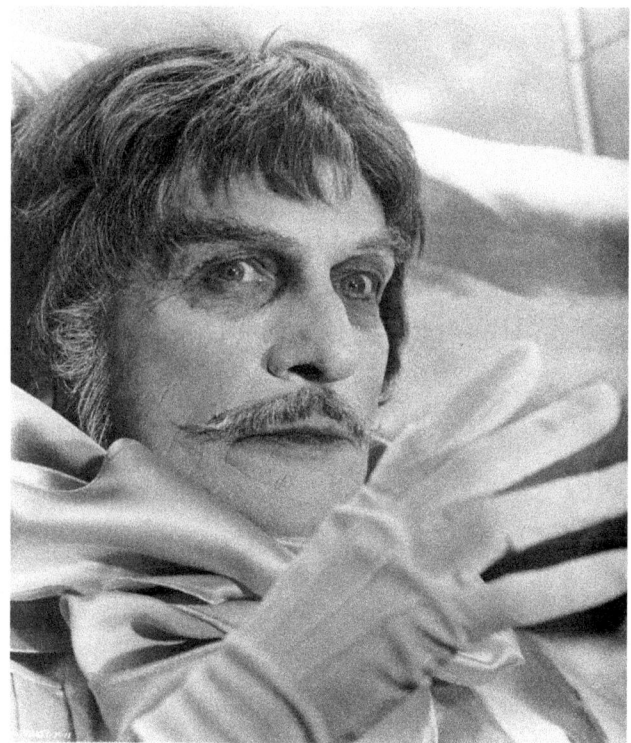

THE SCRIPT

[Author's Note: For more information about the early drafts of *Dr. Phibes Rises Again*, please refer to "The Unphilmed Phibes" chapter elsewhere in this book.]

Fuest began building his story to tie in with the British Museum's Treasures of Tutankhamen exhibit, which was to begin on March 30, 1972. Designed to commemorate the fiftieth anniversary of the discovery of King Tut's tomb, this enormously popular exhibit drew over a million visitors in less than a year. Having established Phibes' fascination with Egypt in the first film, Phibes and Vulnavia actually traveling there was a logical progression.

The sequel, *Dr. Phibes Rises Again*'s, plot took the structure of the original *Dr. Phibes* and inverted it: instead of killing in the style of curses visited upon one of the Pharoahs, Phibes killed the script's tomb raiders in the spirit of the legendary curse Tutankhamen supposedly visited upon the defilers of his tomb. The fact that King Tut's tomb had been discovered in 1922, only a few years before the events of the original *Dr. Phibes*, made an archaeological milieu all the more apropos.

Rises Again would be loosely structured like *Dr. Phibes*, but matching its predecessor's symmetry, cleverness, and wild invention was a tall order. Instead of having a definite pattern, they could easily just end up being wacky killings . . . which they ultimately did. As horror historian Kim Newman noted, the script Fuest filmed "lacks the beautiful ruthlessness of the plot of *The Abominable Dr. Phibes*, which is structured around the twelve plagues of Egypt . . . Without this structure, this goes a bit haywire . . ."

William Goldstein observes, "Basically, *Phibes Rises Again*, while it has measurable production values that look good on the screen, it has pretty good performances from both leads– it misses what has come to be known as the key ingredient of a Phibes story: it doesn't have the death geometry. It has killings in it, but they're disconnected, they're random, they're doctrinaire– they're not all that inventive. Other than that, it did okay." Though there was ultimately no hard framework to *Rises Again*'s murders, most of them have a distinctly Egyptian flavor, involving snakes, scorpions, sand, etc.

One deft shift from *The Abominable Dr. Phibes*, though, was to give Phibes a worthy opponent: the centuries-old, brilliant Biderbeck. Phibes had faced very little resistance from the bumbling detectives of the first film. Here the seemingly insuperable Phibes was pitted against an archrival very nearly—but not quite-- his equal.

Fuest was a major music enthusiast, and particularly liked trumpeting-- "[Fuest] liked his jazz," composer John Gale said. As he wrote, Fuest named many of the film's main characters after famous

Robert Fuest and the film's sarcophagus.

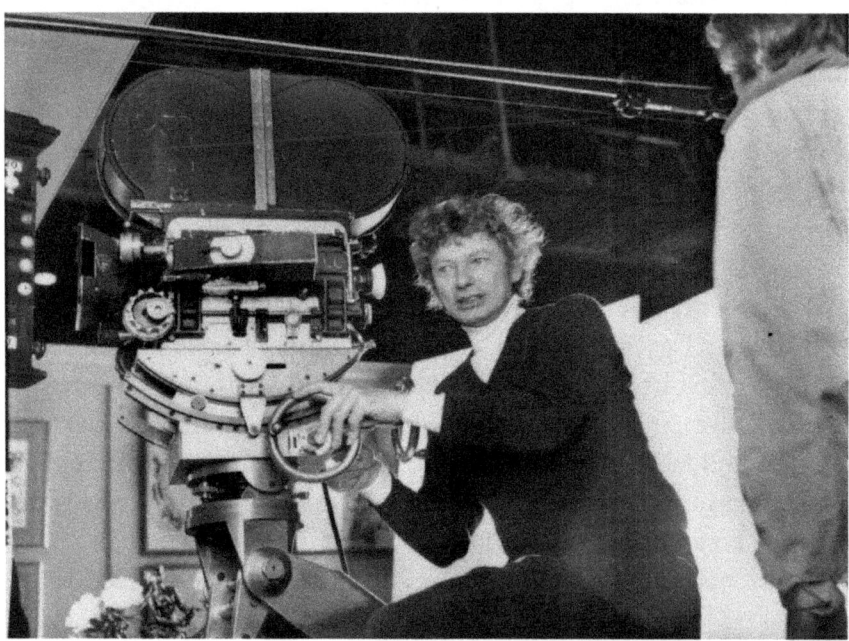

Fuest filming.

Fuest confers with a script person.

(L-R) John Cater, Peter Jeffrey, Fuest, and Terry-Thomas.

trumpeters: Biderbeck after cornetist Bix Biederbecke; Shavers was named after Charlie Shavers; Baker, after Chet Baker; Hackett, after Bobby Hackett; Stewart, after Rex Stewart; Lombardo, after Guy Lombardo; and though not a trumpeter, Ambrose was possibly named after the English bandleader Bert Ambrose. Fuest also said that he added in a line, "Hackett, meet Biederbeck," because Bix Beiderbecke had, in reality, heavily influenced Bobby Hackett.

Two literary jokes in the script may also have originated with Fuest. Just before a victim is crushed by a screw-like device, he sets down a copy of Henry James' *The Turn of the Screw*. And when Phibes' Clockwork Wizards are relocated to Egypt, they are renamed "The Alexandrian Quartet"—a play on a group of books by Lawrence Durrell.

But the single, and seemingly most logical, plot point that was never used (and may have never even been brought up) was this: Why doesn't the film end with Victoria returning to life? The opening scene firmly posits the film in a near-fantasy realm: the embalming fluid in Phibes' veins pumps out as he refills with blood, followed by Vulnavia's entrance from some netherworld, setting a tone of life eternal—these are obviously *deathless* creatures. (The same (almost) goes for Biderbeck, who is a kind of Jazz Age Dorian Gray.) *Rises Again* is a film about rebirth: it begins with these resurrections and ends with Phibes seemingly poling off to immortality with Victoria's body, with Vulnavia joining them. In a film so full of unreal plot convolutions, why isn't Victoria revivified?

Prior to all this, William Goldstein and James Whiton had written a sequel of their own, *Phibes Resurrectus*, which differed wildly from Fuest and his eventual co-screenwriter, Robert Blees's, script: It was "Totally [different]," Goldstein says. "A 180 . . . But I should say this: the thinking was at AIP that Phibes was going to be a five-picture franchise and that was one of the reasons I picked up my family and moved to [Los Angeles].

"AIP commissioned [*Phibes Resurrectus*]-- it was in our contract– we thought, as we were developing the story with Bob Blees, who was the story editor at AIP, all we knew was that our script was going to be the next Phibes film."

In working with Blees, Goldstein found him to be a "Very low-key, laid-back type. He actually looked a bit frail when we worked with him. When you're working with a story editor, you have regular meetings, but never in any of those meetings did we get any inkling that he was developing another story."

Looking back on AIP using a completely different script, Goldstein remains philosophical: "That's the business ... Here's another cliche: you really can't look back. I mean, I could and feel bad about it, but that wouldn't serve any purpose ...

"We had weekly working sessions with Blees, and we thought everything was going along swimmingly. The script– and I've read it recently– is tight. We were in this groove– we found our groove, partly because the first film was still in release, AIP was really excited about it, and in this business, real excitement is rare, and there was real excitement, so everything seemed to be working."

Goldstein puts the basic flaws in the Phibes follow-up as filmed down to "Sequelitis!" He adds, "I just saw *Phibes Rises* a couple of weeks ago, and it does have more 'flat' than it should have."

Co-producer "Deke" Heyward explained Tom Weaver how Blees was brought on the project: "I brought out from L.A. a writer named Bob Blees, a dear friend; he did for me one of the best emotion-laden pictures ever made, *Magnificent Obsession* [(1954)]. And he also had a sly sense of humor which I felt would fit in with Phibes. Now, Bob Fuest wanted to write this second film, and the two of 'em did not see eye-to-eye on anything. They were two men with great senses of integrity, but one protecting director's viewpoint and the other protecting writer's viewpoint. The visions that Fuest enjoyed were in his head; the visions that Blees had were on paper—and easier to handle. So suddenly you were referee, placed in a position you did not want to be in because they were both right. It was a question of allowing them to as far as they could, and then saying to yourself, 'Don't worry, there'll be a rewrite at the end and we'll straighten out whatever doesn't seem to work.' That's of course what followed."

Blees himself told Denis Meikle: "The boys who'd written the first one [Goldstein and Whiton] turned in something that just didn't work. AIP had a commitment with Vincent Price for $75,000 to

Fuest and Beryl Reid.

The director and cast of Fear in the Night visit Price during a break. (L-R) Jimmy Sangster, Ralph Bates, Price, and Judy Geeson. (Courtesy of Andy Roffey.).

do the sequel and, to Sam [Arkoff] that was an awful lot of money ... The instruction was basically, 'Give us eight reels, and every reel has a guest star and a horror/comedic payoff.'"

While Fuest wrote his version at home, Blees crafted his in a London hotel. There wasn't much interaction between the two; Blees flew back to America; and Fuest cobbled together a new, and by his own estimation, "schizophrenic" version of the two. On another occasion, Fuest told Sam Irvin: "AIP immediately approached me to do a sequel. I wrote the script to the second one, and sent it to AIP for approval. They had one of their writers change a few things, and the sequence of events was rearranged. I got it back and was relatively pleased."

Fuest also got input during filming from his dear friend and brilliant collaborator, production designer Brian Eatwell. "We started filming," Fuest told Tony Earnshaw, "and we'd done the first week, but we hadn't got the ending. Brian came round to my house at about ten o'clock at night with a huge bottle of wine and said, 'Listen, I'm not going home until we've sorted out this ending. I've got the art department on my back.' And we sat down in my living room and worked through the night. Neither of us went to bed. It's madness to start a film without actually having an ending."

In Fuest's shooting script—likely containing various ideas from Blees—the moon and stars are in proper alignment, setting the machinery of Phibes' house in motion through "a window of most extraordinary shape and design ... a complex glass skylight set in the roof of PHIBES' shrine room." From within the earth comes "a primeval howl almost shattering the eardrums" as the Moon on Phibes' tomb begins a glowing "heart-like beat." The embalming fluid is pumped hydraulically out of Phibes' veins and his blood rushes back in.

Three years have passed since Phibes' disappearance, and he awakens to carry his beloved Victoria to Egypt to resurrect her and find eternal life for them both. Vulnavia enters, as in the first film, in "an ecstatic burst of unreal glow" to join him on his quest. Phibes climbs out of his cellar (he rides the organ up in the finished film) only to discover "Absolute desolation," a "wrecking vehicle," and a demolition sign. "If the world has done this to him whilst he and his beloved slept," the script ran, "he shall have revenge and victory!" (Vincent Price wrote "Needs line" next to this in his script. In the final, reedited film, new expository dialogue was added here.)

The next scene begins with the erudite Biderbeck's hand "stabbing into" what at first appears to be Egypt, but is actually a scale model. (Fuest had used a similar visual trick in his *Just Like a Woman*.) Biderbeck is described as "a man with infinite interests and the income to indulge them" who is planning a trip to Egypt of his own in search of the legendary tomb of King Amenophis, which he is certain "leads to the River of Life... and the secret of immortality." He reveals to his associate Ambrose that he has almost all the pieces of the fabled Osiris Papyrus, which is apparently critical to their finding the tomb. Ambrose describes Biderbeck as "Acclaimed as certainly the most brilliant mind in the Western hemisphere."

Biderbeck, Ambrose, and Biderbeck's lady-love, Diana Trowbridge, go out for the evening, with Biderbeck's house left guarded by his massive manservant Bruno (Cheng, in the film). Phibes murders Bruno and makes off with the papyrus. Bruno/Cheng plays pool by himself and is startled by a group of snakes. He kills one and discovers it's one of Phibes' clockwork creations, but another snake proves to be all-too-alive and poisons him. He races to the phone and is impaled from ear-to-ear by a golden snake-shaped spike in the earpiece. In a very funny deleted gag, Bruno/Chang's body's police chalk outline had marks indicating the "protuberances" of the golden snake that penetrated his head!

Phibes is shown preparing for his trip by adding an elegant hammock to Victoria's tomb. A scene of Biderbeck overseeing two dockworkers loading his crates of gear aboard ship was later dropped. Phibes travels with "The Most Magnificent Calliope": "A mobile steam organ built on the lines of a fairground trailer. This is not a mere mechanical organ, but has incorporated into it various devices like snare drums, tambourines, trumpets and clarinets. Miniature mechanical men appear to be playing the instruments themselves. The gold and silver and scarlet paints are most elaborate and delightful." In a gorgeous, fanciful segue from Phibes' house's ruins to their ship, mist envelopes him and Vulnavia as they dance, then clears, revealing them on the deck: "As we pull back from this close-up we discover that Vulnavia is in a different dress! As we pull back further – the massive keel of a lifeboat appears in the frame – we read the name plate on the side – 'The Empress of Quebec.'"

Phibes and Vulnavia are aboard the same ship that Biderbeck, Diana, and Ambrose are taking. Ambrose discovers Victoria's calliope coffin and is thrown overboard in a giant gin bottle by Phibes. When his body is discovered in the film, a line was added during production: "He's corked, sir."

Waverly and Trout are once again on the case. Much of Waverly's very British comic dialogue throughout was cut, such as: "A man in a bottle? A bit unusual, yes, but he was washed up in the Channel, now, wasn't he? Across from France, you think of that, Trout? A typical Frenchie kind of homicide, eh? Bizarre... absinthe... wine for the kiddies, eh, Trout?"

Trout immediately realizes that Phibes is once again at work: "The golden asp business (an uneasy pause) I would describe that as typically Phibesian, sir." But, dense as ever, Waverly completely blows off Trout's theories about Phibes' connection to the murders and Trout's plan to travel to Egypt in search of him, but their boss, "the Old Man," thinks Trout is dead on the money. Waverly tries to play it off: "And listen, Trout. I've come to a decision about this Phibes matter. I've got the Old Man to give in to me as he usually does when I'm on the scent of something important. Ever been to Egypt? Thought not. Can't waste time. We'll go out on a flying boat, R.A.F. *Calshot*, eighteen hundred hours tonight, right? Don't just stand there, man, draw your tropical gear, get cracking!" (This entire segue was either never filmed or cut.)

Meanwhile, in Egypt, Phibes and Vulnavia stop for an elegant lunch: "An umbrella has already been set up. While Vulnavia is busy at the calliope, opening its cargo doors, Phibes has just started to utilize his famous BRIAN WORMSCREW, an item about four feet long, it appears, and about eight inches in diameter. Phibes sticks its sharp point down into the sand, then unlocks the handles at the other end. These handles are golden, and for decoration are in the shape of two jackals' heads. By turning he handle, the screw bites into the sand, presenting a practical support for a table top."

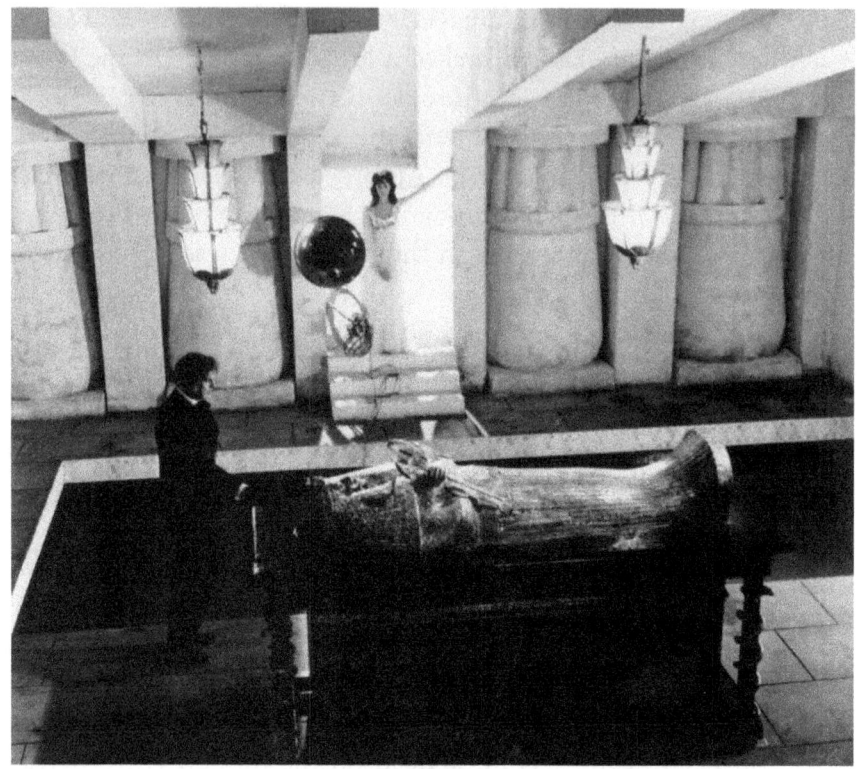

An uncropped set still revealing the set's upper edge.

Phibes opens the calliope, revealing a series of alphabetically labeled drawers. Under "C," he pulls out a bottle of champagne.

Phibes arrives at the hidden mountainside entrance to his Egyptian lair, where, in horror, he spots tire tracks in the sand, memorizes their tread pattern, and the shot jumps to the actual tires, on Hackett's truck. (This effect was similar to visual segues in *Dr. Phibes*.) As Phibes dusts off his lair, he ironically plays "The Sheik of Araby" on his organ.

As Biderbeck and his men make camp, his associate Shavers discovers Phibes' lair—Phibes and Vulnavia see him, he turns tail and runs, and she sets an eagle after him. It kills him, then the scene shifts to a "Rocky Crag" on the mountain: "For a moment the screen seems filled with huge black wings, until we discern that it is Phibes himself, with a great swoop of cloak, making his way to the top of a mountain crag, where, lying hidden in a secret place of its own, is

Phibes' meteorological and observation post. An anemometer and such like are there, most of them covered (like the furniture) with protective wrappings. Phibes tears away the covering of the largest object to reveal a telescope. He looks through it...adjusts the focus. ..moves in on its massive tripod to look to..."

... Biderbeck's camp, in a scene that introduces Shavers, Stuart (later Stewart), and the rest of his company, first seen sitting around playing poker and grousing, and wondering why they are "here" when they could be after Tutankhamen's tomb-like riches: "Right now, we could be in the Valley of the Kings," gripes Stuart.

"Can't get in, old chap," Baker replies. "Everybody's going there. It's fully booked."

"They're standing in the Nile," says Stuart.

Shavers and Stuart are bored at the camp and tell Hackett that they want go to on "a little walkabout," but he reminds them of Biderbeck's strict instructions to remain in camp.

Diana and Biderbeck talk, and she mentions some background information that is missing from the film: she has been with him "Ever since I was put in your care after that horrible accident." Diana complains that Biderbeck is "so callous now ... d'you honestly care what I really think? Do you?"

In Phibes' lair, he arranging his main laboratory: "Phibes has set up his research lab, the principal feature of which is what we shall call a 'Moon Clock.' This ornate panel, beautifully adorned with ancient and contemporary devices, features the signs of the Zodiac, the Planets in the heavens, the Sun and the Moon. There are definite similarities in style between all this and the lid of the crypt in Maldine Square, with its heavenly bodies." One important feature is a "window," like the part of a dial of a calendar-watch, which shows numbers in decreasing order (like a countdown). In fact, even as we watch, the number "8" is slowly passing from view and "7" is taking its place. A series of ancient wall paintings explaining how the Egyptians would flood and drain these tombs, explaining why they were undiscovered, were never filmed (or possibly cut).

Phibes discovers Amenophis's sarcophagus chamber which has "decorations which make descriptions folly!" As Biderbeck and his men venture into the mountain, one of Fuest's best sight gags has

"Phibes in his bare skull" burying himself among the skeletons of ages-old dead slave workers so that he can covertly observe Biderbeck and his party.

That night, Phibes uses Vulnavia as bait to lead Stewart into a trap. Disguised as an old Bedouin, Phibes collects money from Stewart so he can see Vulnavia dance (and potentially screw her). Her dance "almost justifies an 'X' certificate," the script goes.

Originally, Stewart sits in a scorpion chair whose claws trap him; spikes driving into his wrists were added in the film. Phibes takes the key to the chair and drops it in "An intriguing pottery item, a container of some sort, more or less round, with a slot in the top its only opening"—which, in the film, became the EMI "His Master's Voice" dog. (EMI owned Elstree Studios at the time.)

Shavers body was originally discovered when an old Arab worker goes to raise a Union Jack over Biderbeck's camp, only to have the corpse flop down with a golden eagle impaled in him, its talons driven into his eye sockets. Cut to Phibes triumphantly playing the organ and Vulnavia doing a victory dance.

Waverly and Trout spot Stewart's body seated on its fatal golden throne, which Waverly refuses to believe is anything but a mirage: "What's it look like, eh? Some bloody beggar baked to a crisp sitting in some ridiculous golden throne arrangement! That make any sense at all? You think you're actually seeing that? It's the sirocco, Trout, that and the foreign food we've had to put up with. . ." They investigate only to make a gruesome discovery akin to Nurse Allan's corpse in *Dr. Phibes*: "Scorpions are still feeding on choice tid-bits. Eye sockets are empty.

Bone is showing. Dried blood. (It might be well to provide First-Aid personnel in the theaters during this footage.)"

"Sir," Trout ventures, "if I may say so, this also looks to be typically--

"Not yet," Waverly tensely replies. "Don't mention that name to me just yet."

As they move the throne toward the camera, a visual segue connects the throne and the sarcophagus Phibes and Vulnavia are transporting. Phibes hooks up his throat-mic and assures his deceased beloved that, in two days, he will find the hidden River of Life: "Until then, my darling, sleep your dreamless sleep. . . and await your true awakening!" Inadvertently, Phibes discovers the key to the River of Life—he is ecstatic.

Back at the camp, Biderbeck delivers the "Amen" at Shavers' funeral service. His Arab bearers are visibly alarmed by the murder. (The script reads: "(PRODUCTION NOTE: Covering close-ups depending on first or second unit work, availabilities, etc. To be specified by R.F. [Robert Fuest] and A.F. [Albert Fennell]") Waverly and Trout arrive with Stewart's corpse on the throne and, to Biderbeck's horror, the Arabs desert him en masse. Waverly hands Biderbeck an i.d. disc: "Knew he was with your expedition by this. (a pause) Fortunately scorpions can't devour aluminum."

Trout and Waverly explain the situation to Biderbeck, and tell him about Phibes. "I'd almost like to meet him," Biderbeck "ruefully" says—a clear indication he realizes Phibes is his match. Waverly reveals he has withdrawn Biderbeck's permission "To explore in this area" from English government officials in Egypt, "And as a result of my full and complete delineation of the entire Phibes matter, a Battalion of the Scottish Fusiliers is even now en route by forced march to this very spot. . . to hunt Dr. Phibes--or whoever it may be--to hunt him out no matter where he is lurking!"

Biderbeck resists, but Waverly insists that the Fusiliers will "smoke" Phibes out of the "rabbit warren" of tunnels within the mountain. Hackett and Baker are eager to pull up stakes and leave. Biderbeck asks for the approximately thirty-six hours it will take the Fusiliers to arrive to continue with his work, and Waverly grants it to him.

Cut to Phibes' Moon Clock: "A projection of the Moon is slowly coming into perfect register with the golden moon of the device. . . and other rays of light (as if in a planetarium) are also converging toward several intersecting lines embossed on the face of the panel. . . so that, if the image of the moon continues in the same way, and the lines continue to move in the same ways, EVERYTHING will be in perfect register. (R.F. [Robert Fuest] and B.E. [Brian Eatwell] have this all worked out.)" Phibes and Vulnavia delightedly observe Biderbeck's camp being struck through their telescope.

The alarmed Diana packs and Biderbeck coaxes her into staying. Back in Phibes' main chamber, Vulnavia weaves a massive tapestry while Phibes plays some "at home" music like "Who's Sorry Now?" (Unlike the first *Dr. Phibes*, there was, in the end, very little in the way of period music, despite these specific song choices by Fuest.)

The next day, Biderbeck and company head into the main corridor within the mountain. Waverly and Trout scan the surrounding area for anything suspicious. "That's the way he works, damn it," Waverly says. "Underhanded. Least expect it. Foreign descent, I wager. Couldn't be British." As the group goes further into the mountain, Biderbeck anticipates a *Raiders of the Lost Ark*-like booby trap, which he triggers, causing a small cave-in. It reveals a hidden ramp and chamber, which they enter.

Phibes and Vulnavia watch the Moon Clock ticking down, then "He takes her hand... a gesture not dissimilar to Biderbeck's with Diana, incidentally." They enter the secret chamber only to find that Biderbeck has smashed through a wall and taken the sarcophagus. Phibes' response is mute horror.

Biderbeck and company toast their victory with beer back at their campsite. Biderbeck is elated: "Probably the greatest find of the Century. If I can... unravel... all the secrets locked in there... it will be more important than—Tutankhamen... perhaps more important than the Rosetta Stone..." Alone, Biderbeck examines the sarcophagus and to his amazement and utter delight, he discovers that it contains an undisturbed mummy.

"SMASH CUT" to the furious Phibes, speaking to a photograph of Victoria through his "Moon Clock jack." Phibes dashes off. That evening, using a massive "propeller wind machine," he creates a sandstorm that plays out much as it does in Fuest's film. To kill Baker, "Phibes is now using the famous Brian [Eatwell] wormscrew, first seen at the picnic, for a much more fiendish purpose." Phibes crushes Baker in the vice-like device, which feature a jackal's head that was subsequently deleted. With Baker dead, Phibes enter his tent and using a remote control, jacks the propeller machine up from "Medium" to "Maximum." He triumphantly unveils the scarcophagus and, with Vulnavia at the wheel of the truck it rests on, the two drive off with it.

The next morning Biderbeck and a tearful Diana discover Baker's remains: "There have also been two busts of Egyptian royalty--gold and purple designs, elaborate headdress--on a table of their own. Now, next to them, as a CAMERA ZOOM POINTS OUT, is what remains of poor Baker... a normal-sized head, to be sure, but below that a 'body' only one foot square, comprised, so car as we can tell, of a compressed sleeping bag and cot." Waverly demands that they strike camp and leave in ninety minutes or less; they will join Major Braff and his Fusiliers at a nearby oasis.

Within his "condominium," Phibes speaks comfortably to Victoria's corpse: "I will keep you by my side for these next three hours... and then will be revealed to us the true meaning of the conjunction of the Moon, the spirits of Isis and Osiris, and the secret of the Mountains of Ibiscus! We shall wait together... We shall find together the River of Life... Together we shall unlock the door to Reincarnation and Eternal Life!" Again, Biderbeck disrupts his plan: The key has vanished.

Back at camp, Biderbeck fondles the key as the others pack. He desperately tries to calm the unsettled Diana, who is becoming increasingly deaf to Biderbeck's entreaties. Waverly enters and in his usual inarticulate, utterly British way tries to assuage Biderbeck's annoyance: "Realize it's a disappointment, naturally, suppose it's like getting a great monster salmon right up to the net and having him break the line, what? But there's more fish in the sea, right? Now I must insist, sir." Diana decides to leave with Waverly and company in their first truck.

Major Braff of the Scottish Fusiliers shows up on a motorcycle, with his men an hour behind him. (Braff's scenes, like so many others, may or may not have been filmed—it's likely they weren't. Either way, excising his character undercut the buildup to a later gag involving the Fusiliers.) Along the way, he had a "Most unusual experience, maps all show permanently dry waddy eleven miles back. Monstrous depression. No reason to doubt military maps, what? Plunged down the bank, found myself up to the hubcaps in water. Absolute flash flood, queer, eh?" He adds: "Seemed like that whole bloody mountain sprung a leak." Biderbeck is elated—this is exactly the eleventh-hour clue he needed. (Fuest used a similar ironic device in *Dr. Phibes* when Lem offhandedly mentions "the great organists" and tips Vesalius off to Darrow. Fuest was parodying the mystery fiction chestnut of having a character casually provide an integral clue.)

Braff goes on to conveniently say: "Incredible, whole river of water, probably seep away by the time you go back. Old Bedouin on a camel on the opposite bank, very poor English, matter of fact, but finally made sense of him, going through all sorts of rigmarole about superstitions and legends, last time it happened four hundred, five hundred years ago, some fanciful myth..."

Braff's other dialogue was 100% pure British Fuest humor. The Major intends to use explosives to smoke Phibes out: "Understand this fellow's probably skulking about that mountain? Bloody big pile. Done it before. Big bang... couple of dozen sticks should do it... bastard comes out." Waverly and Braff discuss striking camp and Braff loudly demands that Diana leave immediately, for her own safety. From afar, Phibes observes them and eavesdrops using another of his wild gadgets: "He is fiddling with a special attachment to his ear mechanism... a miniature copper aerial, suspended about eight inches from miniature pole to miniature pole, the whole linked to his audio-sensory unit." Using this surveillance device, he can hear the conversation back at the camp. Phibes is pleased.

Diana—at first stoically, then tearfully—leaves with Hackett. As they travel through the desert, they hear blaring bagpipes and marching feet and see the Fusiliers heading in the wrong direction. The camera reveals that the Fusiliers are in fact Phibes' Clockwork Wizards in kilts, with one of them carrying a Victrola playing bagpipe music with marching sound effects.

The car's door opens, revealing Vulnavia. Diana remembers her from aboard ship: "Oh--! You came out on the Empress of Quebec, too! (extends her hand) I know we were never introduced, but I'm Diana Trowbridge!" Vulnavia reaches toward Diana, with something in her hand.

Meanwhile, Hackett races over the dunes to the "Fusiliers" while Phibes is briefly seen putting something in the car's engine. Hackett discovers Phibes' trick and darts back to Diana's car in time to see Phibes' Rolls-Royce driving off. He reaches the car, with no Diana in sight. He starts the ignition: "One of the instrument dials is blown off and from its aperture comes an unending rush of sand under great pressure." Hackett is hit full-force and is sandblasted to death—a variation on Phibes' Curse of Hail murder and yet another Phibes murder involving facial disfigurement.

Back at camp, Braff pulls rank on Biderbeck and demands that they strike camp. Diana's car comes racing back and crashes into another vehicle. "You actually see this man Hackett's driver's permit?" Braff asks Waverly. They discover Hackett's sandblasted face and Diana missing. Braff tells Trout "Take care of... him. Probably comes under a Special Situation Section, military burial, right?" Biderbeck finds a flawless miniature of the sarcophagus on the car's seat, perfect down to the snake's head lever. He pulls it and the lid opens, revealing a note: "COME ALONE."

Biderbeck sneaks off to see Phibes, who, meanwhile, is (ironically) playing "Somebody Stole My Gal" on his organ as Vulnavia dances. Biderbeck and Phibes square off in Phibes' organ room-- he demands that Biderbeck give him the key. As they argue, Biderbeck says "Your wife is dead!" "And once was I!" Phibes retorts. "But I live now! And so shall she!"

Phibes reveals that Diana is trapped in a "Bicylinder" where she will be boiled in oil if Biderbeck can't make his way through the mountain's inner maze and free her with the key. Biderbeck works his way through the maze, which Phibes has booby-trapped with snakes and a tarantula. Biderbeck saves her in time and Vulnavia snatches the precious key from him, passing it along to Phibes. Phibes, Victoria's corpse, and Vulnavia float triumphantly down the hidden River of Life: "Farewell... in some other time... some other world... we may meet again!" Phibes shouts back.

As Braff, Trout, and the others show up (naturally, too late), Biderbeck explains the otherworldly situation to them. Phibes is leaving on...

"A royal barge... sailing on the Egyptian equivalent of the River Styx," Biderbeck says. "The River of Life, of Immortality... and in a few moments, Dr. Phibes will know all the secrets which lie at its end."

Then I'll bring a gunboat upriver!" Braff replies. "Man has to come out someplace, what?"

"Quite useless, Major..." says Biderbeck. "Dr. Phibes will appear only when he is ready ... and where he wishes."

The film's largely deleted dance number begins.

Part of the dance number's deleted elegant transition.

As Biderbeck prepares to walk away, he begins to age rapidly, hideously. Suddenly, he is "Even older than Dorian Gray in the tenth reel." He and Diana exchange their farewells; she closes with "Till death do we part." As he dies in her arms, Phibes paddles away triumphantly with an orchestral version of "Somewhere Over the Rainbow" blasting. He remains invincible.

THE CAST

Journeyman actor Robert Quarry, who had recently had a major drive-in success headlining American International's *Count Yorga, Vampire* (1970), was cast as Biderbeck. This was a somewhat thankless role as Biderbeck is a sour, humorless character in a film populated mainly by winning comic ones. Quarry wasn't particularly well-suited for the role, which might have been far more effective in the hands of, say, Christopher Lee. Quarry's Biderbeck comes off as unsympathetic, bitchy, effete, and haughty. His protestations of love for Diana seem hollow and forced—it would have been much wiser to make Biderbeck genuinely as passionately in love with Diana as Phibes is with Victoria to give his character equally intense motivation to match their nearly well-matched intellects.

Co-star John Cater was very impressed by Quarry's approach: "I thought he was marvelous. He avoided every temptation to play his role for laughs. He played it absolutely straight and I think much of the picture's strength comes from his performance. There was always the temptation to jazz it up, but he resisted."

Unfortunately, Quarry's presence caused a certain tension between him and Vincent Price. Price's days at AIP were numbered: the kind of Gothic fare he had starred in so profitably for the company for so long was going out of vogue, and Price himself was wearying of his identification with horror. The discomfort between Quarry and Price began when "This one 'marvelous' press agent came up to Vincent at a London promotional party," Quarry told Anthony Petkovich, "and said, 'I understand Robert Quarry is being groomed to take over your roles.' So [makes quick razor-slicing motion across his throat] Krrrpt!—the resentment on Vincent's behalf immediately set in. After that, Vincent tried to pretend we were friendly but he wasn't really that nice ever again."

"There *was* a kind of tension [between Price and Quarry]," Robert Fuest recalled. Fortunately, though, "They rarely met because they don't see each other too often in the film. They're too busy killing other people," he laughed. Whatever differences they had caused no major problems during filming. Fuest wasn't thrilled by him: "He was very nice to me. He was just not a very good actor. He was all right."

However, Price's annoyance with Quarry did rear its head periodically. Fuest often spoke of the time Quarry was singing on-set and remarked to Price and the others "I'll bet you didn't know I was a singer!" to which Price replied, "Well we knew you weren't a fucking actor!"

The absolutely stunning English actress Fiona Lewis was cast as Biderbeck's girlfriend, Diana. Lewis had already appeared in Roman Polanski's *The Fearless Vampire Killers* (1967), among other films. Her striking features were ideally suited to the '20s era fashions she wears in the film. Diana is deeply bored and annoyed by the film's Egyptian voyage and Lewis nicely conveys her character's "Let's-get-this-over-with" attitude toward the proceedings.

Lewis recalls her audition: "I remember very well. I didn't have a car in those days in London and I took a train at six in the morning to get out to Pinewood to have an audition. It was just like a regular audition and I got the part... I didn't really do anything but talk to [Fuest]... I didn't read. In those days, you didn't read and thank God, because I was never a good read... I just went in and talked to him."

"Smashing girl, very funny," Robert Fuest said of Lewis. "I remember we had lunch once or twice and she used to wear... She just turned up in a sort of negligee– black underwear– and really sort of stopped the traffic. I liked her very much. She was a very funny girl. And curiously enough, I tried afterwards [to find her] because I had gone to things that I was doing that I thought she would be good [in], you know."

Lewis didn't see any sparks fly between Quarry and Price: "I don't think so. That's not really how any English person would behave. I think it was more that he was American so there was a certain—not remove, but a certain difference... [Quarry] was a very nice, polite man, so if there was tension, he wouldn't have shown it, I think...

"I remember [Quarry] being very personable and very nice, slightly removed," Lewis says. "A really nice guy. I don't think I got to know him very well on the picture. He was a nice man with nice manners. But he was American. When you have an American within an English group of people, the English aren't always... They were slightly alien in those days, an American on an English set. He was treated like the star, but I don't think he went to the pub at lunchtime."

Reprising the roles of Trout and Waverly were Peter Jeffrey and John Cater. Together, they continued the first film's exquisitely British use of ludicrous comic asides, like when Waverly hears that someone has brought an organ aboard the ocean liner bound for Egypt. "Organ music," he idiotically muses, "bound to go down well with all those Arabs."

Another master of asides, Terry-Thomas, returned from the first film in a new role as shipping agent Lombardo. The actor delivered some of the film's funniest throwaway lines, like Lombardo's response to the detective's inquiry about whether or not any of his ship's passengers seemed strange: "Well, the whole ruddy lot of them... Well, that's a slight exaggeration..."

Hugh Griffith-- the first *Dr. Phibes'* Rabbi, a veteran of Fuest's *Wuthering Heights*, and an AIP stock player-- was also cast in an alternate role, as Biderbeck's associate Harry Ambrose. Griffith's drinking problem had been a concern on *The Abominable Dr. Phibes*. In a sadly ironic touch, Ambrose's character is a heavy drinker who dies as he lived: Phibes strangles him and buries him at sea in a giant Miller's Gin bottle. (In an almost eerie reflection of Griffith's life, the actor is framed with the huge gin bottle prop looming over him. Gazing at it, Griffith says "Empty, I suppose. Pity.") In one of the film's many morbid puns, the ship's captain (Peter Cushing) discusses Ambrose's disappearance with Biderbeck and inquires if Ambrose "never touched the bottle?"

Fuest only worked with horror great Peter Cushing one day in his entire career, when he filmed the actor's single scene for *Rises Again*. Cushing had recently lost his beloved wife, Helen, and was shattered from grief, which had earlier led to him bowing out of playing Dr. Vesalius in *Dr. Phibes*. Though Cushing was notoriously gracious and good-humored, Fuest recalled him being icy and almost brusque—completely understandably the result, no doubt, of his enormous loss. Cushing, however, delivered a first-rate performance in his brief role as the ship's Captain.

Venerable British actress Beryl Reid essentially cameos as Ambrose's sister. Keith Buckley, who had appeared in Fuest's *Wuthering Heights*, plays one of Biderbeck's party, Stewart, the scorpion victim. Silently returning as the late Mrs. Phibes was the gorgeous Caroline Munro. And hulking ex-wrestler Milton Reid, who had become a fixture as brutish thugs in Hammer films like *Camp on Blood Island* (1958), *The Stranglers of Bombay* (1959), and *Blood of the Vampire* (1958) was cast as Biderbeck's lackey, Cheng. As was usually the case with Reid's roles, Cheng is mute.

Since Virginia North had gotten married and was pregnant, she was replaced as Vulnavia by Australian model and beauty contest winner Valli Kemp. The Clockwork Wizards were played by Richard Luck, Jack Dearlove, John Clarke, and Michael Clarke. (Dearlove was later Harrison Ford's stand-in on the first three *Star Wars* and *Indiana Jones* movies.)

Phibes and the new Vulnavia (Valli Kemp).

THE DÉCOR

Fuest and Blees' script described Phibes' Egyptian lair as follows: "The decorator must have been the same as furnished Maldine Square." And this was literally true: Fuest called upon his dear friend Brian Eatwell to design Phibes' world with him. Eatwell rises again, as it were.

The comically arcane inventiveness that the pair had shown in *Dr. Phibes* returned in full force for *Rises Again*. They created new sets every bit as stunning and absurd as those in the first. Their standout creations include a mirrored corridor that Vulnavia wafts along for her grand, ethereal entrance and exit, and the deranged fairground-midway-style combination coffin/calliope/bandstand where Phibes transports Victoria's corpse and the Clockwork Wizards in. Mirrored surfaces were used more heavily in *Rises Again* than the first film, including the aforementioned corridor, the inner lid of Phibes' crypt, and the ceiling of an ocean liner's stateroom.

Dr. Phibes' surreality was pushed even further in *Rises Again*. Phibes and Vulnavia are almost invariably immaculately dressed, no matter where they are or what they're doing. And Vulnavia's mirrored corridor seems less of this world than of the Great Beyond. (And how would it get from London to Egypt otherwise? And why the hell ask questions like that about a film as bizarre as this?)

Art Deco was ideally suited for an Egyptian locale, since the style itself drew heavily on Egyptian motifs. Fuest and Eatwell played with that connection in Phibes' Egyptian lair, which is decorated in early Busby Berkeley by way of Giza. According to Eatwell's daughter, Joanna, her father broke his rule from the first Phibes of never bringing any of his personal *objets d'art* for set decoration. She recalls a poster hanging in one of the liner's staterooms having hung in their home when she was a child. Eatwell also reused the decorative figural lamp on Mr. Darrow's desk from *Dr. Phibes* on the back of Phibes' barge during the final sequence.

Various set pieces and costumes from the first film were economically recycled, including the same organ, Phibes' crypt, various pieces of the Maldine Square mansion, and the Clockwork Wizards' masks. Reusing the first film's sets meant they could allot more

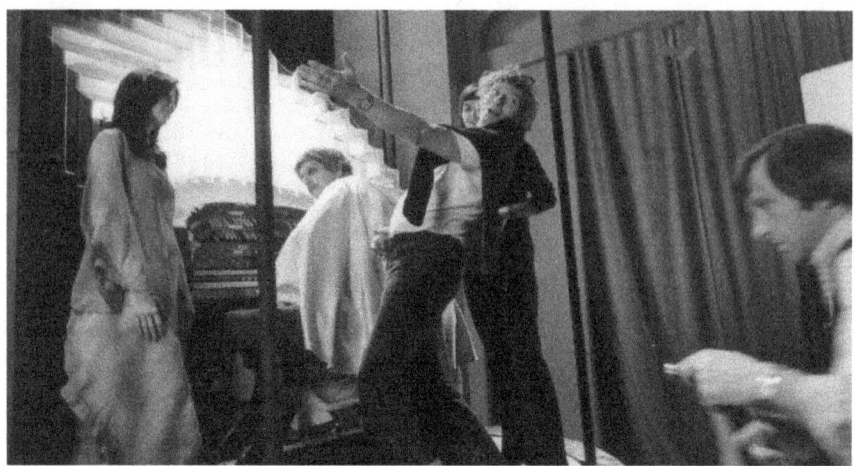

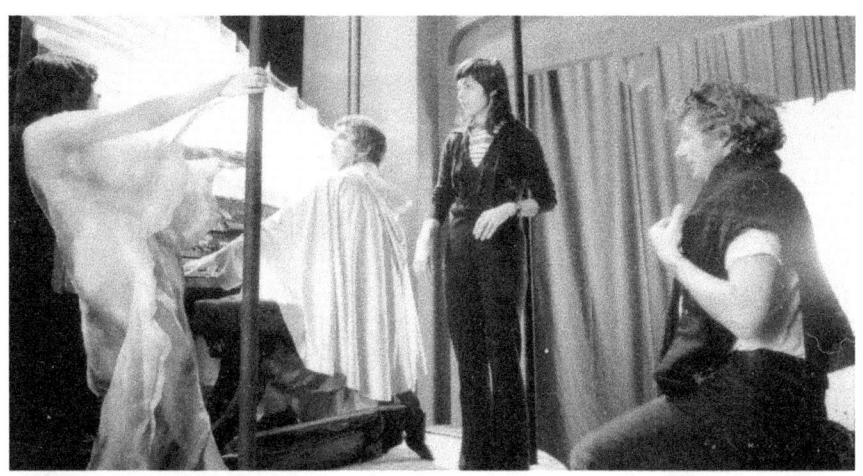

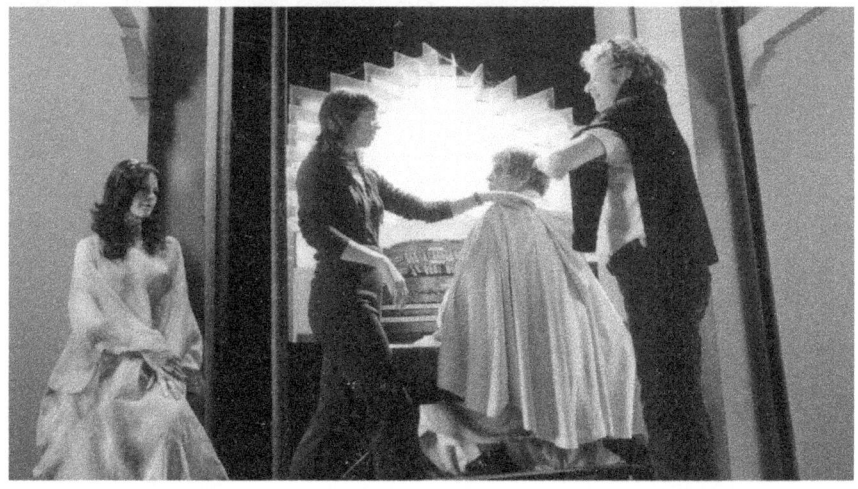

money to new, more elaborate ones. For the chamber where Diana faces impalement by spiked snakes, Eatwell and Fuest redressed the same drained pool where Dr. Vesalius had operated on his son in the first film. The bizarre prop requirements of a Phibes opus were apparent on call sheets requesting items like a "Scorpion throne with practical arm clamps."

Fiona Lewis was stunned by Eatwell's sets: "Even though I wasn't smart enough to know how clever he was, I did remember thinking

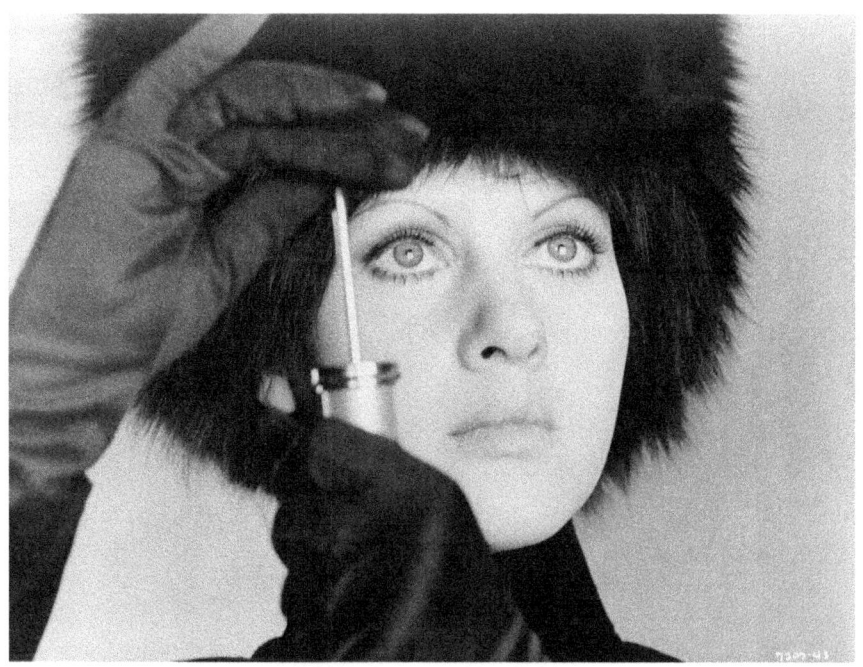

Vulnavia delivers the coup de grace.

Phibes at sea.

The Captain (Peter Cushing) and Biderbeck (Robert Quarry).

Peter Cushing.

Diana (Fiona Lewis).

Fiona Lewis vamping at Phibes' organ.

it was quite brilliant. Everybody knows about Deco now—knows what it is and they've seen places like decorated like that, but in those days you hadn't really seen it. I thought it was ingenious, what he did, and on a low budget managed to pull off. It was fabulous. He really did create sets that put you in the time and place. I thought [Eatwell] was a brilliant man."

THE CREW

Various veterans of the first *Phibes*' crew returned, including choreographer Suzanne France and sound editor Peter Lennard. In Norman Warwick's place was cinematographer Alex Thomson, who had formerly been cinematographer/director Nicolas Roeg's camera operator and would go on to shoot Roeg's *Eureka* (1983) and *Track 29* (1988). Thomson and Eatwell had previously worked together on *The Strange Affair* (1968). Thomson continued on to a notable career, shooting moody fantasies and horror films like *Raw Meat* (aka: *Death Line*) (1972), *Excalibur* (1981), *Legend* (1985), *Labyrinth* (1986), and Kenneth Branagh's *Hamlet* (1996). Thomson shot the film well, but often lit it more flatly than Norman Warwick's painterly approach to the first film's look. Various shots strongly show Fuest's compositional touch, like the image of Phibes' face framed within a phonograph's arm in the foreground of the shot—a classic example of his Bryan Forbes-like style.

Trevor Crole-Rees once again crafted Price's makeup. In January, 1972, Crole-Rees was interviewed during filming along with Price by the *Evening Standard*. "The makeup looks simple enough when it's on," Crole-Rees said, "yet it is one of the trickiest I've ever had to do in the thirty-seven years I've been in the business... The face, you see, is terribly brittle. It is made of melted wax, applied hot and then covered with a special plastic skin, which adheres to the wax before it sets.

"It has to stay put on Mr. Price throughout the day's filming, which means 8 ½ hours. And there's always the danger it may crack. If that happened, it could cause anything up to a two-hour delay in shooting." Of this uncomfortable makeup, Price said: "Under that wax and plastic skin, my face sweats and itches horribly in the

Phibes and Vulnavia in an artistic mood.

hot studio lights. Sometimes I want to tear it of, or go mad. But I daren't even touch it.

"But my biggest danger is my nose. I daren't blow it. And I daren't sneeze. To do either could cause real facial havoc!

"During lunch breaks, one of my biggest fears is that I shall encounter in the restaurant one of my comedian friends, like Max Bygraves, Tommy Cooper, or Frankie Howerd. A joke or gag from them could set me laughing uncontrollably, and that could crack my make-up like a shattered windscreen!"

In conversation with Sam Irvin, John Cater noted Price's commitment to his role: "Although I never actually did any scenes with him, I met him on the set many times and was amazed with his serious dedication toward his work. He would always insist on doing every bit of his part himself, always resisting the temptation to let a stuntman or stand-in do it. One part I remember had a shot of a bunch of skulls. It just so happens that one of the skulls is Phibes and you see his eyes move. Well, I expected to see a stand-in get down in the ground, with this skull mask on to do the scene. All you can of the person is the eyes. But Vincent insisted on doing it himself, and I admired him for that."

Crole-Rees also had to give Robert Quarry the Methuselah treatment at the film's end. "The makeup process was broken down into various stages of aging," Quarry told Anthony Petkovich. "So for each of the various stages, I'd swim back and they would put this makeup on me, and then I'd have to get back into exactly the same position deep in the water for the camera. But in-between the makeup changes, it was like an hour to an hour-and-a-half, and I'm still soaking wet because there was simply no time to change. It was hard fucking work... For one week I was sopping wet from the moment we started to do that scene. I could take the shirt off but not the pants. Clammy."

THE FILMING

The majority of *Rises Again* was shot, like *Dr. Phibes*, at Elstree Studios. Some location work was filmed in Las Ramblas in Ibiza, Spain, a popular location also seen in films like *A Fistful of Dollars* (1964). On-set photos from *Rises Again* almost invariably show Fuest and his cast laughing and obviously having a wonderful time. Fuest is occasionally pictured making his signature expressively broad arm gestures. The shoot's generally comic mood is indicated on the call sheet for Friday, December 24, 1971, when part of the scorpion scene was being shot: "GENERAL NOTE: YOU ARE REQUESTED NOT TO FEED THE CROCODILES OR FALL IN THE TANK ON STAGE 4."

As Fuest recalled: "What was the worst thing... in [*Phibes*] 2 was the scorpions. The second unit shot that on a VERY long lens," Fuest laughed. "It was about a hundred yards away on this guy's chest! I'm exaggerating, but they were a hell of a long way away. And this guy was pulling these scorpions out and saying, 'They'll be all right,' because once they sting they die or something ridiculous. I've forgotten everything I know about scorpions."

Valli Kemp's recollections of working with Price attest to the set's light-hearted tone: "It's difficult having to keep a straight face through some of these scenes, because just before a shot Vincent is likely to pat me on the bottom and say 'Go on' and joke with me and I'm supposed to go on and be serious.

"I did one scene with Vincent and I was playing the violin. He took a grape from the fruit bowl and shoved it in my mouth. He then gets another grape and shoves that in my mouth. So I have two grapes in my mouth and I daren't swallow them because if I did, I'd burst out laughing. The he picks up a pineapple and went to put that in my mouth as well, but then he shakes his head when he realizes it's too big—the pineapple that is—and he puts it down. This is all in the film and it's hysterical as it was complete improvisation. I didn't know anything about it."

Fuest and Price added various other impromptu bits of business throughout the film, like when Phibes first rises from his tomb and adjusts the crick in his neck, and when he cracks his knuckles and dusts the organ before playing it. (However, the wonderful shtick where Phibes "daintily withdraws a nasty fishbone" from his throat via his socket was scripted.) Phibes became funnier and less sinister in *Rises Again* than he had been in *Dr. Phibes*—audiences had liked him so much that Fuest, Price, and company were doing their best to make the good doctor more likable still.

John Cater's recollections of shooting the movie echoed Kemp's: "I loved the day we shot the scene with Beryl Reid, and I really loved the next day when we did the scene with Terry-Thomas. If you will notice in that scene, that every time they cut, it is as much as we can do not to break up laughing. Peter and I seemed to make him laugh as much as he made us laugh. We ruined countless shots by bursting out laughing; it took us hours and hours to do it. We had to really strain. Finally, the producer came down and said, 'Now, come on guys, we've only got Terry-Thomas for one day and he is very expensive."

In another interview, Cater said, "When we were called onto the set, [Terry-Thomas] flourished Robert Fuest's script, said he hadn't learnt it but that he'd got a few ideas. He had of course read the text many times and his vesion was very funny as can be seen in the film. (He cut phrases rather than added to them.) What can also be seen is the rather rapid editing from shot-to-shot sliced a bit too thin. This is because we laughed at one another so much we were already breaking up before Bob said 'Cut'. . . . At about 5:00 pm Albert Fennell, executive producer, came down onto the floor nervously looking at his watch; by this time our ribs were aching from the effort of trying to repress the giggling, and word had got upstairs." Cater mentioned that Terry-Thomas wore one of his own suits in the film and recalled the experience as "The most enjoyable and glorious day's work I've ever been privileged to do on film."

Fiona Lewis remembers Fuest warmly: "He was great fun, that's what I remember—very enthusiastic. Very personable. In fact, what I remember about the whole shoot was that everybody was having a good time. Doing movies back then in the '70s, because movies were cheaper to make, there wasn't the sort of desperation like there is now and corporations weren't running everything. So there was a much more relaxed attitude: 'Let's have fun on this movie and who knows if it will work or not, but isn't this great fun?' And Vincent Price was definitely one of those people that was going to have fun. He was very funny on the set and made everybody relax. And it was London, still the swinging sixties even though it was the 1970s because the swinging sixties didn't really end until about 1973.

"And it was just fun. There was no pressure. And we just had a really good time. And lots of laughs, I remember, on the set. . . I think it was very smooth. There were certainly no arguments on the set, which usually there are on a movie. Everybody had a good time. I think it was really one of those movies where everybody really loved doing it. And, as I said, Vincent Price was funny and very friendly, [with a] 'We're going to make this fun' kind of attitude, which having played a variation on that part many times, he was still extremely enthusiastic about it."

Lewis also vividly remembers laying around as bait for Biderbeck in the final sequence: "I remember that it was very cold. They were filling up the tank with water and I remember it was pretty chilly and we had a long day in this tank. But it was funny: there I was, fully made-up in my wig and nightie or whatever I was wearing, under chicken wire. It's hard not to find it amusing."

The Turn of the Screw.

Stewart (Keith Buckley) gets his.

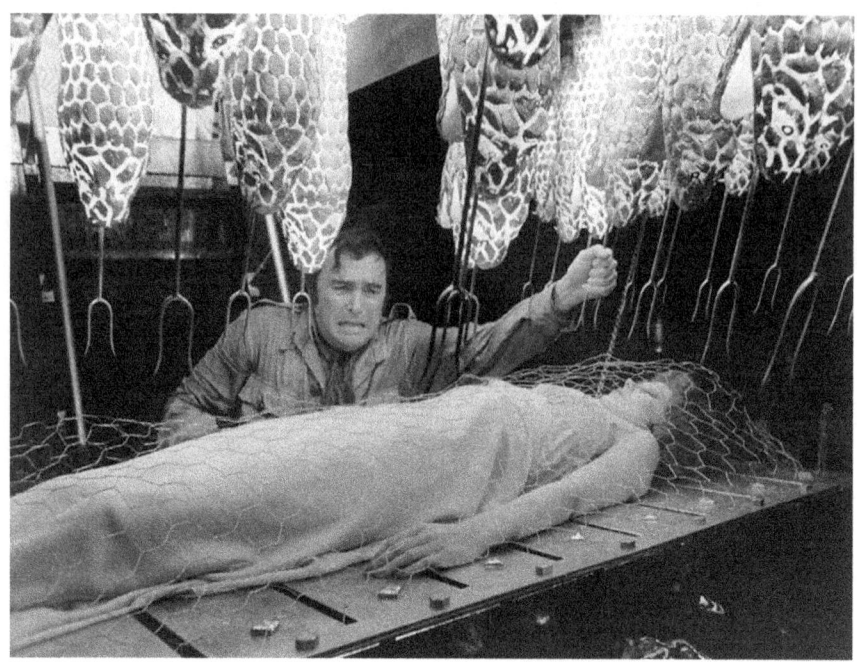
Biderbeck desperately tries to save Diana.

THE MUSIC

Rises Again's score would take on a substantially different sound than the previous film's. Instead of Basil Kirchin's askew jazz performed by a small combo or period tunes, Fuest got a full orchestral score of operatic intensity, complete with choral accompaniment. Fuest called in John Gale, who had provided very memorable musical cues for *Dr. Phibes*; his "Vulnavia's Theme" was so good, in fact, that it was reused in *Rises Again* for the new Vulnavia's otherworldly entrance.

As Gale recalled, he and Fuest loved working together: "It was great, it really was. I went along to one or two of the film shoots with him and sat in the editor's room quite a bit. He was fantastic. We both had the same sort of sense of humor. We were always giggling and laughing.

"I can remember we were having a gin and tonic or something in my office once and he popped by and we were having lots of laughs. He was trying to think of another movie and we both hatched up a funny plot, because I was ex-RAF, in my youth, and I said, 'I've got an idea—you know that the RAF used to scramble during the War?' Do you understand that? All the pilots would be waiting outside the hut with a telephone and they were waiting for the call to scramble— you jumped in your airplane, get up there, shoot the Jerry down, and all the rest. I said, 'Suppose we did a film like that, a scramble film, but it's all the old RAF boys and they've all got model planes!' We were rolling on the floor laughing about it."

The recording for Gale's "Vulnavia" tracks from *Dr. Phibes* had been recorded at CTS Studios in Kensington, London, "And that's where the main music of *Dr. Phibes Rises Again* was done, too," in May, 1972, Gale recalled. "And I used a BIG orchestra for that and a big choir."

Gale employed the London Bach Choir, approximately forty singers who worked on a kind of volunteer basis: "Let me explain that to you: all choirs over here, with few exceptions, are amateur singers ... There's a thing like the BBC Singers but they're employed by the BBC, you know what I mean? But the big four orchestras over here in London—the London Symphony, the London Phil, the Royal Phil, and the Philharmonia— they all have a choral side locked and they would all be amateurs. But when you hire a choir like the Bach choir, you do a deal and you pay a check to their [charitable] fund."

"And I'll tell you a funny story about that. Bob said to me, 'Look, send it all up, if you want to' ... And English choirs—you can never understand what they're singing about, whether they're singing in whatever language, even English! So I thought I would sing the titles in Latin, you see. And the only trouble was I didn't know any Latin. And my stepson, who was about fourteen, had just started 'big school'—boarding school—and I contacted him and I said, 'Are you learning any Latin yet?' And he said, 'Yeah, we're learning Latin.' So I sent him the *Dr. Phibes Rises Again* and things and he translated it into Latin for me! So the translation was by a fourteen-year-old schoolboy! It was very funny."

Though Fuest had played music on the set of *Dr. Phibes*, he didn't try to have Gale pattern his music after any particular compositions: "No, no. The only thing [Fuest] ever said was, he liked Sibelius, I think it was. Sibelius tends to use running-around violins and things, so the opening—the resurrection bit—I used a lot of running-around violins like Sibelius. Also, I took a leaf out of Wagner's book. As you might know, in his operas, he had a thing called a leitmotif, so I treated the film as an opera basically. And I wanted a leitmotif to run through the film. And I said to Bob, 'I feel a bit like Schnozzla Durante because I'm trying to look for the Lost Chord.' And I found that by . . . I called it (Bob laughed) 'My pregnant thirteenth'–I used a bass guitar and a bottom 'G' sort of thing and then four horns playing 'F' seventh above it and things. And that was Phibes' leitmotif. Which the editor on the DVD has mucked-about a bit."

Composer Paul Lewis worked for many years with Gale, beginning in the 1960s at ABC Television; working from Gale's instructions, Lewis orchestrated much of the *Rises Again* soundtrack (except for the critical opening and closing pieces). Lewis discussed the "Phibes Chord" that Gale mentioned, in an interview with composer Jason Frederick: "John wanted to write a motif for Dr. Phibes himself but, in fact, Phibes isn't always there long enough to hear a theme or even a motif. Sometimes he just appears in the background or John needed to indicate his presence even offscreen. So really it became just one chord. Now, because Dr. Phibes, although he is a lunatic mass murderer, he's also a very sympathetic person. The whole point of the killings is to avenge the death of his wife. It is in a way a bizarre love story. So John decided a rich, warm chord on French horns, a minor ninth—that note added at the top—now, John did a very clever thing, that's a very romantic chord, but to make it sound ominous, he took that note from the top and he gave it to a bass guitar, so you have the richness of the French horns and the bass guitar, which is almost a dead sort of sound. It doesn't ring on richly like a plucked string bass . . . And that very romantic ninth played right down the bottom becomes strangely ominous and disconcerting. All is not well with Dr. Phibes. I thought it was very clever at the time, and I still think it's very clever whenever I hear it."

Both Dr. Phibes films climaxed with versions of "Over the Rainbow" that were orchestrated in keeping with the endings' respective tones. The first film required a bittersweet version, but *Rises Again* demanded something really triumphant. "Now, that's an interesting thing," Gale said. "Bob wanted 'Over the Rainbow' so I said to Bob, 'Let's give it a big Elgarian classical feel, like 'Pomp and Circumstance,'" you see. And he laughed, he said, 'That's a great idea–do it.' So I scored it out as an Elgar piece. But at some time after I was finished, somebody must have asked Vincent Price to sing along with it, so I wasn't in with that."

Fuest was absolutely elated by Gale's score, as he told Sam Irvin: "I thought it was magnificent . . . the best film music I ever had. The first Phibes film was scored by Basil Kirchin, who really did not do the best job in the world, for my tastes. I rang up a guy I had known from my days of working on commercials. His name was John Gale. He had never done a film. I paid him $500 to write some addition music for the first Phibes film. He did thirty minutes' worth of music for that film, and we were so pleased that we hired him to do all of the music for the second one. He wrote over sixty minutes of music for *Dr. Phibes Rises Again* and it was great. We got the London Philharmonic Orchestra and the Bach Choir; we had more than ninety people packed into the recording studio wondering what in the hell they were doing. He wrote some mock-Tchaikovsky and the orchestra was arguing about what Tchaikovsky piece it was. They all thought it was the real thing. He had the choir speaking in Latin.

"And he did the most incredible version of 'Somewhere Over the Rainbow' that has ever been recorded. I had a meeting with John about this number. I told him that I wanted it to be so spectacular that it would blow the audience's mind. He asked me to sort of hum it out for him. So I went into a frizzy in the office, booming out the tune to 'Over the Rainbow,' and before long John was joining in. Secretaries kept popping their heads in, wondering what on God's earth was happening. Well, John made a recording of us screaming it out, and literally transferred it to sheet music for the London Philharmonic and the Bach Choir. I was at the recording session, and believe me, it was absolutely unreal. I just creamed: I came!"

(Of the "booming" that went on between Fuest and Gale, Gale commented: "One of my disadvantages in life is that I'm not a very good pianist, so I would 'boom' things at him, so he probably 'boomed' things back to me.")

Gale also worked a few popular standards into the film, like "Moonlight Sonata" and the Clockwork Wizards' wheezy version of "Ach du Lieber Augustin." "Apart from the clockwork musicians," Gale noted, "where they were playing standards, apart from that, there were two scenes where I resorted to library music. One was the Scottish pipe band out in the desert–that was a piece of library music. The 'Ach du Lieber Augustin' on the steam organ was a piece of library music which I oversaw via my library. And the 'Toccata and Fugue'–Phibes plays it on the organ doesn't he? I've done lots of the arrangements of the 'Toccata and Fugue'– I've got a symphonic one, too.

[Author's note: In transcribing interviews, I seldom find words that I absolutely can't make out, but Gale used a musical term that eluded me. I have listed it in brackets phonetically. If anyone can tell me what this specific term is, please write and let me know! –JH] "You know the bit where they go down into the tombs? I think I wanted to have the sound of what I would call an Egyptian [Moshe] band sort of, of yonderyear, and with this big orchestra there I just wanted to have it as a fanfare with brass. And I said to the brass section, 'I want it quite raucous like an ancient [Moshe] band sound I'm looking for.' So the lead horn player stood up . . . Horns are normally called French horns, but in actual fact, horn players play what they call German horns. And he said, 'I'll tell you what, John: we'll all unscrew our bells,' and all the horn players, all four of them, unscrewed their bells, put them on top of their heads, looking like Chinese coolies, [laughs] and they let up a lovely rasping noise! So that's how I got that noise.

"On the singing front, there's a sarcophagus, so I got some singers from St. Paul's Cathedral to do that bit in a sort of Gregorian chant way."

Gale recalled that the response to his excellent score was generally positive: "Well, the generalization–a very good one. More late in life [than] at the time. For instance, when we were doing all the recording of it and everything, there were talks about releasing a record–that would have been an LP in those days, of course. And I think whilst all the musician side was contracted to include the record, nothing happened and I think that was probably at the time there was the contretemps going on [with AIP] so it all died a bit of a death.

"Anyway, I can tell you that . . . Let's say twenty-five years ago, I was approached by a British record company that wanted to release the soundtrack for it. And I said, 'I'm not absolutely certain,' because I didn't do the paperwork side of booking all the orchestras and things like that, that was done by the production office, you know. I said, 'I'll have to just look into the question because over here, there are all sorts of restrictions and rights that unions demand and all the rest of it–how we stand on that.' I wrote to the London Philharmonic and they said, 'It's not really our decision, it's the Musician's Union's decision.' And they came back and said, 'The Musician's Union says 'We've all got to be paid again.' So the record producers wouldn't have that. So I said, 'Look, I've got a great idea: let's give a donation to the Musician's Benevolent Fund of a thousand pounds'- or whatever it was- 'and let's get on with it.' And the Musician's Union refused. So it died a death.

"And then something like ten to fifteen years ago, I had a call from Perseverance Records in the States and they said they want to release it. So I said, 'Look, as far as I'm concerned, if it's a USA release, the paperwork side has nothing to do with me.' As far as I can remember everybody was paid for a record release anyway and this was to be a CD thing, fifteen years ago. So fortunately, I kept all the quarter-inch masters, so I sent them over to Perseverance Records in the States and they put out a CD of it all. Lucky I kept those tapes, wasn't it?" Gale laughed. He passed away on December 27, 2015.

THE MUTILATION

In the late 1960s and early 1970s, American International had developed an ugly habit of recutting certain productions. Outstanding examples include Roger Corman's *Bloody Mama* and *Gas-s-s-s* (both 1970), the latter having been recut so badly that Corman severed his longstanding ties with AIP over it. Fuest's *Wuthering Heights* had also fallen prey to AIP's editor's talons. Creative differences led to some of these various films' cuts, but trims were often made for economical reasons: film canisters are heavy and transporting them is expensive—the fewer film canisters, the cheaper shipping them is. Also, the shorter the film, the more screenings a theater can cram into a single day. But with *Rises Again*, AIP had a different reason: to them, the film was just *too British*.

"I made the film pushing for even more comedy than before," Fuest told Sam Irvin. "In fact, it was a sendup of the first one. I loved the film I made but you have not seen it. AIP violently cut it up and subdued the comedy to a great extent. I guess because it was full of subtle 'British humor,' but contrary to what AIP thinks, I feel that Americans not only understand, but enjoy British humor … Of course, I don't dislike *Dr. Phibes Rises Again*, but the original print I made was better."

"On *Rises Again*," John Cater told Irvin, "Bob wrote a huge amount of English jokes for me and Peter [Jeffrey] to say. When I saw the AIP version when it opened at the New Victoria Cinema here in London, most of these jokes had been edited out. I understand Bob Fuest has an uncut version, and I was invited to a screening of it, but had to decline because I was working on [*Captain*] *Kronos* [*Vampire Hunter*]. Bob was very pleased with the cut he had, but something happened to his film between there and the New Victoria; I don't know just what. Somebody at AIP evidently thought that the American public would not understand British humor, and I frankly think that could not be more untrue."

As Fuest told Anthony Petkovich, "The problem was that Arkoff and Nicholson had been working together as a team for some twenty years, and they'd had an argument, with this sequel ultimately falling victim to their quarreling. Whole scenes were exactly cut out, but they were shortened so that the niceties of the thing were lost. I think times have changed now, but the during the early '70s, they wanted this in-your-face stuff; a really kind of slap-bang-wallop, he-gets-hit-with-a-pie sort of thing. Very few subtleties. Nicholson and Arkoff just wanted to do it, make their money, and to hell with everything else. The movie does have its moments, though. But it was rearranged and chopped and changed and, well, it's just not the same as my originally planned version." "Laugh-In" announcer Gary Owens recorded opening narration over the opening recap of the previous film's events. Expository lines spoken by Phibes—glaringly in scenes where he's not hooked-up to his neck jack—were added to bridge gaps, just as AIP had done to smooth the flow of Fuest's *Wuthering Heights* with Nellie's narration. One positive alteration was adding Price singing "Somewhere Over the Rainbow" over John Gale's monumental orchestration of the song. (In the film's initial video releases, the song, including Price's singing, were annoyingly removed due to rights issues.)

One of the outstanding mutilated scenes was the stylish segue from the ruins of Phibes' house on Maldine Square onto the *Empress of Quebec*. In the final release version, just as Phibes and Vulnavia are packed and preparing to leave, for barely a second or two, a spotlight hits them, followed by a sharp cut to stock footage of an ocean liner. In the scene as filmed, the spotlight held on the two as they danced and were engulfed by fog. They elegantly drifted through it, and as it cleared, they were suddenly dancing on the ocean liner's deck. This scene was shot, and its stupid and intrusive deletion added nothing to the film.

At various points in the film, lines were dropped, one of which wound up in the film's trailer, when Biederbeck warns Trout: "Then, Inspector, we're faced with an impossible task. Well, there's no force in the world that could win a fight against such a supreme opponent." Rumors that there were additional deleted scenes with Terry-Thomas and Beryl Reid appear to be just rumors; the two were only on-set briefly, additional scripted scenes haven't surfaced, and the likelihood of any of their work having been excised seems doubtful. (Author's note: If anyone can conclusively prove me wrong about this, please do!)

According to a letter to AIP's post-production supervisor Salvatore Billitteri from Tristam Cones in England, Price redubbed his lines with Billitteri at Ryder Sound Studios in Hollywood in mid-April, 1972. "As far as I can remember," sound editor Peter Lennard says, "the only thing that was added was lines from Vincent Price. They had a separate music and effects track which they could use to fill in where the new lines were inserted if needed.

"The only thing that did not match the original Phibes dialogue was the equalization. I don't know how hard they tried to match our equalization. Equipment was not so good in those days so they could have had trouble re-mixing the new dialogue." The newly-recorded interstitial lines sounded 'off' not only because of the difference in sound quality, but, as previously mentioned, also because Phibes was speaking at times without his signature Victrola speaker.

One egregiously unnecessary line comes when Vulnavia is making her dazzling and wistful exit during the finale. Instead of simply letting the scene silently speak for itself, as it were, AIP inserted a blatant expository line where Phibes invites Vulnavia to join him and Victoria on the other side. The hypnotic beauty of this brief but unforgettable scene was broken.

The cover of AIP's promo standee for the film.

Several Dr. Phibes stills "cameo" in a scene from Price's final AIP film, Madhouse. Phibes himself never committed butchery so ghastly.

THE RECEPTION

AIP's usually savvy publicity department dropped the ball with *Rises Again*, showing little of the ingenuity lavished on *Dr. Phibes*. James Raker and other AIP ad men produced a dreary, generic, unappealing one-sheet poster and ad campaign featuring a model being menaced by a phony rubber spider and skeletal hands. Another ad featured odd artwork centered around a face composed of various exaggerated versions of scenes and characters from the film, done in the style of the painter Arcimboldo; AIP had used this technique much more effectively in their ad art for Price's *The Masque of the Red Death* (1964). At the very least, the film's trailer was solid. (In Mexico, the film was retitled *The Return of the Abominable Dr. Phibes*, which was odd considering the first film's Mexican title was *The Satanic Dr. Phibe*. Other retitlings include *Dr. Phibes Vuelve a la Tumba* (*Dr. Phibes Returns From the Grave*) and, in Finland, *Vampyyri Nousee Haudastaan* (*The Vampire Rises From the*

Grave). But the nuttiest retitling of all was in Italy, where it was simply called *Frustrazione* (*Frustration*)!)

A high point of the film's ad campaign was a coffin-shaped, fold-out standee featuring photographs from the film and some purple ad copy extolling the film's virtues: "Sparing neither expense nor talent, American-International Pictures has filmed these LATEST and GREATEST adventures in all their evil splendor. From the vaults of the British Museum to the underground tombs of the ancient Pharoahs, AIP has gathered prop and set, location and trick of cinema magic to bring Anton Phibes once more to a waiting world- in the FIRST HORROR SPECTACULAR EVER FILMED."

Meanwhile, the press coverage included a "split-face" image of Phibes' masked and skeletal faces, taken by famed British photographer Brian Duffy, who would go on to photograph David Bowie for his "Aladdin Sane" and "Ashes to Ashes" albums. Meanwhile, Price himself appeared on a Halloween episode of "The Dating Game," where both Dr. Phibes films were both mentioned on-air. Clad in a Phibes-like toga, Price grilled bachelors on that episode on behalf of starlet Janit Baldwin (*Ruby*, *Prime Cut*).

This would be Fuest's final film for AIP, sadly. "AIP had a lot of films scheduled for me to do such as *House of Seven Gables*," Fuest recalled, "and of course they hoped the Phibes thing would keep me busy for years. I suppose for a while, it looked as though I was going to be AIP's new Roger Corman." Sadly, *Rises Again*'s box-office performance undid Fuest's career at AIP. (Note: Patrick Tilley, screenwriter of Fuest's *Wuthering Heights*, recalls writing a script of *The House of Seven Gables* for AIP without his involvement.)

Fuest was offered the job of directing the Vincent Price classic *Theater of Blood* (1973), which was directly patterned after the Phibes films. Fuest said that he turned it down because he didn't want to get typed as the guy who makes the Vincent-Price-theme-killings movies. Douglas Hickox directed the film, which is excellent in its own right.

As for Vincent Price and American International, Price did one last movie for AIP, the lame *Madhouse* (1974). Co-starring Robert Quarry and Peter Cushing, the film followed macabre doings surrounding horror star Paul Toombes (Price) and his return to acting after hideous personal tragedies. Toombes' trademark character is "Dr. Death," and several photos from *The Abominable Dr. Phibes* appear in a display of stills from the fictitious Dr. Death series. AIP monkeyed with the film to no one's satisfaction and it remains a sad coda to Price's marvelous association with AIP.

Though *Dr. Phibes Rises Again* was by no means a masterpiece, it remains a very enjoyable piece of work and an incredible example of filmmaking economy and ingenuity. Price, Fuest, and Phibes deserved better, but it was still worthy. Though it was Price's swan song as the good doctor, Phibes' nefarious career was far from over.

VHS video box art by artist Bill Morrison, now Editor of Mad magazine. (Artwork courtesy Bill Morrison. Reprinted with his permission.)

Chapter 3

The Unphilmed Phibes: From *The Fingers of Dr. Pibe* to *Somewhere Over the Rainbow*

By David Taylor and Sam Irvin

In the real world, there were only ever two Dr. Phibes movies – *The Abominable Dr. Phibes* and *Dr. Phibes Rises Again* – made by American International Pictures over the course of two years in the early 1970s.

However, in the often dreamlike world of the cinema, there have been any number of bizarre proposals, abandoned projects and unrealized movies that have helped keep the good doctor's name alive for more than four decades. In the ensuing years there have been sequels, prequels and – as per that peculiarly 21st-century concept – re-imaginings placed on the table, only to be brushed aside.

On May 9, 2012, columnist Liz Smith at the website wowOwow.com revealed that director Tim Burton and actor Johnny Depp had expressed a keen interest in mounting a big budget remake of *The Abominable Dr. Phibes*. Other reports placed the project on the production slate at Warner Bros, the studio for whom Burton and Depp were about to resurrect another forty-year-old cult horror icon, Barnabas Collins, in a lavish big screen update of the *Dark Shadows* TV series. When *Dark Shadows* underperformed at the box office, the proposed *Phibes* remake quietly slipped back into the vault.

It wasn't the first time that a *Phibes* project had withered on the vine and is unlikely to be the last. This is an attempt to exhume all those lost *Phibes* movies: the ones that could have been, the ones that should have been and the ones that we're probably glad never were.

* * *

In the beginning, there was no Dr. Phibes. Instead, there was Dr. Pibe.

In the earliest drafts of the screenplay that was to become The Abominable Dr. Phibes, two former school friends from New York,

William Goldstein and Charles Whiton, devised a fiendish genius named Dr. Pibe, who sought vengeance for the death of his wife on a hospital operating table by murdering the various medics responsible, using as his modus operandi the G'tach, the ten curses visited on the Egyptian pharaoh by Moses in the Book of Exodus. Pibe is never given a Christian name in these initial drafts, although his primary adversary is identified as Dr. Anton Vesalius, which was later changed to Henri Vesalius in the shooting script.

Goldstein has stated that the original title for the film was The Fingers of Dr. Pibe, in reference to a scene where a rabbi imparts an ersatz slice of Hebrew theology which describes the ten Biblical curses as "the ten fingers of God". It's noticeable in the early drafts that Goldstein and Whiton place great emphasis on Pibe's fingers – described as "excessively long and tapered" – whether they are playing the pipe organ or manipulating one of his elaborate death machines.

American International Pictures snapped up the screenplay. "It caught on very quickly at AIP," Goldstein said, "and within six months after they had the first look, they were in preproduction. They picked it up with the idea that there would be a series – we were told in the beginning perhaps five pictures."

Robert Fuest, who had just reworked Emily Brönte's Wuthering Heights for AIP, was assigned to direct. His observations of the original draft of the Goldstein and Whiton screenplay were that it was extraordinary, but impractical given the budget the film had been allocated. In an interview with Bizarre magazine, he said: "In the original script, there were 17 flights of stairs to Dr. Phibes' dungeon under the ballroom. Well that blew the art department's budget right there, so I knew that there was going to have to be major rewriting." He also commented on the script's length: "It was 275 pages long! The average script only has about 100!" (William Goldstein has challenged the allegation that the original screenplay was overlong, saying that Fuest had been misled about its length due to the fact that it had been typed using double-spacing. However, to be fair, even a single-spaced 137-page script would still have been well beyond the scope of a typical AIP production. The industry standard for measuring script length is that, on average, one page equals one minute of screen time. Given that *The Abominable*

Dr. Phibes clocks in at 94 minutes, an 137-page script would have been deemed too long by nearly 50%.)

By the time shooting commenced, the title of the screenplay had been changed to *The Curses of Dr. Pibe*, possibly to make it more obvious to potential audiences that it was a horror movie, although pre-release trade advertising was already promoting the movie as *Dr. Phibes*, before AIP finally settled on *The Abominable Dr. Phibes*. Whether or not Whiton and Goldstein were responsible for these title revisions, not to mention the changing of the name of the central character, is unclear. Director Robert Fuest did extensive uncredited rewrites to the final shooting script, transforming the plot, characters, dialogue and, most crucially, the tone of the piece, placing the emphasis on quirky black comedy rather than straight horror. Those rewrites continued during shooting. "Most of it was actually rewritten day by day on the set," Fuest admitted. And there was a second, uncredited writer who played an important role in shaping the final shooting script, in particular the climax of the story, but more about him later.

It wasn't only the screenplay that underwent changes prior to filming. Peter Cushing had been contracted to play Henri Vesalius in the movie and his name appears prominently in the pre-production advertising. However, Cushing's wife, Helen, was in very poor health and, in order to care for her, he bowed out of the production (as well as from Hammer's *Lust for a Vampire* and *Blood from the Mummy's Tomb*, both released in 1971, where his roles were filled by Ralph Bates and Andrew Keir respectively). Joseph Cotten, whose illustrious Hollywood career in the 1940s and 1950s had by this time been reduced to guest roles on television and cameo appearances in movies, came to London to take on the Vesalius role, then stuck around in Europe long enough to also make *Lady Frankenstein* (1971) and *Baron Blood* (1972).

Similarly, the pre-production advertising bears the line "And Introducing Vulnavia", suggesting that AIP was planning to cast an unknown actress in the enigmatic role and keep her true identity a secret, in much the same way as Paramount Pictures had promoted Kathleen Burke, a one-time dental assistant from Indiana, as The Panther Woman in *Island of Lost Souls* back in 1932. In the end, the role went to up-and-coming actress Virginia North, who had already made appearances in the two 'Bulldog' Drummond escapades, *Deadlier Than the Male* (1967) and *Some Girls Do* (1969), as well as the historical epic *The Long Duel* (1967) and the James Bond movie *On Her Majesty's Secret Service* (1969). What most likely clinched the role of Vulnavia for North, however, was her ethereal, non-speaking performance as the Devil's daughter, despatched from the underworld to spread a sexually-transmitted plague to mankind, in a controversial 1970 revival of Oscar Panizza's allegedly blasphemous stage play *The Council Of Love* in London's West End.

Whereas the Whiton and Goldstein screenplay for *The Curses of Dr. Pibe* opens in 1925 with the curse of boils, depicting a sequence where Pibe releases a swarm of bees into the exotic hothouse of Dr. Wister Dugdates to sting him to death, in the completed film this event is referred to as having already transpired. In fact, in the screenplay, two murders have already been committed by Pibe prior to the opening scene, already fulfilling the curses of the firstborn and of frogs. The curse of the firstborn refers to the son of Dr. Vesalius, who was found drowned in a swimming pool, and the curse of frogs refers to Dr. Hargraves (this is later amended to Hargreaves in the shooting script), who was found dead of fright in his Chelsea home after it had been overrun with frogs (the exact specifics of why Hargraves should be so terrified by frogs is never made clear and seems fairly ridiculous, which is perhaps why it was altered by Fuest to having him being killed by the constricting frog mask in the finished film). The decision to change the nature and chronology of the early murders in the movie seems arbitrary, although it was perhaps partly dependent on what the special effects team felt could be achieved effectively. The screenplay makes a great deal of the fact that Pibe is accurately replicating the Biblical curses in sequence, but in reality neither it nor the finished film follow the order of the plagues as they occur in *The Bible*. Both also chose to ignore the plagues of lice and flies, instead substituting bats and rats.

The rest of the death scenes in the finished film follow their description in the screenplay, with only minor changes to specifics. In the screenplay, the death by rats of Dr. Kitaj takes place aboard his yacht in Falmouth harbour; Fuest changed this to an aircraft because he felt it would have been too easy for Kitaj to escape the rats simply by jumping into the sea. The plague of locusts in the screenplay actually results in the death of two nurses – Jean Allen and Mozella Williams – both of whom were in attendance during the operation on Victoria Pibe. And there's one other small change to this sequence: in the screenplay, in addition to releasing the swarm of locusts into the room, Pibe also unleashes an army of voracious red ants to help with the job.

Significant alterations were also made to the characters between screenplay and film. In the screenplay, Harry Trout is a rookie reporter for the *London Chronicle*, who tags along with the police and teams up with Vesalius to solve the murders, while Vulnavia (only ever referred to in the screenplay as The Girl) is revealed to be a clockwork automaton that Pibe activates by winding a device in the nape of her neck. There is also an intimation in the script that she has been built to provide some sort of sexual services, as she is described as displaying a sexual wantonness when activated – an idea that is never really explored. Somewhat confusingly, at the climax of the screenplay, her false face is ripped away to reveal her to be another living corpse like Pibe, although no explanation of how she came to be that way is ever offered. In addition to Vulnavia, the screenplay also gives Pibe another automaton sidekick – a 10ft tall effigy of an Etruscan warrior that he uses to randomly choose the next victim in the cycle of killings. And the Clockwork Wizards play a much more prominent role in the scripted climax, dropping their musical instruments for a huge battle with Trout, Vesalius and the amassed police officers when they storm Maldine Square.

It was this ending that gave Fuest the most trouble when he was doing his rewrites, knowing that the budget couldn't stretch to accommodate the amount of action and special effects specified in the script. Help came from an unexpected quarter: writer and producer Brian Clemens, who had worked with Fuest on both *The Avengers* TV series in the late 1960s and his feature film debut *And Soon the Darkness* (1970), and who was working on the Hammer film *Dr Jekyll & Sister Hyde* (1971) at Elstree Studios at the same time as Fuest was there filming *Phibes*. As Fuest revealed in an interview with *Psychotronic* magazine: "I knew we needed a different ending but couldn't think of one ... Well, since Brian Clemens and I were working in the same studio at the time, I remember talking with him about how difficult it was to film this ending and how I couldn't figure it out. And the next day – lo and behold – Brian came up with the way to do it. 'I've got a great ending,' he said. 'Supposing that Dr. Phibes kidnaps the boy and they put key inside him, etc, etc.' I mean the whole incredible conclusion to that film is down to Brian, which he did in one evening."

Yet for all the changes made to the screenplay by Fuest and Clemens, it is the manner in which they fleshed out and refined the title character that was to have the most impact on the film. For all its imaginative flourishes, Whiton and Goldstein's screenplay was pretty much a straightforward horror thriller and Pibe simply an archetypal madman bent on revenge. A few clues are dropped as to his background: born in Paris to British parents who had made a fortune in banking, recipient of doctorates in both music and biophysics, but otherwise notable for being a recluse and, as is revealed in one sequence, a cocaine addict. Pibe has surprisingly little to say for himself in the original screenplay – indeed, he emits little more than callous laughter until his first proper line of dialogue at what would be approximately 30 minutes into the movie. There is an attempt to give him the aura of the doomed romantic in a lengthy sequence where he recites John Donne's poem *The Good Morrow* in his shrine to Victoria, but there's little of the sense of wounded nobility and ironic wit that Vincent Price would eventually bring to the role.

One of the more intriguing aspects of the original screenplay is that Maldine Square houses one of Pibe's strangest inventions: a pair of enormous gyroscopes which, when set spinning, create an air corridor between them through which any object that passes is rendered invisible. The presence of a Foucault pendulum near to this device seems to indicate that Pibe is conducting some strange experiment to affect the world's rotation and that this will play a part in the delivery of the final curse. But despite a few teasing hints – Pibe announces plans "To move the Earth its final step" – the exact nature of the machine is never explained, and even when it is activated at the climax it doesn't appear to do anything. The rewrites dropped this science fiction aspect of the story; despite his handiness at constructing peculiar murder machines, Phibes is said to have received his doctorate in the field of theology.

If Goldstein resented the changes made to the screenplay written by Whiton and himself, he didn't show it. For the release of the film in May 1971, he wrote the accompanying movie tie-in novelization, published by Award Books. The novel follows the plot as revised by Fuest and Clemens, even going so far as to flesh out events prior to and during the narrative, including introducing a handful of new characters to populate the back stories of the doomed medics.

What is most surprising about the book is the way in which it pushes the title character into background. Phibes makes only a few fleeting appearances following a lengthy opening chapter describing how he has driven his Hispano-Suiza off the road in the Jura mountains in Switzerland and miraculously survived the accident (the specifics of how Phibes recuperated from the car accident and made his way back to London would eventually be revealed in Goldstein's novelization of *Dr. Phibes Rises Again*). Vulnavia becomes even more of an afterthought in the novel, putting in her first appearance on page 74, almost halfway through the book.

While Goldstein sticks to the revised plotline established by the movie, he does insert a few of his own ideas. One is to restage the murder of Nurse Allen so that she is consumed by both ants and locusts, as per his original screenplay. The second is not to have Vulnavia doused in acid at the climax of the movie, but rather to commit suicide by stabbing herself with a dagger across the keyboard of Phibes' pipe organ (this self-sacrifice was an idea that obviously appealed to Goldstein as he was to reuse it several times, as we will see). For all that, the book is reasonably well written for a movie tie-in, many of which are simply tossed off with as little imaginative effort from the author as possible, and Goldstein obviously undertook a lot of historical research to paint a reasonably authentic background of 1920s London. Only occasionally does the prose jar noticeably, such as when Schenley describes someone as "a sonofabitch", an oath that is more Bowery than Battersea.

After *The Abominable Dr. Phibes* proved to be the hit that AIP had hoped it would be, Goldstein and Whiton were commissioned to produce a screenplay for the first sequel, taking a leaf from James Whale by titling it *The Bride of Dr. Phibes*. Picking up in 1934, ten years after the events of the first film, it has Phibes emerging from his secret burial chamber under Maldine Square, ready to take advantage of the advances in medical science to revive his beloved Victoria. After a brief detour to liberate Vulnavia from the St. Daffodil's Home for the Criminally Insane and spending some time rebuilding her acid-scarred face, Phibes then sets about his primary task.

Unfortunately, he discovers that Victoria's body has been kidnapped by a group of eccentric Satanists who are hiding their occult experiments under the guise of the Institute of Psychic Phenomena and are planning to use Victoria as a touchstone in various arcane pursuits. Phibes and Vulnavia then stalk the members, dispatching them in a variety of inventive methods, only belatedly discovering that their playboy leader, Emil Salveus, is actually an anagrammatic mask for none other than the grown-up Lem Vesalius, Henri's son, who has engineered the entire plot as a ploy to draw Phibes into the open so that he can wreak revenge on him for destroying his father and ruining the family name.

By the time he has vanquished the various members of the Institute of Psychic Phenomena and recovered Victoria's body, Phibes discovers to his dismay that her heart has been surgically removed and has fallen into the hands of Inspector Trout. Trout arranges a trap to catch Phibes by luring him to, of all places, Wembley Football Stadium for a handover. But Phibes has the last laugh by sending a clockwork doppleganger in his place and sneaking in disguised as a policeman, before grabbing the heart and stealing a police car for a short car chase back to his country estate, similarly decked out to Maldine Square with a hidden vault and another set of Clockwork Wizards.

While Goldstein and Whiton successfully manage to tap into the macabre but elegant sense of humor that Fuest had brought to the first movie, the story doesn't have the same narrative cohesion. The murders are appropriately intricate but have no guiding logic: one character becomes food for leeches while attending a health spa, another drifts off tied to a balloon, yet another finds he's sharing his bed with a nest of cobras. It's also noticeable that the screenplay attempts to substantially raise the gore quotient with a sequence wherein a fallen priest is disemboweled with a primitive vacuum cleaner, not to mention the Grand Guignol showdown in an elaborate home abattoir built by Salveus/Vesalius.

The other problem with the *Bride* script is that it never really makes much sense. It's not entirely clear why Lem Vesalius feels to the need to reinvent himself as Emil Salveus except to provide a late-breaking surprise for the audience. Phibes' motives are similarly opaque: having triumphed over all manner of adversity and finally succeeded in reviving Victoria at the end of the film, he then proceeds to cryogenically freeze the pair of them in readiness, presumably, for the next sequel. Poor Vulnavia is given even shorter shrift – having helped fight off the police with a bow and arrow alongside the Clockwork Wizards in a rehash of the ending of *The Curses of Dr. Pibe*, she stabs herself to death across the keyboard of Phibes' pipe organ just as in Goldstein's *Dr. Phibes* novelization.

Perhaps unsurprisingly, AIP passed on *The Bride of Dr. Phibes* and instead went with *Dr. Phibes Rises Again*, based on a screenplay by Robert Fuest and Robert Blees. However, this was not before another concept had been brought to the table...

The Abominable Dr. Phibes had not been AIP's only success of 1971. A low budget contemporary vampire story, *Count Yorga, Vampire* (which had been filmed by writer/director Bob Kelljan as *The Loves of Count Iorga, Vampire*; some prints of the movie still bear this title and have a slightly extended running time), had also proved to be a sleeper hit for the company and had transformed its lead actor, the dapper Robert Quarry, into a new star in the horror firmament. At some point in late 1971, someone at AIP came up with the brainwave of rolling these two hit franchises into one: *Dr. Phibes vs. Count Yorga*, if you like. Thus the first *Phibes* sequel would also serve as a *Yorga* prequel.

But there was an ulterior – and rather spiteful – motive for the proposed *Phibes/Yorga* mash-up. It was no secret that Vincent Price had an increasingly acrimonious relationship with Samuel Z Arkoff, vice president at AIP, and was infuriated by his constant penny-pinching when it came to negotiating contracts and budgeting features. Price felt that, as he had earned a considerable amount of money for AIP thanks to a lengthy string of hits throughout the 1960s, he received scant respect for his efforts, much less a decent remuneration. Given the popularity of Robert Quarry with horror fans, not to mention his ability to exude suave villainy, AIP saw him as a way to get Price to fall into line. Even after the *Phibes/Yorga* proposal had (thankfully) imploded in a welter of creative difficulties, they brought Quarry on board as Darius Biderbeck (he's originally named Jonathan in early drafts) in *Dr. Phibes Rises Again*, then made sure rumours began circulating that he was being groomed as Price's successor. This led to a well-publicized rancor between the two actors during the making of the film.

Robert Fuest's initial screenplay for the sequel, titled just *Phibes Rises Again*, does not seem to have had Quarry in mind for Biederbeck (as it is originally spelled; a variant spelling of one of Fuest's favorite jazz musicians, cornetist Bix Beiderbecke). In this early draft Biederbeck is not the scheming villain desperate to extend his lifespan, but simply a committed archaeologist seeking to unravel the mysteries of the Egyptian temple complex of Ibiscus, unaware that Phibes has transformed the ancient tomb into a mountain stronghold, while Diana Trowbridge is his daughter, not his lover. It wouldn't be a stretch to imagine Peter Cushing as Biederbeck in the script as written.

The other big surprise is the absence of Vulnavia. Instead, a new female assistant named Andrea is conjured up by Phibes, although she bears all of Vulnavia's traits of mute resolve, cool sexuality and absolute devotion. It was Fuest's idea to recruit this new assistant, arguing that Vulnavia had been killed at the end of the first film, but the powers that be had other ideas. As Fuest said: "AIP wanted Vulnavia back; they wanted several continuing characters because they planned to make a series of these *Dr. Phibes* films. So Andrea became Vulnavia. She is so mysterious that it is not really illogical that the acid did not really destroy her in the first film."

The initial stages of Fuest's script feel a little clumsy. After Phibes is revived in Maldine Square in 1935, the action abruptly jumps straight to Egypt and the so-called Phibes Mountain, where Phibes is using a periscope to observe a pair of archaeologists, Shavers and Hacket (as his name is spelled in this version; it is amended to Hackett in the shooting script), as they explore the underground temple. He unleashes an eagle to kill Shavers in the same manner as depicted in the finished film (this murder scene, along with the later death of Ambrose by being encased in a giant gin bottle and dropped in the ocean, are the only two set pieces that would be retained for subsequent drafts of the screenplay). The action then shifts back to London as Hacket returns to report to his boss, Biederbeck, with Phibes and Andrea in hot pursuit. Hacket is subsequently killed in a manner that reuses one of the concepts that was dropped from *The Curses of Dr. Pibe* (although it made a brief reappearance in Goldstein's *Dr. Phibes* novelization) – consumed by a swarm of red ants – before Phibes recovers Victoria's body and everyone then sets off back to Egypt again.

In the revised screenplay by Fuest and Robert Blees – which gains an exclamation point to become *Phibes Rises Again!* and sets the story in 1928, just three years after the events of *The Abominable Dr. Phibes* – the repeated to-ing and fro-ing between Egypt and England is simplified into a single trip, and it jettisons a lengthy subplot that has Biederbeck's team transporting Victoria's sarcophagus back to Cairo in the mistaken belief that they have found an ancient relic. It also dispenses with a number of alternate death scenes – Stewart being lured by Andrea into a giant web and being attacked by poisonous spiders, Baker being decapitated by a ceiling fan – and the climactic duel of wits between Phibes and Biederbeck is far more elaborate than the ending in the completed film. In order to distract Biederbeck from attempting to stop Phibes and Victoria crossing the River of Life, Diana is kidnapped and locked into a golden throne at the apex of a giant pyramid, beneath a tube that is slowly filling with boiling oil. Biederbeck has to work his way up through a glass maze inside the pyramid, fight his way past a number of booby-traps – including snakes, scorpions and venomous spiders – in order to release Diana before she is boiled alive. Andrea has two different fates, depending on the script: in Fuest's initial screenplay, she ends up falling into the boiling oil, but in the Fuest/Blees version she sails off down the River of Life alongside Phibes and Victoria.

If the eventual film of *Dr. Phibes Rises Again* is closer to the Fuest/Blees draft than Fuest's solo effort, the screenplay is actually little more than a template. Virtually none of the scripted dialogue remains in the movie, replaced with a lot of apparent improvising and throwaway lines. There are also a number of scenes – such as a short appearance by the veteran comic actress Beryl Reid as Miss Ambrose – that don't appear to have been scripted at all.

Fuest has said that he felt he had to smuggle much of the humor in *The Abominable Dr. Phibes* past the AIP brass, who had hired him to craft a straight horror movie. Bolstered by the popularity of the first film, however, Fuest felt confident enough to bring the humor to the forefront in *Rises Again*, devising surreal visual gags and encouraging the cast to have fun with their characters and dialogue. Unfortunately he seriously overestimated the amount of freedom he had to indulge himself. When he turned in his cut of the film, AIP responded by re-editing the film, excising much of the comedy in order to emphasize the horror.

There is certainly a feeling with *Dr. Phibes Rises Again* that there are scenes missing from the story as it jerks along with little concern for logic or continuity. A number of crucial questions – such as how Phibes and Biderbeck (as the name is now spelled) know each other, or indeed how Biderbeck discovered the elixir of youth that has been sustaining him for all these years – remain unanswered. Whether these gaps were ever filled in the director's cut of the film is unknown as that version has never surfaced, but they certainly aren't addressed in the Fuest/Blees script.

Despite having had no hand in the *Rises Again* screenplay, William Goldstein came on board again to write the movie tie-in novelization published by Award Books in 1972. It quickly becomes obvious that Goldstein based the book on the Fuest/Blees script rather than the finished film since it includes numerous episodes that never made it to the screen, such as the climactic scenes inside the glass pyramid. It also restores a character that was excised from the movie – Major Braff of the Scottish Fusiliers, who is a late arrival at the archaeological camp in Egypt and becomes part of the force trying to stop Phibes from crossing the River of Life – and, as per the screenplay, there is no sign of the character of Miss

Ambrose. The novel also confuses matters with yet another variation on Biederbeck/Biderbeck by naming him Jonathan Biderbeck throughout.

The strength of the novel is that it does attempt to clarify some of the holes in the plot. A lengthy opening section set circa 1330 B.C. depicts the efforts to build a tomb for the pharaoh Akhenaton by flooding a temple complex and thus establishing the River of Life. The dying Akhenaton bequeaths a gift to one of his faithful servants: a scroll that is actually a map to finding the River of Life and two vials of life-extending elixir to help the servant join his master in the afterlife. The scroll and vials are then stolen by tomb raiders and separated. Centuries later, Biderbeck has found the vials and is using the elixir to keep himself alive long enough to recover the scroll and find a way across the River of Life.

The novel also tries to redress one of the criticisms that has been leveled at the sequel: that the character of Phibes is rendered somewhat less appealing in *Rises Again* because he insists on murdering essentially blameless characters such as Biderbeck's manservant Bruno simply because they happen to get in his way. To make such murders seem less callous, Goldstein devises back-stories for the victims that try to justify their deaths – such as making Bruno a brutal killer who's under Biderbeck's protection.

* * *

Throughout the making of *Dr. Phibes Rises Again*, plans were definitely afoot for another sequel. In a set report for the Summer 1972 issue of *Cinefantastique* magazine, Chris Knight and Peter Nicholson reported on discussions about a third film in the series that would have propelled the story into the late 1930s and pitted Phibes against Adolf Hitler. It's unclear whether this concept ever got beyond the planning stages, but no treatment or screenplay has ever surfaced.

Robert Fuest also toyed with his own treatment for a third film in the series, entitled *The Son of Dr. Phibes*, which would have featured Phibes and his offspring battling to save the environment. He told *Psychotronic* magazine in 2004: "In the Seventies, AIP had an actor who looked exactly like a younger version of Vincent Price, and I thought 'Wouldn't it be wonderful to put both this younger guy and Vincent in the same movie together?' The story concerned Dr. Phibes and his son waging green war on pollution and oil companies and petroleum and gas. Guys would die in oil, others would die from all the various resources of the earth; you know, like the tide coming in and killing some guy. I had some nice murder scenes in it too, like this one guy who was standing, tied up, upon a huge piece of cheese, and he had this loose fitting noose around his neck. There's be lots of mice crawling over the huge wedge of cheese and eating it, with this guy standing on the wedge, his feet giving way under him, and ultimately hanging himself.

"Anyway, I had a few ideas for a third Dr. Phibes entry, but the thing never came to fruition. Truthfully, I think we managed to just about get away with the ironic gag in *Rises Again*. If we'd done a third film, it would have taken a miracle to get it off the ground because it would have been very difficult to top the first one and the sequel."

Fuest never got the chance to try and pull off that miracle. By the time of the cinema release of *Dr. Phibes Rises Again*, the grand plan for a five-movie cycle had bitten the dust. *Rises Again* underperformed at the box office, leading AIP to question the enduring popularity of the character. It didn't help that the company was in a state of flux at the time – although they never entirely abandoned the low budget exploitation movies with which they had made their name in the 1950s and 1960s, they did have ambitions to develop more prestigious mainstream projects such as *Shout at the Devil* (1976), *Force 10 from Navarone* (1978) and *Meteor* (1979), many of which proved to be costly flops and helped sink the company. By the end of the 1970s, AIP had been absorbed into Filmways, Inc. which was, in turn, bought by Orion Pictures in 1982. AIP became little more than a registered trademark and a back catalogue of movies that has been changing hands ever since.

With AIP turning away from the horror genre, Robert Fuest also decided the time had come to move on. After *Rises Again*, he was approached to team up with Vincent Price again for *Theater of Blood* (1973), a black comedy very much inspired by the *Phibes* movies that has an embittered classical actor, Edward Lionheart, bumping off his critics one by one, each murder being inspired by a different Shakespeare play. Worried that he might become typecast as the go-to director for comical multiple murder movies, he opted instead to mount an ambitious adaptation of Michael Moorcock's experimental sci-fi novel *The Final Programme* (1973), the first in a series of books and stories featuring Moorcock's enigmatic secret agent, Jerry Cornelius. Sadly, cinema audiences in the early 1970s were not quite ready to embrace the cynical, polysexual Cornelius and the film was dismissed as an ambitious misfire.

Goldstein and Whiton, however, kept the faith. They dusted down *The Bride of Dr. Phibes* screenplay, made a few tweaks to bring the story into line with the chronology established by *Dr. Phibes Rises Again*, retitled it *Phibes Resurrectus* and presented it to AIP alumnus Roger Corman over at New World Pictures (which had also made a game attempt to find an audience for *The Final Programme* in the US under the title *The Last Days of Man on Earth*). The amendments made by Goldstein and Whiton to *The Bride of Dr. Phibes* were fairly cosmetic, the most notable being a revised opening sequence in which Phibes returns to England in a hot air balloon upon which is emblazoned the motto 'Non omnis moriar', a quote from the poet Horace which translates as "I shall not wholly die."

Corman displayed some interest in the project and even went so far as to assemble a wish list of actors for the film, including David Carradine as Phibes and songwriter Paul Williams as Emil Salveus. This was the first time that Williams, who had caught horror fans' attention playing the Mephistophelean record producer Swan in Brian De Palma's *Phantom of the Paradise* (1974), was mentioned in connection with a *Phibes* movie. It wouldn't be the last.

As various Victims and Interested Parties, Corman also floated such tasty casting choices as Orson Welles, Roddy McDowell, Sam Jaffe, Donald Pleasence, John Carradine, and, somewhat surprisingly, Coral Browne. After all, Browne had been married to Vincent Price since 1974, having met him on the set of *Theatre of Blood* (1973), in which she had played one of the theatre critics gruesomely dispatched by the vengeful Edward Lionheart.

With Coral Browne in the mix, it strongly suggests that Vincent Price was still being considered to play Phibes, despite talk of David Carradine taking over the role. After all, Corman and Price had worked together many times in the past, most notably on Corman's popular series of Edgar Allan Poe adaptations for AIP. This theory is further supported by Corman's gimmicky proposal of casting Forrest J. Ackerman, editor of *Famous Monsters of Filmland* magazine, as the clockwork doppelgänger of Phibes that is used to fool the police at the climax. For years, the resemblance between Ackerman and Price had been played up in the pages of *Famous Monsters*, so there would been no point in casting the magazine editor as a double for David Carradine. Given Corman's reputation for being tightfisted, it's possible that all of this came down to simple economics, with Corman floating the idea of Carradine as Phibes simply as bargaining ploy to get Price to reduce his asking price, in much the same way that AIP had used Robert Quarry partly as a lever to get Price to tow the line during the making of *Dr. Phibes Rises Again*.

Whatever the case, despite New World giving *Phibes Resurrectus* a provisional release date of 1977, it ended up being pushed further and further back in the studio schedule before being quietly dropped.

While New World was dithering over *Resurrectus*, another Phibes project reared its head from an unlikely quarter, as reported in Ed Sikov's book *Mr. Strangelove: A Biography of Peter Sellers*. In the wake of the success of *The Return of the Pink Panther* in 1975, which had successfully brought the bumbling French police detective Jacques Clouseau back to the screen after an absence of 11 years, Peter Sellers and director Blake Edwards were throwing around ideas for a fourth Clouseau comedy. One of these concepts would have cast Sellers in multiple roles a la *Dr. Strangelove* (1964). In addition to Clouseau, Sellers would reprise his turn as James Bond (aka Evelyn Tremble) in *Casino Royale* (1967) and pit the pair against the insidious Dr. Fu Manchu and Dr. Phibes. Even had Edwards managed to navigate the numerous copyright issues over usage of the different characters, Sellers pretty much put the kibosh on the idea by signing up to play detective Sidney Wang in *Murder*

By Death (1975); following that comedy with yet another caricature Chinese impersonation seemed like a bad idea. The film that emerged from this creative process, *The Pink Panther Strikes Back* (1976), bore little resemblance to the early outline, although Sellers would eventually resurrect the Fu Manchu idea with *The Fiendish Plot of Dr. Fu Manchu* in 1980, with disastrous results.

By 1978 it had become apparent that *Phibes Resurrectus* was not going to be made at New World, so William Goldstein and James Whiton decided to set their own sequel in motion. They formed The Phibes Production Company with a view to making *Phibes in the Holy Lands,* based on a draft screenplay by one Solomon Bolo. It transpired that Bolo was actually a pseudonym for – who else? – Goldstein and Whiton, and apparently amused them because every second letter was an 'O'. As Goldstein explained: "'Solomon Bolo' was Jim Whiton's invention. He used it on certain pieces; and he liked the notion of cutting through the writer's many headwinds with his bolo." (It's worth noting that 'bolo' is a term coined in the Philippines to refer to a type of machete commonly used to hack down sugar cane.)

Set in the 1930s and pretty much ignoring the events of *Dr. Phibes Rises Again, Phibes in the Holy Lands* follows on from the first film by having Phibes and Vulnavia arrive by railroad handcar at a residence on the edge of the Sea of Galilee, where the good doctor is planning to complete work on The Lady Phibes Concerto in an effort to immortalize the memory of his beloved Victoria. Unfortunately his presence attracts the attention of his neighbour, Lord Gabriel, an insanely egotistical composer who believes he is on a divine mission to produce celestial music and who will let nothing stand in the way of his self-proclaimed genius. He declares war on Phibes and unleashes a number of assassins – including a homunculus with a spear, a flamethrower-wielding biker and the mummified remains of his own brother – to destroy his rival.

It is perhaps telling that the first person to be signed up for the *Holy Lands* project was songwriter Paul Williams, who had earlier been pegged to play Emil Salveus in *Phibes Resurrectus.* The character of Lord Gabriel had obviously been written with Williams in mind, being an even more extreme version of Swan from *Phantom of the*

Paradise, and also provided him with the opportunity to compose all the music for the film (The label to which Williams was exclusively contracted, A&M Records, which had released an LP of his score to *Phantom of the Paradise*, was, according to Goldstein's investors' prospectus, committed to release a soundtrack album of Williams' score to *Phibes in the Holy Lands*). The trouble was that this reduced Dr. Phibes to little more than a supporting player in his own movie, simply reacting to events rather than using his superior intellect to engineer them. For much of its running time, *Phibes in the Holy Lands* plays like a live action version of a *Road Runner* cartoon with Gabriel as Wile E. Coyote, devising ever more elaborate schemes to vanquish his detested rival, all of which are doomed to failure.

Even at just 75 pages, the screenplay for *Phibes in the Holy Lands* feels as if it is struggling to make up its running time. Gabriel's ranting monologues are amusing at first, but quickly become repetitious. And the inclusion of a pair of hangdog police detectives in Jerusalem feels like filler, as they hover on the edges of the action, doing little more than ruminating on events that have already happened, including providing an unnecessarily detailed rehash of the murders from the previous films.

For all its shortcomings, *Phibes in the Holy Lands* did attract the interest of Vincent Price. In an interview with *Cinefantastique* magazine, Price enthused: "It's a marvelous script, a very funny script. I wanted Bob Fuest to direct it. He is the only person in the world who is mad enough to direct the *Dr. Phibes* films. He's a genuine, registered nut. He even looks like a madman. He's all over the place, like an unmade bed. What an imagination he has. They were all his ideas." It's unknown whether Goldstein and Whiton approached Fuest to direct the film, but the project was eventually abandoned.

More promising was a further treatment by Goldstein and Whiton that emerged in the early 1980s. Titled simply *Dr. Phibes* it was an attempt to reboot the series in a contemporary setting, reviving Dr. Phibes in the present day and sending him, Vulnavia and the remains of Victoria to New York aboard an ocean-going yacht, in search of a means to revive Victoria in America. However, once Phibes and Co. are ensconced in a Manhattan penthouse, they find themselves up against the members of the Wormwood

Institute, a sinister corporate think tank of eminent scientists. When their perverted leader, Hector Wormwood, smashes Victoria's crystal coffin, her body shrivels, forcing Phibes on a search for the essential salts to restore her. Along the way he gets revenge by killing off the various members of Wormwood Institute – including a pedophile astrophysicist, a gluttonous germ warfare expert, identical twin transvestites who develop nuclear weapons and a 12-year-old physics genius – using suitably ironic modus operandi that exploit their various personal and sexual peccadilloes. In the right hands, *Dr. Phibes* might have actually made for an admirably twisted and blackly comical satire of the Reagan Generation, but there is no indication that the treatment was ever worked up into a full screenplay.

It's also unclear whether it was this *Dr. Phibes* outline that was announced as being in production at Laurel Entertainment in 1984 or simply another renaming of Goldstein and Whiton's earlier *The Bride of Dr. Phibes/Phibes Resurrectus*. In 1984, trade ads appeared in magazines such as *Variety* that presented Laurel's production slate for 1985, among which was a project entitled *Phibes Resurrected*. Although it was rumoured that the celebrated George A. Romero had been brought on board to direct, he has since stated that he had no knowledge of the film. Whatever the case, by the following year, *Phibes Resurrected* had effectively been reinterred.

At this time, Whiton and Goldstein weren't the only members of the original *Phibes* team to actively seek to exercise their rights to create further adventures for the character. Louis M. Heyward, who had produced the first two *Phibes* movies as the head of AIP's London production office, made an attempt to resurrect the character for an animated weekly television series called *The Sinister Dr. Phibes*. Heyward reimagined the character as a modern-day crimefighter with the ability to adopt different disguises using prosthetic masks to cover his skeletal visage. For the purposes of pitching the concept to various television networks, Heyward got the veteran comic book artist Jack Kirby, best known for his work with Marvel Comics on characters such as Captain America, the Fantastic Four and X-Men, to work up a visual concept for the series. Ultimately the series was never commissioned, although it's worth noting the uncanny similarity between Heyward's rough outline and director Sam Raimi's offbeat superhero adventure *Darkman* (1990).

One further feature film treatment emerged during the 1980s, from an unusual source. Paul Clemens, the actor son of Eleanor Parker, and writer Ron Magid developed their own treatment, entitled *The Seven Fates of Dr. Phibes*. Of all the unmade sequels this is perhaps the one that Phibes fans would have most liked to have reached the screen.

The treatment begins with a prologue set prior to the events of *The Abominable Dr. Phibes* with Phibes and Victoria both still alive. Dressed in Grecian robes, they perform an occult rite and outline a grand plan to cross the River of Life. They subsequently travel to the Mediterranean where, with the help of seven antique ivory carvings of characters from Greek mythology, they hope to achieve their ultimate objective. The story proper then begins in the early 1930s, with the duo emerging from a hidden cavern aboard the funeral barge that has carried them across the River of Life, disembarking in what is eventually revealed to be the fabled Elephant's Graveyard. From there they return to London to retrieve the ivory carvings, which are secreted in an underground chamber in Maldine Square, and put the final stages of their grand plan into action.

In London, however, they discover that a hotel has now been built on the ruins of Maldine Square and that the hotel manager has discovered the ivory carvings and sold them to various wealthy individuals, keeping one of them – a statue of Polyphemus the Cyclops – for himself. He informs Phibes and Victoria that they aren't the first people to inquire after the carvings; a certain Professor Grayson Norquist has also been attempting to track down the antiques, having so far only managed to obtain one of them, a statue of the Minotaur.

With the help of the ever faithful Vulnavia, Phibes and Victoria set about tracking down and murdering each of the current owners of the carvings in elegantly macabre fashion, each killing mirroring the nature of the ivory effigies: Medusa, Arachne, Icarus, Cerberus and the Trojan Horse. These sequences also feature some of the most elaborate Phibes inventions to date, including a three-headed clockwork dog and a huge metal sculpture of Medusa that spews liquid cement. Needless to say, dogging their footsteps are the bumbling Trout and Waverly, not to mention the mysterious Professor Norquist.

The story climaxes on the island of Crete, with a showdown between Phibes and Norquist in the labyrinth of King Minos, where a bizarre pact is struck. Norquist hands Phibes the final ivory carving in exchange for an occult necklace that will give him dominion in Hades, then allows Phibes to kill him so that he can assume his throne in the underworld. With Vulnavia finally revealed to be the living incarnation of Athena, goddess of wisdom, strategy and just warfare (and finally getting her first lines of dialogue in the series), she helps Phibes and Victoria to achieve their ultimate objective of joining her in immortality on Mount Olympus. The trio is last seen ascending into the heavens aboard Phibes' art deco pipe organ to the strains of *Over the Rainbow*.

The Seven Fates of Dr. Phibes is wildly overblown in the best possible way. More than any other writers, Clemens and Magid really tap into the macabre, offbeat humor that Fuest had brought to the earlier films. The murder set pieces are bizarre and intricate, exploiting Phibes' genius for mechanical invention and warped sense of poetic justice. And they wrap up the innumerable loose ends left dangling by the earlier films neatly, logically and satisfyingly, while also finding time to pepper the scenario with obscure in-jokes – the hotel manager who is holding the Cyclops effigy is named Dekker, obviously in homage to Albert Dekker, star of *Dr. Cyclops* (1940) – and arcane literary references to Edgar Allan Poe and H.P. Lovecraft. It's the work of two men who don't just like the Phibes movies, but really *love* them.

Vincent Price obviously concurred. In a letter to Paul Clemens he wrote: "I love your new adventures of Dr. Phibes! It's well conceived and just preposterous enough to be equal fun with the others. I think it exactly the right time to do it as the out and out horror has been done to death, and a laugh or two – or in this case many more – is what people want. Keep in touch – I'm ready to go anytime."

One can only imagine what might have transpired had Robert Fuest joined Price, Clemens and Magid for one last waltz round Maldine Square.

[Editor's note: In 2003, Dave Elsey and Jon Groom wrote what is, for my money, the best unfilmed Phibes script, *Phibes Lives!* In it, they wittily recaptured the elegance and gallows humor of Fuest's films. -JH]

*   *   *

"They haven't built the coffin that can hold him!" ran the tagline for *Dr. Phibes Rises Again*. That has certainly proved to be the case.

Over the years, Phibes fans have been amused to find the good doctor popping up in the most unexpected places. Director John Carpenter paid homage to the character in his 1980 ghost story *The Fog*, with a medic named Dr. Phibes, played by Darwin Joston. Writers Steven Knight and Mike Whitehill introduced a sinister pathologist named Dr. Phibes for an episode of the British TV comedy series *The Detectives* (1993-1997), with Richard O'Brien, creator of *The Rocky Horror Show*, cast in the role and ghoulishly grafting a plastic troll doll to the head of comedian Jasper Carrott. Oscar-winning screenwriter/director Roger Avary pronounced himself a fan by creating an eccentric emergency room doctor named Phibes for his 2002 film adaptation of Bret Easton Ellis's novel *The Rules of Attraction*; in a further twist on the history of the series, Avary cast Paul Williams in the role, finally fulfilling the songwriter's ambition of becoming part of the *Phibes* saga. And writer Steven Sessions created a recurring supervillain named Dr. Phinias Phibes, an evil scientific genius with a prosthetic hand, for the animated TV series *Shaggy & Scooby-Doo: Get a Clue* that ran from 2006 to 2007.

The music world has similarly thrown up innumerable tributes, the most prominent being the English psychedelic rock trio Dr. Phibes & the House of Wax Equations, who produced two LPs and a handful of singles and EPs between 1990 and 1995, and the band The Clockwork Wizards. Phibes has also been name-checked in songs by The Misfits, Angel Witch, Murderdolls, The Busters, Overmamba, The Company Band and Madre Del Vizio. Punk band The Bollock Brothers used a photo of Phibes and Vulnavia on the picture sleeve of their 1983 single *Horror Movies*, released under one of the group's numerous pseudonyms, The B.B.s. Meanwhile, the song *13th Floor Vendetta* by The Damned opens with the line "The organ plays to midnight on Maldine Square tonight". And in one of those bizarre nuggets of pop culture trivia that you really couldn't make up, it has been established that Keith Moon, drummer with The Who, was watching *The Abominable Dr. Phibes* on television on the night that he died of a drug overdose in 1978.

Then as the new millennium dawned and it seemed that perhaps the world really *had* heard the last of Dr. Anton Phibes, a familiar figure emerged from the shadows...

In 2008, the Spanish science fiction novelist Felix J. Palma published *The Map of Time*, the first volume in an ambitious steampunk trilogy, which took delight in mixing up pseudo-scientific charlatanry and genuine temporal paradoxes in Victorian England as H.G. Wells, Jack the Ripper and Queen Victoria all become haplessly involved in a time-bending love story. Making a sneaky cameo appearance in one of the numerous alternative timelines that crisscross through the novel is Dr. Phibes, an amazing chess-playing automaton (or, if you prefer, clockwork wizard) who becomes a popular sideshow carnival attraction until his dark secret is uncovered.

Just a year later, the Brazilian comic book artist Adriano was given free rein to create a brand new Phibes adventure in graphic form for the *Vincent Price Presents* series published by Bluewater Productions. Adriano's story, *The Dark Comedy*, was published in issue 13 in November 2009. Set just after the events of *Dr. Phibes Rises Again*, it has Phibes returning to London after his Egyptian foray, having discovered that the River of Life had not enough power to raise Victoria from the dead. Instead, he begins to tap into a new scheme to raise a Lovecraftian elder god, whose immense strength may help him to generate the energy to revive his dead wife. Opposing him is the long-suffering Harry Trout and a mysterious figure named Thanatos, eventually revealed to be Victoria's father. In a cute in-joke, passing reference is also made to another serial killer plaguing London at the time: one Edward Lionheart, the deranged Shakespearean actor from *Theatre of Blood*. *The Dark Comedy* is a nice concept and Adriano has an evocative visual style, but the story seems a touch perfunctory. Adriano has intimated in interviews that he had originally envisioned the story as a three- or four-part mini-series, so condensing the entire story into a single issue makes for an ultimately unsatisfactory instalment in the saga.

Bluewater continued the Phibes theme in issue 14 of *Vincent Price Presents* in December 2009 with the first part of an untitled Phibes adventure written by Mel Smith, Clark Castillo and Paul H. Birch, with art by Nadja Smith. This adventure has Phibes being transported from the 1930s to 1999 by an unexplained time vortex that separates him from the now-revived Victoria. Under cover of a bizarre series of murders, Phibes has been stealing ancient artifacts as part of yet another scheme to return Victoria to his side, a rite that entails the human sacrifice of a pair of identical twins on the top of the World Trade Centre as the world enters the new millennium. Although the story is entertaining enough and throws in a few neat ideas – including a Pink Floydian inflatable pig floating over NYC – Phibes seems out of place in the 21st Century. It didn't help matters that the second half of the story wasn't published until issue 28 of *Vincent Price Presents* in March 2011, at a point when most people had given up hope of ever seeing it concluded. For the second episode, Mats Engesten and Andrew Dodd provided the artwork. The story leaves room for a further sequel, but whether any further instalments will be forthcoming remains to be seen.

Following publication in *Vincent Price Presents*, both of these comic book stories were adapted for the radio by the Colonial Radio Theatre. Operating out of Boston and broadcasting on XM/Sirius satellite radio, this repertory company has a long history of presenting fantasy and science fiction works by authors such as L. Frank Baum, Ray Bradbury and William F. Nolan. The unnamed two-part story that appeared in issues 14 and 28 of *Vincent Price Presents* was given the title of *The Seven Lives of Dr. Phibes* for its radio presentation and the subsequent audio book release of the show. Bluewater Productions also used this title when they brought together all three comic books for an omnibus edition published in 2013.

Another offbeat theatrical adaptation debuted in 2011 as part of the Vincentenniel celebrations in St Louis to honour the birth of Vincent Price, one of the town's most famous sons, on May 27, 1911. Magic Smoking Monkey Theatre, a comedy troupe specializing in stage parodies of cult movies, performed *The Abominable Dr. Phibes – in 3-D!* at the Regional Arts Commission Studio Theatre in University City from May 13-21. For this stage production, Richard Lewis was cast as Anton Phibes, Luke Lindberg played Vesalius and the overworked Scott McMaster had the thankless task of playing ALL of the victims. [Editor's note: I sent Bob Fuest a link to a video clip of the *Phibes* stage production and he said he enjoyed it greatly.]

And even this essay's co-author, filmmaker Sam Irvin, paid tribute to the Phibes universe in his made-for-television whodunit *Open Marriage* by including a character named Vulnavia, an enigmatic sex club proprietress, played by the exquisitely offbeat Debra Wilson of *MADtv*.

[Editor's Note: In 2017, comedian Kumail Nanjiani built a scene in his Academy Award-nominated comedy *The Big Sick* around *Dr. Phibes*. Nanjiani, as himself, excitedly tells his new girlfriend about *The Abominable Dr. Phibes*... and gets nearly every detail of its production wrong! He tells her that Metro-Goldwyn-Mayer produced it, that Price was their biggest star, that *Dr. Phibes* was made to recoup losses from M-G-M's expensive flops, all in 1969! The menu screen from the Scream Factory BluRay appears, and clips from the film play while Nanjiani and costar Zoe Kazan make out. Nanjiani's facts might have been off—he needs to read this book!--but his affection for the film is strong, undeniable, and welcome. In an interview with Nanjiani quoted in *The Denton Record*-Chronicle, Nanjiani said: "I originally wrote that scene as a way to share something I love with Emily. Then, [Gordon] rewrote the scene as a way to show that I am testing her tastes by having my character stare at her while she watches the film. I realized that I hadn't seen a moment like that before in a movie, yet it's such a relatable thing to show others what we love as litmus test of sorts." Ironically, I have been using *Dr. Phibes* as a similar "litmus test" for years! Nanjiani is a man after my own heart. –JH]

* * *

Yet even after all this time, it turned out that the world had not heard the last of William Goldstein ...

In July 2011, Goldstein reasserted his co-ownership of his and Whiton's characters by self-publishing the novel *Dr. Phibes – In the Beginning* as an e-book available through amazon.com, following this a few months later with e-book reissues of his movie tie-ins of *The Abominable Dr. Phibes* and *Dr. Phibes Rises Again*.

In the Beginning follows the chronology set by the films (well, sort of . . . in the new novel, Goldstein writes that Anton and Victoria meet and marry in 1928, which would be three years after the events of the first film in the accepted timeline). Most of the book is a sprawling collection of ephemera including a history of Phibes' military career as a regimental corporal during World War One and his work as a diplomat after the war, his courtship of American debutante Victoria Regina de Guine at a country estate in the Lake District in the north of England, his recuperation and reconstruction following his car accident at the Klingenstein Clinic near – Sherlock Holmes fans take note – the Reichenbach Falls and his first failed attempt to restore his beloved Victoria to life. This also includes digressions into Henri Vesalius's wartime experiences, a brief history of Maldine Square and a look at how rose quartz is mined in Brazil.

The novel also delves into the origins of Vulnavia and the Clockwork Wizards. It explains how Phibes expanded on the principles of Charles Babbage's 19th-century proto-computer, the Difference Engine, to create what are referred to as "androbots", semi-synthetic people. The Clockwork Wizards are his earliest creations, later refined into Vulnavia. The book also introduces a further evolution of the process: Sophie, the first androbot capable of speech, who is the singer with Clockwork Wizards and the final step in a process that he hopes will resurrect Victoria.

All of this is book-ended by the investigations of police detective Valor Pretorius and news reporter Willow Weeps into a bizarre string of murders in modern-day New York in what is eventually revealed to be a variant on Goldstein's film treatment for the *Dr. Phibes* reboot of the early 1980s. Instead of the Wormwood Institute, Phibes is up against the Ponce de Leon Society, an elite club of wealthy socialites seeking the secret of eternal youth, who have stolen the body of Victoria and the androbot Sophie in order to harvest their DNA for further experiments. Phibes plots the murders of the Society members according to the principles of the Seven Deadly Sins, although the individual victims are never really fleshed out as characters and sadly there isn't much detail as to the processes by which the murders are committed.

The book concludes with a teaser for *The Real Androbots*, a forthcoming graphic novel by William Goldstein and his son Damon, which would chart the continuing adventures of Sophie and the Clockwork Wizards.

In 2012, a year after *Dr. Phibes – In the Beginning*, Goldstein Sr dashed out another book in the series, entitled *Vulnavia's Secret*. At just 86 pages, it is essentially little more than a bridge between the events of *The Abominable Dr. Phibes* and *Dr. Phibes Rises Again*, and despite what its title might suggest, Vulnavia appears only fleetingly.

The opening chapter lifts a scene directly from the screenplay for *The Bride of Dr. Phibes*, with Phibes springing the acid-burned Vulnavia from her cell at St. Daffodils Home for the Criminally Insane, before whisking her back to Maldine Square for some groundbreaking facial reconstruction that he has developed through a lengthy correspondence with Alexander Maximov, the eminent Russian scientist who pioneered stem cell surgery in the early years of the 20th Century. Maximov is just the first of several real-life historical figures, including fashion designer Christian Louboutin and Mustafa Kemal Ataturk, the founder of modern-day Turkey, who are referenced in the book. The rest of the story then provides a flashback to Phibes' first visit to Egypt, setting into motion his search for the River Of Life, with a digression of a few pages to catch up with Harry Trout, at this point having been drummed out of the police force and living rough in the seaside town of Margate.

If *Dr. Phibes – In the Beginning* often seems more like a miscellany of Phibes lore than a genuine novel, *Vulnavia's Secret* is even more ephemeral, an exercise in tying up a few loose ends and filling in gaps in the established chronology of events. What remains unexplained are some cryptic references to a heavily fortified Velocity Room in Maldine Square and a chapter detailing a mysterious earthquake that partially collapses the building and is later discovered to have resulted from a pressure wave emanating from the house itself and moving in a direct line down to the centre of the earth. It isn't unreasonable to conclude that all of this has something to do with the unexplained gyroscopes and the plot "To move the Earth its final step" mentioned in the screenplay for *The Curses of Dr. Pibe*. Whether Goldstein will ever resolve this continuing mystery remains to be seen.

Vulnavia's Secret concludes with yet another teaser for *The Real Androbots* graphic novel – which was still forthcoming in mid-2016 – but it also added another wrinkle to the Phibes saga with an invitation to fans from William and Damon Goldstein to invest in a Kickstarter project to develop a showreel for a new movie that would centre around the character of Sophie. The idea seemed to be that the showreel would be used to attract investors to the film. However, a visit to the relevant Kickstarter website page reveals that the project failed to achieve the necessary goal of raising $19,999 and was cancelled in June 2013.

With the proposed Tim Burton/Johnny Depp remake of *The Abominable Dr. Phibes* currently in limbo and the Goldsteins' Sophie spin-off project an apparent non-starter, one might reasonably conclude that the cinematic history of Phibes, Victoria and Vulnavia had come to an end. Then, in 2015, the Goldsteins issued a press release announcing that they were developing a new movie, *Forever Phibes*, with Malcolm McDowell attached to play the vengeful doctor and a proposed release date of Halloween 2016 (although it seemed unlikely even then that the film would be greenlit, crewed up and completed in just over a year). Whether or not this latest production proves to be a new beginning or another false ending, it does prove that there is still life in the good doctor yet.

Non omnis moriar, indeed.

Chapter 4
The Irreplaceable Mr. Fuest: A Remembrance of Robert Fuest

By Justin Humphreys

Miss Brunner: What are you going to do now?
Jerry Cornelius: Well, for a start, I'm going to sit here and get smashed out of my mind. And I also have it on very good authority that the world is coming to an end. I thought I'd go home and watch it on television.

- Dialogue from Robert Fuest's *The Final Programme* (1974).

Director/designer/writer Robert Fuest died early on March 21, 2012, peacefully in bed, at home with his loving family. He leaves behind a visionary legacy in fantastic cinema. Along with his fellow maverick English directors, Ken Russell, Joseph McGrath, and Nicolas Roeg-- whose directorial careers, like Bob's, began in the late 1960s and early 1970s-- Fuest fearlessly rewrote the rules of moviemaking. Their work even intersected: Roeg shot some early commercials that Fuest directed, Fuest and McGrath worked together at one point, and Russell's visit to the gigantic human pinball machine casino set from Fuest's *The Final Programme* (1973) directly inspired the design of his own *Tommy*.

Most famously, Fuest altered the face – no pun intended – of modern horror movies with his beloved *The Abominable Dr. Phibes* (1971). It plays like a hybrid of Poe's "The Raven," *The Phantom of the Opera*, and *Ten Little Indians*, with a healthy dose of the madcap experimentation of Francois Truffaut's *Shoot the Piano Player* (1962) mixed in. (However, Fuest and the film's screenwriter, William Goldstein, both denied any such conscious influences on it.) Like Truffaut's film, *Dr. Phibes* was an exhilarating cinematic curveball, deliberately flaunting genre conventions while wildly, affectionately reinventing them.

And reinvent horror, Fuest did. His titular vengeful madman didn't skulk around a hackneyed Old Dark House or Gothic castle (unlike in the film's shooting script)– he strolled suavely around an immaculate, vibrantly colorful Art Deco palace. And Phibes' assistant was no ordinary, cookie-cutter, hunchbacked male slob– she was the horror cinema's Helen of Troy, the supremely cool Vulnavia (Virginia North). Bob had no interest in worn-out horror tropes– he was concerned with unaffected painterly elegance, gallows humor, and, above all, imagination. And Fuest's imagination was boundless.

Dr. Phibes' star Vincent Price immediately recognized that in Bob. The film broke the mold for Price's work– its freshness and artistic vitality appealed immensely to him and won him over. (Fuest deliberately avoided the stale look of director Gordon Hessler's period horror films– he deemed Hessler's work "as subtle as an air raid.") During the film's shoot, Price described Fuest as "the best young director I've ever worked with, he's so creative and brilliant." In later interviews, Price inevitably brightened at the mention of Fuest's name and spoke just as effusively of him.

Fuest truly is the architect of *Dr. Phibes*– its original screenplay and shooting script were nearly dead serious. Almost all of the film's beloved asides and comical exchanges were absent, like Terry-Thomas' hasty explanation that the screen he's watching a stag movie on is "a new thing on the market... It keeps out draughts..." I knew Bob Fuest well and, after speaking to him for five minutes, you could spot the sense of humor that permeated his *Just Like a Woman* (1968), *Dr. Phibes* and *The Final Programme*. A typical exchange: Me- "Hey, Bob. What are you up to?" Bob- "Hatching a fiendish plot!"

Bob and his set designer, Brian Eatwell originated Dr. Phibes' signature Deco design. Bob's background in art direction permeates the film. In the screenplay, Phibes' mansion was decorated busily in Louis XIV style. Bob scratched this description out in his shooting script and scrawled one word over it: "BOLLOX."

Robert Fuest and Brian Clemens confer during the filming of And Soon the Darkness.

Fuest at work on And Soon the Darkness.

Probably the greatest joy of being an interviewer is getting to know your favorite filmmakers and discovering that they are even more marvelous than their work. Such was the case with Bob. Whenever I spoke with him, he was an unfailingly upbeat, incredibly funny, witty, vital, interesting, and extremely supportive person— a great listener who would exclaim "That's fan-tastic!" whenever I'd mention some new positive development. As mentally sharp and energetic as he was, it was very difficult to imagine him being an octogenarian. And he giggled, constantly and infectiously.

Bob looked every bit the eccentric artist with his huge mop of hair (worn long before Tim Burton patented that style) and his frenetic energy, but he was askew in the best way. When Bob really got going, he was a virtuoso of utterly wonderful weirdness. In Fuest's movie worlds, nuns calmly play slot machines while the world collapses offscreen. A satanic cult melts into bubbling pools of tapioca. An eminent surgeon is impaled by a brass unicorn in the heart of London, forcing police detectives to ever-so-politely unscrew his corpse from a gentlemen's club wall. A brooding Nobel Prize-winning physicist, his nails neatly polished black, lives on a diet of Bell's whiskey and chocolate biscuits. (This little bit of business, says Fuest's widow, was somewhat "autobiographical": Fuest "loved his whiskey and chocky bikkies," she says.) In the remains of a Nazi stronghold, that same physicist merges with a woman to become the new Messiah: an apeman. Within his personal artificial nightclub, a disfigured murderer genteelly sips champagne through a throat socket while life-size clockwork musicians serenade him and his gorgeous assistant.

But Bob wasn't eccentric for eccentricity's sake, or merely eccentric. His thriller *And Soon the Darkness* (1970) was shot straightforwardly, largely in scenic, sun-drenched outdoor settings. "Remember the way Hitchcock kept you on the edge of your seat?" the film's posters asked, which was highly appropriate, considering that Bob's widow says he favored a *North By Northwest*-style approach: horrifying scenes, he felt, often worked best in idyllic locales. This idea was reminiscent of Bob's favorite element of John Cassavettes' movies: their calm surfaces masked darkness.

As heavily as music figured into Bob's best films, long stretches of *And Soon the Darkness* are eerily silent or set only to the sounds of nature, accentuating the isolation of the film's heroines within the sprawling French countryside. Radio music plays dimly behind one of the film's suspense highlights: when actress Michele Dotrice

Fuest directing Wuthering Heights.

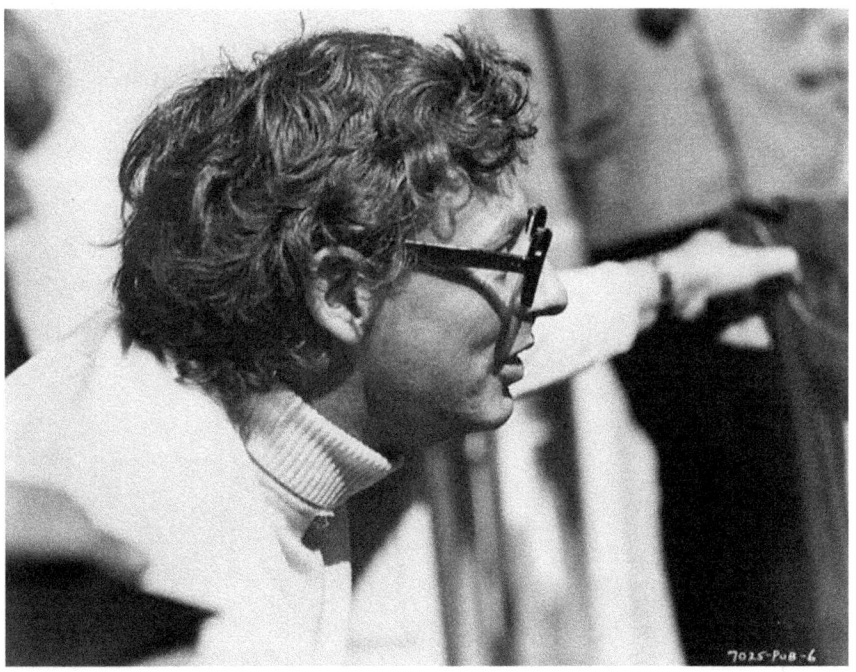

Directing Wuthering Heights.

A deleted scene from Wuthering Heights.

Another excised shot from Wuthering Heights.

Directing Wuthering Heights.

is silently stalked while sunbathing. Just before she later awakens, the music on the radio becomes garbled, maybe from its batteries dying-- subtly, aurally giving the impression that the situation is distinctly out of whack– just as, even subtler still, the unidentified stalker's shadow passes over Dotrice's face, seen in close-up.

Bob proved his versatility early on with *And Soon the Darkness* and his next film, *Wuthering Heights* (1970), which made it abundantly clear that he could make an outstanding straight drama. The film is particularly well-cast, with Timothy Dalton nailing Heathcliff's feral, Gypsy mien, and Anna Calder-Marshall giving Cathy the perfect edge of mental instability. Bob's sweet tooth for casting oddball character actors is apparent in all of his early films.

At heart, *Dr. Phibes* and *Wuthering Heights* are surprisingly similar. Both are epically romantic tales of love beyond death, of brooding anti-heroes inseparable from their mates who are eventually united with them in un-death. The films' protagonists' professions of love are almost interchangeable. "Let God take vengeance on the wicked," serving girl Nellie tells Heathcliff. "Why should he get all the satisfaction?" Heathcliff snarls. Dr. Phibes would agree.

American International Pictures produced some of Bob's finest films, but they also carved around 40 minutes of footage out of *Wuthering Heights*, and the film cries out for restoration (and will probably never get it). (For detailed descriptions of the missing scenes from Bob's *Wuthering Heights*, listen to my audio commentary on Twilight Time Video's 2017 BluRay release of that film.)

Bob had very mixed feelings about AIP: "If they were making hubcaps, they'd make more hubcaps. . . When I made *Wuthering Heights*, the producers at AIP hadn't read the book. They'd read the comic, but they hadn't read the book." The film was his breakthrough hit, though– it was AIP's "first film to have a run at Radio City Music Hall," Bob said. *Wuthering Heights* was a coup, but it didn't exemplify Bob's style (and it should be duly noted how different, yet distinctly similar, Bob's first few films all look).

More than any of Bob's films, *The Final Programme* showcased his off-kilter brilliance. The film's French dvd release is in a series titled "Les Films Inclassables"– "The Unclassifiable Films"– and that, as science fiction goes, the film definitely is. Very few directors captured the elusive feel of sf's then-current New Wave as well as Bob, or even attempted to. The film takes unprecedented risks, exploring dark, bizarre, and crazily inventive ideas that took full advantage of the creative freedom that its limited budget afforded it. The final response to The Final Programme has been wildly mixed– it confused as many people as it has hardcore enthusiasts.

While making *The Final Programme*, Sterling Hayden asked Bob how he should approach his character, a jovial, utterly amoral arms dealer, "Wrongway" Lindbergh. Bob told him, "He's a used car salesman in a Hieronymus Bosch painting." That bit of direction nicely encapsulates not only that film, but Bob's personal style. Bob frequently fused seemingly completely unrelated things together to create brilliant new ideas and insights, while incorporating his extensive art background.

Art was central to Bob's life, which was symmetrical– he began his career as a painter and art teacher, and ended it as a film professor and painter. I have seldom encountered an artist who was such

Jerry Cornelius (Jon Finch) and Miss Dazzle (Julie Ege) at the stylized casino in Fuest's The Final Programme.

an enthusiastic cheerleader for his fellow artists without ever coming off as a Pollyanna or as someone who lacked critical acumen. Among directors, he loved Cassavettes. He lovingly reminisced about Bert Stern's documentary *Jazz on a Summer's Day* (1959), which he hadn't seen in decades but still adored. Bob would wonder why Ben Shahn, who was like "a god" to him in art school, he said, could become so neglected.

Among artists, Bob seemed to like few better than actors, and actors loved him– even the notoriously bitchy Robert Quarry.

Among his favorites was the inimitable British character actor Ronald Lacey, who Bob used briefly but unforgettably in *The Final Programme*. Bob recalled Lacey wearing fur coats and sporting a cane, looking something like a '20s lumber baron– in other words, just ripe to appear in a Fuest movie. He and Lacey had planned on making a film together that Lacey was assembling– an Agatha Christie-like whodunit directed by Bob, starring Bette Davis, with Lacey co-starring and producing. Bob found Lacey incredibly funny and warned him, "We can't make it– we'll spend the whole time laughing!" Bob was amazed when I told him that Lacey had physically suffered later in life as a result of having part of his intestines removed. "It says that on the Internet?" Bob exclaimed. "'Ron Lacey had part of his guts taken out'?" Oddly enough, one of the few actors that Bob recalled being nonplused by was Peter Cushing during their one-day working relationship on *Dr. Phibes Rises Again*. Bob said that Cushing being cold, distant, and overly businesslike, due no doubt to his having only recently begun the lifelong process of grieving his one-and-only wife, Helen.

On the other hand, Bob completely took to Ernest Borgnine. He said that every morning on *The Devil's Rain* (1975), Borgnine would show up, fully prepared, greeting him with a jovial, "Good morning, guv'nor!" Though even Bob himself freely admitted to walking around the set asking people what the hell the movie was about, Borgnine brought an impressive level of sincerity to his performance. As the demonic Corbiss, Borgnine seems to be the only character in the film that fully understands what's going on. Shooting at breakneck speed as they were, Bob said that he regretted never having time to tell Borgnine, "You were so good in *Marty*!" Decades later, writer/historian Courtney Joyner was doing a signing with Borgnine and I had him pass along Bob's sentiments to Borgnine.

Among his collaborators in creative areas closer to his own, Bob adored production designer Brian Eatwell, who he remained close friends with until Eatwell's death in 2007. (See Chapter 5.) Not only did Bob coax Eatwell into working in films, but described their relationship as "Art directors on heat!" Like Nicolas Roeg after him, Fuest found in Eatwell an almost supernaturally perfect collaborator– theirs were monumentally feverish imaginations that had finally met their equal. Bob's family and Eatwell's would vacation together and were extremely close— so much so that Eatwell's daughter Joanna recalls thinking of Bob as a second father.

Bob also regularly credited those who had helped him, encouraged him, and trained him. While working with lighting cameraman Norman Warwick early in his career, Warwick graciously took the extra time to show Bob how a movie camera worked, how to load film, etc. Bob vowed to use Warwick when he made features, and he did with magical results. Warwick's knack for lighting gave *Dr. Phibes* and *The Final Programme* the painterly look that Bob was after.

Amazingly, as good as cinematographer John Coquillon's photography in *Wuthering Heights* is with its gorgeous autumnal palette, Bob was disappointed by it. He said that, during production, Coquillon actually approached him and apologized. "If I ever have a fortune," Coquillon said, "I will pay for you to shoot this movie over."

Dr. Phibes was Bob's favorite of his own films, and he was well aware that it was practically my all-time favorite movie. 2010 was a vicious kick in the teeth for a lot of people— for me, it brought my father's death in late winter. That summer, I received a package— Bob had sent me his personal shooting script to *Dr. Phibes*. He had inscribed the title page: "Dear Justin- This is my script which I'd like you to have (and I'm quite sure Phibes would have wished the same). And so now- just you take care of yourself my dear friend." I nearly cried— it was an indescribably beautiful gesture of solidarity and friendship. I felt like I'd been knighted.

Around that time, Bob and I got in a long talk about our late fathers. He said that his working-class father, a railroad man, had never understood his artistic career choices. "He was disappointed that I didn't become a footballer or something, I think," Bob said. Bob's memories of his childhood sometimes came up at the oddest moments. When I brought up the toy train in Dr. Vesalius' (Joseph Cotten) house in Dr. Phibes, Bob wrote, "Growing up during the war years, there were no toy trains like this and I would have killed for this model."

In November, 2011, among my usual barrage of questions about *Dr. Phibes*, Bob brought up several of his unrealized films. One such project was a proposed adaptation of Colin Wilson's *The Philosopher's Stone*, a vehicle for tv psychic Uri Gellar, commissioned by pop producer Robert Stigwood, which he was paid to write for six months. "What a waste!" Bob laughed. "I met Uri Gellar a number of times," Bob said, "and the man is very strange. He has got something going on there– he's not just all [smoke] and mirrors. He does stop your watch– when you talk about him, things a million miles away fall off... He really is a strange man. I've heard many stories about him, which I can vouch for.

"The idea was that we only use one-third of our brains or two-thirds of our brains– there's an area of the brain which is there, but nobody uses it. This company has got this scientist and his arrangement [where] they think they can get some people, maybe half a dozen guys, Uri Gellar and some guys, they can give them an extra kind of something that nobody else had... You know roughly what I'm talking about . . . Something where, in a business meeting, they had the edge over everybody because they were just that much more smart.

"So that was that and I met Gellar and I did a lot of research... The amazing stuff that I found, which is all written up and researched– there are a whole lot of people who can look into the lens of a camera and make an image on a film, which seems to me extraordinary. Not a reflection of themselves, but a fishing boat or something like that, which is extraordinary– take a plate camera, then when it's pulled out, there's an image there. Work that one out..."

Bob also opened up with a film professor's usual complaints. "When I was at the London Film School," he said, "I found that most of the students really... because it was a private school, they were very rich and basically they just wanted to do it in order to make a film and get into the business. And they weren't into anything– script theory, imagery– except maybe the difference between 16 and 35, the kind of nuts and bolts and that particular thing...

"And another thing, they were all INCREDIBLY ignorant, it seemed to me! They had no idea! I'd ask them to name a few directors. They'd say, 'Spielberg,' mainly, and there'd be a long pause. And in a fucking film school!"

Bob and I talked for a while longer, and he said something that touched me deeply: "I really admire you tremendously, Justin, and I'm very fond of you!" We parted soon after. I was very busy over the next several months and didn't have time to call Bob, but, that Christmas, I had about ten of my fellow Fuest aficionados sign a card for Bob with affectionate notes. Dr. Phibes' creator, William Goldstein, praised Bob on the "classic elegance" of the film's opening waltz sequence. Author Darius James called Bob's work "Fucking genius." Brian Eatwell's widow sent her regards. And, naturally, I chimed in. When the card reached them, Bob's wife said that it delighted him.

In January and February, Bob's health declined. He was hospitalized several times and was plagued with anemia. We sent each other our love through Bob's wife regularly. In late February, I discovered an extraordinary essay by writer Laurie Ede on Bob's and Eatwell's designs– it was easily the best writing that I had (and have) ever seen about the Dr. Phibes series. Bob got it, read it, and was (I was told) pleased.

In mid-March, Bob's wife told me that he had been diagnosed with secondary bone cancer. Knowing that Bob existed tenuously and that he was unavailable by phone, I sent him a card, letting him know how important he was to me and how deeply I cared about him. I closed the card with a doodle of Phibes and mailed it immediately. Meanwhile, Bob was going home– a blessing, because he was a very spry octogenarian and loathed hospitals. "Get me out of here," he told his wife. "This place is full of old men!"

The next Monday, Bob's wife told me that the doctors were giving him weeks, not months, to live. I tried calling him very early Wednesday morning and was only able to leave a message. Two hours later, emails arrived, first from Bob's wife and then Eatwell's family: Bob had died at around four or five in the morning, peacefully in his sleep. The next day, I found out that my card had reached Bob on the last day of his life– his son told me that Bob had been "quite touched" by it.

Variety's obituary for Bob was, as usual, cursory, pat, and ignored the fact that Bob had directed John Travolta in his first film role. But Bob's collaborator and longtime friend Brian Clemens has written a gorgeous eulogy that more than makes up for their utilitarian copy: "Yes, dear Bob has gone, but of course he will live on through the tangibility of his work and, inevitably, there will one day come the 'season of,' 'reappreciation of', and hopefully his wonderful painter's eye for a set up will be recognized at last, along with that gentle, coaxing way with actors, and an altogether personal style.

"I have worked with some great and glorious directors, but never one as mercurial as Bob. As surprising. As rewarding... but finally it is the man I will miss, with his mop of boyish hair, giggly sense of humor and, best of all, his love of music, from jelly roll New Orleans to Mozart. The kind of memories he bequeathed will never die."

Dr. Phibes told his dear, dead Victoria that someday they would sit together "in a secluded corner of the great Elysian Field of the beautiful beyond." If there is an afterlife, I'm sure that's where Bob is now. As for me, I will always remember Bob much like Cathy Earnshaw said she would carry her memories of Heathcliff: "I shall love mine yet and take him with me. He's in my soul."

A dapper Brian Eatwell.

Chapter 5
Abandoning the Obvious: The Brilliant Life and Art of Brian Eatwell.

By Justin Humphreys

It's a sadly true cliche that the film industry's true artists often go overlooked, mainly because they are exactly that– true artists, not self-promoters. Pushy, egotistical showboaters– as mediocre as those real artists are inventive– often overshadow the most profound cinematic talents. This is especially true of technical artists– their names and careers remain unknown to the average moviegoer. Such was the case with Brian Eatwell, one of the most madly creative, unique, and underrated production designers of the last half-century.

Eatwell's designs are immediately recognizable. Though he was capable of working in many milieus, he was at his best when presented with wild material, like in his collaborations with his fellow iconoclasts, directors Robert Fuest and Nicolas Roeg. It was Fuest who pushed Eatwell out of tv work and into the movie arena where he belonged. Eatwell took Fuest's two Dr. Phibes films, and working closely with the director, veered sharply away from horror sets' tired Gothic cliches. Instead of a hackneyed old dark house, Eatwell crafted stylish chrome and glass Art Deco environments for the film. As Fuest pointed out in an interview, he and Eatwell's m.o. was "abandoning the obvious." "He was an absolutely brilliant designer," Fuest said, shortly after Eatwell's death. "He could turn his hand to absolutely anything."

Eatwell typically bonded intensely with his directors, and his intelligence, charisma, and overwhelming enthusiasm helped him lead his crews to new heights of artistic achievement. On a tv movie project, *The Missiles of October* (1974), the crew came to practically worship Eatwell. "When it was finished, I was absolutely astonished," Eatwell's widow, May, says, "because the [crew] had just been doing game shows, hadn't done anything that they thought was of any interest whatsoever ... The carpenters and the painters actually picked him up and carried him on their shoulders because they were so thrilled to have created a genuinely extraordinary set.

"He had the ability to inspire people ... He had an amazing contagious sort of impish quality about him, with a wonderful sense of humor. So you always felt that he was a very exciting person to be around."

Eatwell was born in 1939 in London. His initial interest in theatrics began during his studies at an old English public school, Alleyn's in Dulwich. As Eatwell's widow May Routh recalls: "When he'd [Eatwell] been at school in England, the man who taught English at the school was called Michael Croft was one of those extraordinary people that you just probably meet once in your life. And he actually had an ability to inspire horrible spotty schoolboys to be absolutely intrigued with Shakespeare."

In a production of "Julius Caesar," David Weston recalls, "Brian played a Teddy Boy with a razor who cut up Cinna the poet in the first half and then played a rebel soldier, part of Brutus' Army in the second. We did it in 1960 at the Queen's Theatre in London and in 1961 toured Italy and also performed at the Berlin Frestival just as the Wall was going up. Brian being Brian went through the Wall to check out the Berliner Ensemble and was made very welcome."

Eatwell, Weston, Michael York, and Simon Ward were among the Youth Theatre's founding members. "Michael York did not go to Alleyn's School," Weston continues. "He went to school in Croyden but was an early member of the Youth Theatre ... [Eatwell] began [acting] as a serving man in 'Antony and Cleopatra' and then Alice the French Princess' maid in 'Henry V.' The French Princess in question was played by Simon Ward - who was even prettier than Brian, which was a feat in itself. Brian next played Mistress Quickly in 'Henry IV' - I played Falstaff and he tried to have me arrested for breach of promise to marry - he was very funny - remember, Shakespeare wrote the part to be played by a boy. He was a man at last when we did 'Troilus and Cressida' at the Edinburgh Festival in 1957 - he was a very handsome Paris - all the girls that came to the play fell for him. I was his elder brother Hector, Simon Ward, who sadly died last week, was Cressida."

As for his college education, "Brian studied Fine Art at Camberwell Art School," says Eatwell's daughter, Joanna, "and also dabbled in playing the saxophone. He did I believe go on to do a post-graduate course at Bristol Old Vic Theatre School." (Eatwell's brother, Tony, is also an artist.)

"He was acting briefly," Routh continues. "What he really wanted to do was design for the stage. And so he went to the Bristol Old Vic, and what they studied there ... They all had to be absolutely on-time. There was strict discipline. And they all had to do various things, as does the National Youth Theater– the whole premise of

Eatwell on the set of American Dreamer *(1984).*

the Youth Theater is that they do six or eight weeks in which they sweep the stage, make the clothes, make the props, act– like the leading actor, and the next week they're carrying a spear. It's very much an ensemble. Same thing for Brian at the Bristol Old Vic, that they had to do everything, but he was obviously interested in set design." Of Eatwell's specific sources of artistic inspiration, Routh says, "Brian was very influenced by the Art Deco Exposition, German Expressionist and Modernist, artists and architects. He also loved the work of the Spanish architect Gaudi."

Roy Kinnear, Eatwell, and director/star Marty Feldman on the set of The Last Remake of Beau Geste.

Eatwell's matriculated as a set designer at ABC Television, where he first met fellow art director-cum-director Robert Fuest. (For much more about their relationship, refer to Chapter One of this book.) After helping design Fuest's first film *Just Like a Woman* (1967) in high Pop Art style, Eatwell and Fuest had a major artistic coup with *The Abominable Dr. Phibes* (1971) and *Dr. Phibes Rises Again* (1972). The *Village Voice*'s review of *The Abominable Dr. Phibes* typifies the kind of praise that Eatwell's work was singled-out for, calling the film "A designer's dream in the ultimate sense." In 1976, film critic Elliott Stein called Eatwell a "resident genius" of the English cinema and raved about his "cool, insidiously outrageous ... talent for camp, color, and clutter."

A mirrored hallway with an ethereal beauty wafting down it, a madcap Art Deco fortress hidden within an ancient Egyptian tomb, and a '30s-style coffin sporting the Spirit of Ecstasy, a Rolls-Royce hood ornament– the Dr. Phibes series are laden with visual curve-balls like these, a la Eatwell.

Eatwell's set designs– an integral part of the films' success– were more akin to that of his peers/friends like designer Tony Walton (*Fahrenheit*

451) and far less to horror films past. (Ironically, Eatwell's only prior horror film credit, David Greene's *The Shuttered Room* (1966) offered traditional cobwebby, macabre production design, which hearkened back to its source, an H.P. Lovecraft story. Eatwell worked every bit as impressively in this standard milieu as he did

when bending trends.) Though Eatwell essentially reinvented the look of the horror film, almost no other horror filmmakers aped his designs, probably because they couldn't be surpassed.

Perhaps Eatwell's most widely-known films are *The Three Musketeers* (1974) and *The Four Musketeers* (1975), which were shot back-to-back in Spain. The films' producer, Ilya Salkind, echoes the general description that most of Eatwell's collaborators gave of him: "He would GET IT"— with very little talk or explanation, Eatwell could supply exactly what filmmakers needed.

Salkind describes Eatwell as "extremely charming, funny, quick-witted, intelligent . . . Sometimes, [Eatwell could be] a little bit critical, but I would say in the right way . . . I liked him very much, frankly. I would say even from among all the art directors I've worked with, he's definitely one of my favorite guys to work with."

The Musketeers films were probably Eatwell's most exhausting assignment: over a matter of months, he had to design and supervise the construction of literally dozens of recreations of 17th century French buildings . . . which all had to be designed to be backlit by the sun! "That was David Watkins, who had a special way of lighting, which was pretty impressive, but you had to backlight everything," Salkind says. Further stressing Eatwell out was the lack of interest that director Richard Lester seemed to show in his sets. The job became so taxing that Eatwell's hair began falling out.

"He did an enormous job," Salkind says. "Unbelievable what he did . . . Fantastic job." It was while making the *Musketeers* films that Eatwell first encountered a costume assistant named May Routh. They would work together again on *The Man Who Fell to Earth*, among others, and got married in 1983. They remained together until Eatwell's death in 2007.

As with Robert Fuest, Nicolas Roeg's directorial career blossomed concurrently with Eatwell's rise as an art director. In the early 1970s, Roeg launched an artistic blitzkrieg, visually and narratively

An Eatwell design for the unproduced The Fourth Man.

Director Richard Lester, Robert Fuest, Brian Eatwell, and production designer Assheton Gorton. Courtesy of the Brian Eatwell Estate. Used with permission.

reinventing the cinematic form in startling and astonishing ways. His distinctive, truly experimental style dovetailed beautifully with Eatwell's– the pair both shared a gift for successful artistic riskiness.

As a combination production designer/location scout, Eatwell applied his keen visual sense while choosing striking Australian outback locations for Roeg's solo directorial debut *Walkabout* (1971), and performed similar tasks on Roeg's *The Man Who Fell to Earth* (1976), where he discovered properly alien-looking landscapes in New Mexico. In these films, Eatwell's unfettered imagination devised stunning set after stunning set.

Roeg himself recalls: "The curious thing is, with Brian, the relationship, in terms of working together, which is quite rare . . . we didn't have long discussions. After we talked about a scene or something, he really felt the essence of the piece . . . He could interpret my emotions very clearly . . . Very often, one gets onto a set, and thinks, 'Oh, God, that's missed the point . . . No, no, no! Take that down'– some personal thing from the art department has crept in and is making a statement of its own or another thought. But Brian had a curious quality . . . We didn't discuss it at all. He . . . reflected . . .

"In *Walkabout*, the tree, the baobab tree, was there, but it had a couple of other branches and a couple of other growths next to it by the waterhole. I said, 'That's ok, but . . .' He said, 'I think it would be better without those other two [growths].' I thought, 'This is terrific.' He didn't try to make it anything but what it was and reflect the attitude in the piece. And somehow it completely-- in that deserted landscape, with that one single tree with other little branches, little growths beside it halfway up the thing– once they'd gone, it completely changed the set. Completely changed my thoughts about the attitudes which the kids were in . . . Enlarged [them]: 'The boy ought to just enjoy himself, play with his toys' . . .

On Roeg's *Don't Look Now* (1973), Eatwell made several uncredited, and nonetheless vital, contributions: he helped find two critical locations and also fathered one of the film's key players. The critical opening scene involves Donald Sutherland examining a slide of a church, in which he notices a small figure in red just prior to his daughter's death outside. Eatwell chose Sutherland's house for the film, and the church seen in the photo. "As far as *Don't Look*

A Nazi fortress Eatwell designed for an unrealized film.

Now," Joanna Eatwell says, "there were a series of photographs of the Figure in Red, a portent of doom, taken in a local church. On that occasion I was the figure. Also all the black and white photos in the film were of Christine [Eatwell's first wife] and her family." The Eatwells and the Fuests "were all friendly with the vicar of the church in *Don't Look Now*" prior to the film. Eatwell was forced to leave the film when production shifted to Italy, where limitations were placed on the number of British crew members. (Eatwell was also one of the original art directors on Peter Bogdanovich's *Nickelodeon* (1976), but he chose to leave it during a hiatus in production.)

In *The Man Who Fell to Earth*, just as he had done with horror in the Phibes series, Eatwell flaunted the visual conventions of science fiction, shunning their standard accoutrements and steering the genre's look into uncharted territory– "organic" extraterrestrial hardware, among other innovations. For instance, Eatwell designed an alien vehicle to have peat built into its surface, giving it as anti-mechanical a look as possible. He was doing for science fiction what he had done with horror in the Dr. Phibes series.

"It's difficult to praise him, which I like doing, in the usual terms because we knew each other..." Roeg says thoughtfully. "It's rather like... I don't mean this physically, but a mental love affair. We enjoyed the movie together, we enjoyed that part of it– his involvement." Fuest echoed Roeg's sentiments– he said that his collaboration with Eatwell was "like two art directors on heat!" Another director that Eatwell bonded intensely with was David Greene, who he made several films with in various genres.

What makes Eatwell's work so outstanding isn't merely its catchy, stylish oddness, but the logic behind Eatwell's artistic choices– his choices were well-reasoned. For instance, as a budgetary choice, Eatwell used no exposed controls in the alien Mr. Newton's spacecraft. Instead, the control room is spare-- the closest thing to actual instruments is a glowing sphere in its center and row upon row of cones on its walls. Striking, yes, but intelligent, too: Eatwell stated that, to a society as advanced as Mr. Newton's, this equipment makes perfect sense. And though it confuses we earthlings, it's only because our technology lags infinitely behind Newton's.

"I don't think of [Eatwell] in the normal way of thinking of a member of the crew: 'Oh, he's very clever, very good." Roeg continues. "He was particularly unique. Somehow his interpretation of what I was saying was pretty well spot-on what I wanted. We hardly discussed anything about those sets ... I think you noted the spaceship that Mr. Newton goes in with the bulbs and lights ... I mean, it wasn't just because of limited budget– that would have been [unchanged] if we'd had $100 million! It was absolutely dead-on right." When Roeg was attached to the remake of *Flash Gordon*, Eatwell was brought in for discussions and, after Roeg departed the project, Eatwell discussed working on it briefly with its eventual director, Mike Hodges.

Eatwell and Routh eventually settled in Los Angeles. Veteran art directors (the "grey heads," as Routh referred to them) coldly dismissed him as a youthful upstart. Virtually the only production

Eatwell's stunning mirrored dream corridor from Dr. Phibes Rises Again.

designer who welcomed Eatwell with open arms was William Creber (*Planet of the Apes*). Eatwell would remain a Los Angeles resident and a member of the American Art Directors Guild for the rest of his life. (Eatwell was also active in AMPAS and BAFTA.)

Occasionally, Eatwell was given juicy, bizarre visual subject matter to conjure with, which he rolled with his usual panache. In particular, there were to off-the-wall '70s musicals, *Godspell* (1973) and *Sgt. Pepper's Lonely Hearts Club Band* (1978). The former, directed by David (*The Shuttered Room*) Greene, featured Eatwell's tatterdemalion hippie world— a patchwork landscape far-removed from his earlier films, but still distinctly his and typically colorful. In the all-star Sgt. Pepper, Eatwell's penchant for Art Deco was used to good effect, and Eatwell's pinball-machine-like rock visuals were far stronger than the actual production itself.

(An incident during the filming of *Godspell* in New York deeply amused Eatwell. A derelict approached him on-location and asked what they were doing. Eatwell replied that they were making a movie called Godspell. "Dogsmell?" the derelict replied. "Never heard of it!")

Gradually, Eatwell's films' ubjects became generally more visually mundane, like the Middle-American landscape of *The Onion Field* (1979). "I saw it," Fuest recalled, "and it was a kind of grinding sort of murder [story] set in the backwoods of America. He didn't enjoy it very much. It was just sort of grungy, American-style houses and that sort of thing. There wasn't much that he could do with it."

"I think the thing is that he really got involved very closely with the director and the project," Routh says. "He was always married to them and if you didn't go along with that, you lost out. But I don't know if, when he came to America, if he had that kind of close relationship with American directors and he found a lot of them quite wanting." For instance, on Sam Fuller's *White Dog* (1982), the seventy-year-old Fuller would join Eatwell and others to view the film's dailies and would not only fall asleep, but would loudly snore, much to Eatwell's chagrin.

Eatwell diversified in his later years, acting (in the film *American Dreamer* (1984), which he was also designed), directing a play in Los Angeles, and teaching for one semester at UCLA. He also wrote several scripts in his later years. One screenplay was based on a J.G. Ballard novel—Eatwell and Ballard corresponded-- and another brought his career something like full-circle– *Young Will*, about William Shakespeare's early years.

Eatwell died of cancer in 2007. Michael York quoted from Shakespeare at his memorial, and recalled that during their Youth Theater days, Eatwell, on a dare, had performed his role in "The Merchant of Venice" in Amsterdam while wearing yellow clogs. Ian McShane spoke, and Nicolas Roeg sent a message to be read. The then-President of the Art Directors Guild, Tom Walsh, was among those who eulogized Eatwell: "Brian Eatwell is a designer with a uniquely personal style and he is possessed with powers of invention that are second to none. He is every screenwriter's dream champion because he deeply respects the text and the writer's process, and he will go to great lengths to help the screenwriter in the visual translation of their work, providing as much depth and clarity as is humanly possible." Eatwell is buried at Hollywood Forever Cemetery.

Eatwell is gone, but the vitality of the worlds that he shaped lives on, arresting the attention of generation after generation of viewers who continually rediscover his work. And though his name may not adorn the walls of any real-life monuments in ten-foot-high letters, the extraordinary buildings that he created on film have his distinctive, remarkable signature written all over them. They are memorial enough.

Epilogue: In 2011, I took May Routh to a screening of *Walkabout* in Los Angeles. In the film, the three young protagonists pass by a rundown house with a sweatshop operation outside. In this dingy hovel's tiny bedroom is a gleaming pinball machine, leaping out at the viewer like a diamond tiara atop a compost heap. Seeing it, I turned to May and whispered, "That pinball machine looks like Mr. Eatwell's doing."

"That's TOTALLY Brian," May replied, smiling.

Author's note: For further information about Brian Eatwell, I recommend watching the Criterion Collection dvd of *The Man Who Fell To Earth*, which includes a lengthy audio interview with Eatwell conducted in 2005.

All photographs and artwork in this chapter are courtesy of the Brian Eatwell Estate and used with permission. All rights reserved.

John Jay, Dr. Phibes' *on-set still-man. (Photo courtesy Mark Ferelli.)*

The classic pose, signed to Mark Ferelli by its photographer. (Photo courtesy Ferelli.)

Chapter 6
John Jay: Photographer of Phibes

By Mark Ferelli

During the autumn of 1970, John Jay, still photographer at Elstree Studios just outside London, was assigned to the floor of a new Anglo-American production, *The Abominable Dr. Phibes*, a film made under the inventive hand of British director Robert Fuest. By that time, Jay had become one of Britain's foremost film studio photographers, well-respected among his peers for the quality of his work on many a major film production. Jay was born in 1920 to a theatrical family, his actress mother Elizabeth having shared the stage with the legendary Sarah Bernhardt. John had a natural love and affinity for the company of actors, allowing him to move easily about the complex, often emotionally-fraught terrain of a film set.

He began his career at fifteen as a photographic apprentice, eventually heading the stills department of Gainsborough Studios after World War II. In his remarkable career of nearly five decades, John covered such classics as *2001: A Space Odyssey* (1968), Sam Peckinpah's *Straw Dogs* (1971), and *Star Wars* (1977). His on-set memories of *The Abominable Dr. Phibes* were both vivid and entertaining.

John had found the Phibes skull-face mask, created by make-up artist Trevor Crole-Rees, "very interesting to photograph" and whilst he had strong memories of Price in all his gowned, saturnine glory seated at the mighty Wurlitzer organ, he also recalled "Vincent had quite a sweet tooth, I used to bring in the odd bag of sweets for him between takes. He used to come up and ask, 'What you got today, John?'"

His relationship with Fuest was equally cordial: "Robert was a nice man, a good young director. Once you got the director on your side you'd made it! Some directors would let you call for a shot. Some stills-men were seen as a bloody nuisance, getting in the way. You had to feel the actor's mood, know the right moment for a shot".

During more lengthy breaks in shooting, opportunity for more elaborate portraiture would occur, often in the guise of reference shots for make-up and costume. John agreed that it was probably during such a time that he had directed Vincent Price and Virginia North into the memorable pose used to illustrate the film's tagline, "Love Means Never Having To Say Your Ugly."

Looking back over the many stills John Jay shot on *Phibes*, it is more than fair to say we are fortunate to have not only an invaluable production record of a horror classic, but also a body of work of the highest merit and artistic integrity-- a true and enduring testimony to a great craftsman.

Mark Ferelli presenting his "Phibes Risen" magic lantern show. (Photo courtesy Ferelli.)

JUSTIN HUMPHREYS

Chapter 7
Phibes and the Arts: Phibes Risen

By Mark Ferelli

During a winter's evening in London in early December, 2005, an expectant audience witnessed a unique event at the Horse Hospital, Russell Square, an arts venue known and respected for its adventurous promotion of new and unusual work. "Phibes Risen," a magic lantern show performance set amidst a photographic exhibition of rare stills from the movie *The Abominable Dr. Phibes*, arrived via my longstanding fascination with that film-- in particular, the uncanny promotional still that spawned the byline "Love Means Never Having To Say Your Ugly."

Several years earlier, I had toured both the UK and Europe with another magic lantern work, "Devil Daddy." It had sprung from my long-held interest in British horror cinema that had led to the writing of "The Filmshow Trilogy," a darkly personal series of quasi-fictional chapbooks or film histories, composed of original text and movie stills.

I was keen to find a novel means of conveying these oblique, subjective chronicles other than print-- one that hopefully would immerse an audience in a group experience. Fortuitously, I was introduced to the magic lantern whilst working for specialist antique restorers "The House of Automata."

The magic lantern could be described as "pre-cinema," with its rich historical associations of "phantasmagoria" and early fantastic cinema i.e. Robertson, Robert-Houdin, Melies, et al. It is an evocative working tool whose mere presence and operation is a challenge to the bland visual assumptions of the digital age. And with its blend of flickering, oil-fed images and shadow-play, it wasn't long before I began to experiment, producing my own glass slides and spoken-word script.

That was how "Devil Daddy" was born-- a ghost story drawing upon a visit to the countryside location of Piers Haggard's 1970 terror epic *Blood on Satan's Claw*, designed to spirit the spectator away into a world of Arthur Machen-esque disquiet and poetry. Once of an age too young to see such movies, the stills that appeared in the horror film magazines and movie books of the 'seventies had been an early childhood obsession. Often reprinted was the promotional Phibes and Vulnavia embrace image, a theatrical pose conjuring notions of the Medieval theme of "Death and the Maiden." A fascination with this particular image led me to seek out its legendary photographer, Mr. John Jay, as the basis for my next project.

Through his close friend Vincent Murray, a meeting with John was arranged. It was a rare privilege to spend a day with both, looking through stills, talking of his time on the *Phibes* set and his vivid recollections of working with director Robert Fuest.

Some weeks later, I was saddened to receive news from Vincent that John had passed away at home. He took time to thank me for the pleasure of my visit, one that had given this great craftsman a last appreciative interview on an outstanding career. Putting John's archives in order, Vincent had found a number of 10 x 12 black and white prints, production stills taken during the filming of *Phibes* in the autumn of 1970. Passing them on to me for perusal, the idea of staging a long overdue photographic exhibition came to mind-- tribute to John Jay's long-regarded professionalism.

With the support of Roger K. Burton and James Hollands at the Horse Hospital, I decided the gallery would double as exhibition and magic lantern performance space. A collaboration between the two worlds of stills and magic lantern, my work was to be a meditation on that classic image of Phibes and Vulnavia.

In what was to prove a fated circumstance, author Adele Nozedar, once of eccentric 'eighties art indie band Indians in Moscow, generously took time from writing her extraordinary Secret Language of Birds to contribute a haunting soundtrack for the lantern show, composed of the weird chatterings and cries of Jaybirds, genuine field recordings captured about the rural wilds of her recording studio 'Twin Peaks', an enterprise managed with her then-partner Adam Fuest, Robert Fuest's son.

Weeks of magic lantern rehearsal documented by writer and filmmaker Ali Jacques in a remarkable short movie was followed by the hanging of Jay's photographs. Finally, opening night arrived. Suffice it to say the evening was a remarkable success. The lantern performance, allied to the first-ever gallery exhibition of Phibes stills, gave the night a poignant, elegiac character, ultimately in appreciation of the life and work of John Jay. The event remains both singular and memorable.

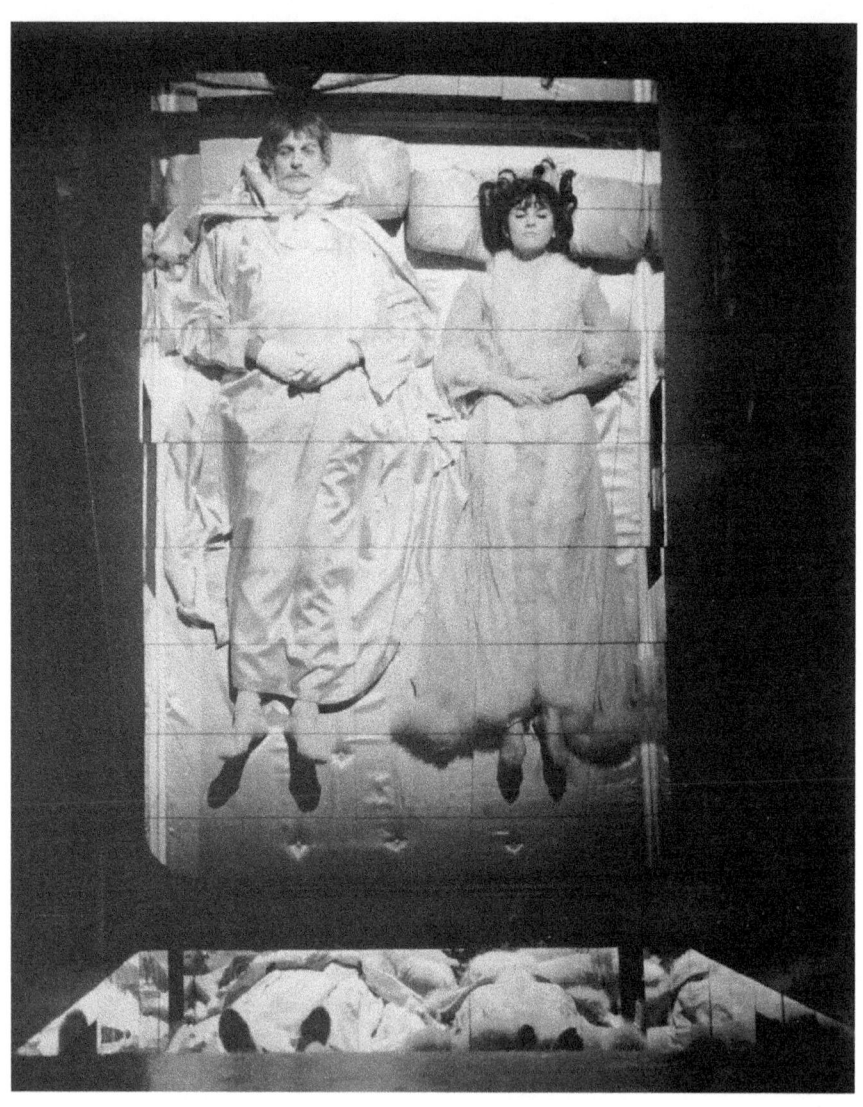

NON OMNIS MORIAR.